Charles Conrad Abbott

Waste-Land Wanderings

Charles Conrad Abbott

Waste-Land Wanderings

ISBN/EAN: 9783337196882

Printed in Europe, USA, Canada, Australia, Japan

Cover: Foto ©Andreas Hilbeck / pixelio.de

More available books at **www.hansebooks.com**

WASTE-LAND WANDERINGS

BY

CHARLES C. ABBOTT, M.D.
AUTHOR OF "UPLAND AND MEADOW" "PRIMITIVE INDUSTRY"
"A NATURALIST'S RAMBLES ABOUT HOME" ETC.

NEW YORK
HARPER & BROTHERS, FRANKLIN SQUARE
LONDON: 30 FLEET STREET
1887

PREFACE.

HAD some sturdy Dutch navigator wandered so far inland from the capes of the Delaware as to see the bold east shore of the river and mouth of Crosswicks Creek, he would doubtless have been charmed with so sweet a spot, and left a marvellous record of his journey. Alas! none came.

Had the plucky Swedish engineer, who, in 1654, mapped the river from the capes to the falls, lost the main stream in some fog, and turned into Crosswicks Creek, what a wonderful account he would have given us of what he took to be the upper regions of the river valley. But there was no fog, and Lindstrom kept straight on until he reached the falls; and it has been recorded by a fellow-countryman of his, that "about the falls of *Assinpink*, and farther up the river, the land is rich, and there are a great many plantations on it. It does not produce much Indian-corn, but a great quantity of grape-vines, white, red, brown, and blue; the inhabitants want only to know how to press the grape in order to have a rich wine country. As to the interior, nothing is known about it, except that it is believed to be a continent: the Swedes have no intercourse with any of the savages but the black and white Mengwes—Iroquois—and these know nothing except that as far as they have gone into the interior the country is inhabited by other wild nations of various races." This nonsense is far less satisfactory than a description of Crosswicks Creek would have been, even if described as the head-waters of the Delaware.

But the mouth of the creek, if I read him aright, did attract him, for it is recorded on his map, very near the mouth of the creek, "Bergs fins Sölfwer Metall," or hills where silver is found; and Campanius adds, "the land is hilly, but not such hills as in Sweden; they are clay and sand hills. Some of them are naturally disposed to the production of metals; for instance, there is a hill at Mekansio Sippus, or creek, in which there is good silver ore, and along the creek the strand is covered all over with flint-stones, some of which are of a round shape, and when broken there are found in them grains of pure silver, some larger and some smaller. Mr. Lindstrom says that he himself has broken more than a hundred of them, and taken out the silver that was therein." The third century is well advanced since this was written, yet this is not a mining country. If Lindstrom left any silver-bearing pebbles, they are still lying on the strand.

Later came the English; and, so far as can be determined, the pleasant valley of this noble creek was a veritable *terra incognita* when Penn's thrifty followers explored, found good, and took possession of it. They certainly knew little and cared less about their red-skinned predecessors, and having no poetry in their souls, gave new and inappropriate names to every important physical feature of the land. It is true that in some cases they Anglicized the Indian name, and the bluffs at Crossweeksung became Crosswicks, as did also the stream that wound thread-like through their meadows.

The Indians were not content with such a paucity of names. One for the pretty hills at Crosswicks must not do duty for miles of meadow and a meandering stream that flowed for leagues through a wilderness of wasteland before lost in the Lenâpé-wihittuck — now Delaware River — so they called the little river Mechentschiholens-sipu, Big Bird Creek. Perhaps, in a succeeding chapter, why it was so called, to what big bird the Indians referred, may be made plain.

It was about 1680 when the earliest settlers in the lower portion of the Crosswicks valley began their frequent journeys to and from the only grist-mill in the neighborhood, and they adopted as their route a certain circuitous path which experience proved to be the least fatiguing to man and beast. For a time no wagons were used, and Stacy's mill on the Assunpink was reached only on horseback or on foot. Finally, when the land was "taken up," this path was officially recognized as a public highway, widened to accommodate carts, and rudely bridged wherever it crossed a brook. From creek to creek the cleared fields were few and small, and there were but three log-houses. All else was an unbroken forest.

To-day every rod of that ancient highway is enclosed, and forms part either of the busy town or of the long line of fertile fields between the site of that old mill and the tortuous, tree-clad valley of Crossweeksung. Not a vestige of the old road remains; not a way-side tree is standing; probably not a person is living who ever travelled it. Except to a few mousers of old records, the fact that another than the present turnpike ever led from valley to valley is quite unknown.

But when this ancient highway was the only one leading from Crosswicks to Stacy's mill — "a most brave place, whatever envy or evil spies may speak of it" —

the creek was a well-travelled water-way, and the only thoroughfare communicating with the then villages of Burlington and Philadelphia. Now, like the old road, the creek as a commercial highway is quite forgotten. For sixty years not a vessel except the hideous hulks of lime-boats has landed at any of its wharves; but, unlike the old road, the stream remains, and, happily for the naturalist and him who loves a quiet outing, has in great measure kept to that condition that made it so attractive to the Indians.

Mechen-tschiholens-sipu, as the redskins called it, is a tide-water stream, and the uppermost of the affluents of the Delaware possessing this feature. When, then, it may be asked, is it seen at its best?—at high or low tide? It is not a mere matter of taste. The two conditions are so unlike as scarcely to be comparable. For myself I should sadly miss either one. At high tide we have a wide stream, with deep green, rushy banks; at low, a narrow, rapid, and more fretful current. The former shuts out the treasures of the stream, and invites to exploration of the curiously nooked and crannied shores; the latter opens up the mysteries of a world beneath the waves, of which, as yet, we have had but casual glimpses. Even animal life that is not strictly aquatic is largely affected by this difference in the tides, and many a creature that we can see at one time is seldom to be found at another. It is always at low tide that I have seen at its best

"The moping heron, motionless and stiff,
That on a stone as silently and stilly
Stood, an apparent sentinel, as if
To guard the water-lily."

There is no rest for these waters. The moment they cease flowing up the valley their downward course commences. This adds another great attraction to the stream: the luxury of floating aimlessly up or down as the tide listeth. It matters not that it is the same stream; as we near the river every bend presents a picture, unlike the varied landscape before us as we return.

What greater joy than floating with the tide? One becomes as the water itself, hopeless as fate, whether borne oceanward or inland. Indeed, we are little else than tide-borne creatures, whatever our calling. Our pitiless surroundings dictate every motion of the hand, every flush of the intellect. Man's free agency is equal to that of the rock-encased toad that a blast in the quarry sets at freedom. Freedom! the toad's first leap will be determined by the nearest fly. But man is practically free who does not feel the chafing of his chains, and should ask no happier fate. Perhaps it may seem trifling and unworthy manhood to thus drift aimlessly along; to be afloat and have no port in view. It is less so than it seems. Who can tell at what moment a passing breeze may lodge us upon a sand-bar; may firmly entangle us among the branches of a sunken tree; may carry us from the main channel to some hitherto unseen stream known far better to the bittern and the muskrat than to man. Are not any and all these ports, if I may call them such, of sufficient merit to be worthy of making? What treasures may there not be there in waiting! The wealth for which we sigh may often be where it is least suspected. If we chance to be caught upon a sand-bar or a waterlogged tree, let it be to the advantage of our patience to await cheerfully for the helpful tide to set us free. His happiness is half assured who has learned to be patient. Suppose it is a sand-bar that has checked our progress. Is this a port that may not be advantageously made? What is a sand-bar? A letter in the short alphabet of geology. It tells in few words of the growth of an island, the silting up of an ancient channel and gradual deepening of a new one. A sand-bar is the initial point in the growth of a foothold for man, for the fructifying sun will soon prompt to vigorous growth the chance-lodged seeds. The aquatic grasses will in time give way to hardier growths. A tide-borne acorn will become an oak, and where in centuries past the Indian floated his canoe, in centuries to come the farmer will guide his plough.

If earth knowledge is desirable, if we would not be strangers in our own land, let us not think ill of the mischance when lodged upon a sand-bar. If we leave it wiser, we leave it happier; and what else, pray, has life to offer?

If the reader has followed me thus far, he knows now the approximate metes and bounds of Mechen-tschiholens-sipu, and, what is of more importance, the author's impelling motive in spending so many days and even nights there and thereabout. I trust that the reader's patience is not exhausted as he turns this page, and hope that what follows may meet with his approbation.

C. C. A.

PROSPECT HILL, TRENTON, N. J.,
January 12, 1887.

CONTENTS.

CHAPTER I.
AT LINDEN BEND.

Characteristic Trees.—Water-thrushes.—Connecticut Warblers.—Natty Fairthorne's Wild-goose Chase.—Traditions concerning the Indians.—Song-thrush.—Quarrels among Birds.—Redstarts.—Yellow-bellied Flycatchers.—Dead Trees.—Epidemic of Yellow-fever, in 1793.—Traces of Indian Villages.—Yellow-breasted Chats . . . . *Page* 1

CHAPTER II.
BUZZARD'S REST.

Miles Overfield.—Weather Predictions.—Animal Weather-lore.—Musk-rats.—Doctor's Creek.—Characteristic Trees.—Kingfishers.—Little Green Herons.—Night-herons.—Color-sense of Birds.—Recognition of Birds of Prey by small Birds.—Turkey-buzzards.—Wild Grape-vines.—Yellow-throated Vireo.—Permanent Mating among Birds.—The Turk's-cap Lily.—August Flowers.—Stone Catfish 21

CHAPTER III.
WATSON'S CROSSING.

Autumn Leaves.—Rocks.—Bowlders.—Faxon's Brook.—August Bloom.—Hopniss: Indian's Use of it.—Flowers.—Old Wharves.—Story of Oconio's Leap.—Anecdote of a Summer Warbler.—Of a King-rail.—Water-snake.—Traces of Indian Villages, Trails, and their Handiwork.—Palæolithic Man.—Eskimos.—Blooming Plants.—Red Admiral Butterfly.—Migration of Milk-weed Butterfly.—Dragon-flies.—Crosswicks Sea-serpent.—Cuckoos.—Night-hawks.—Brood of Winged Ants 63

A*

CHAPTER IV.
SWAMP WHITE-OAK BEND.

Carolina Wren.—Cardinal-grosbeak as a Mimic.—Stranded Fish.—Swamp White-oaks.—A Cunning Musk-rat.—Red-eyed Vireo.—Summer Warblers.—Singing of Birds.—Young Shad.—Indian Method of Fishing: Loskiel's Account; Mahlon Stacy's Account.—Anecdote of a Cat-bird.—Dodders.—Blackberries.—Red-bellied Woodpecker.—Traill's Flycatcher . . . . *Page* 93

CHAPTER V.
DEAD WILLOW BEND.

Dew.—Spring Flowers.—Audubon's Wood-wren.—Water-snake.—Anecdote of Wren.—Willows.—Curious Character met with at the Creek.—Greening of the Willows.—Waste-land.—Bitterns.—Sense of Direction of many Animals.—Coxcomb Grass.—Cove-inlets.—Song-sparrows.—Turn of the Tide.—Indian Relics.—Large Fish: their former greater Abundance.—Tulip-trees.—Beaver-tree, or Magnolia.—Black Snake.—Box-tortoise.—Habits of Young Box-tortoise 116

CHAPTER VI.
THE TWIN ISLANDS.

Old Houses and Furniture.—Florida Gallinule.—Mastodon Bones.—Quicksands: Mink's Opinion thereof.—"Boiling" Springs.—Clay.—Fossil-wood.—Amber.—Gold Claimed to have been Found by the Indians.—Ornamented Minnows.—*Helenium Autumnale.*—Rail-birds.—Corn-crake.—Kingbirds.—Migration of Birds.—Æstivation of Animals.—Showers.—Remarkable Rainfall, and its Effects 153

CHAPTER VII.
MILL CREEK.

A Lonely Sand-piper.—Tree-climbing: its Merits and Disadvantages.—Wood-tattlers.—A Nest of these Birds destroyed by a Bull-frog.—Meadow-mice.—Bush-nests of White-footed Mice.—Etheostomoids.—Mythical Fish described by Early Writers.—Bill-fish.—Sudden Changes of the Weather 190

CHAPTER VIII.
THE LANDING.

Cowpen-birds.—Early Navigation of Crosswicks Creek.—Snowy Owls.—Adventure of Jemmy Cumberford.—Springs: Vegetation Peculiar to their Vicinity.—Golden Club.—Traces of Indian Occupation of the Place.—An Old Beech-tree.—Swarm of Bees.—Mosquitoes.—Velvet Ant.—Burrows of Animals.—Caught by the Tide.—Food of Eels . . . . *Page* 222

CHAPTER IX.
THE DRAWBRIDGE.

Worm-fences.—Drawbridge: on former Site of an Indian Crossing.—Skirmish here during Revolutionary War.—Pearson's Inn: now "White Horse" Tavern.—Plum Point.—Indian Orchards.—Zoology of the Bridge.—Swallows.—Reply to Captious Criticism.—Shrikes.—January Jubilees of the Birds.—Abundance of Birds during Winter.—Catalpas: probably a Native Tree.—Blue-jays.—Vision of Fishes.—Voice of Fishes.—Conclusion 255

INDEX 303

WASTE-LAND WANDERINGS.

CHAPTER I.
AT LINDEN BEND.

IN the long, low, level line of the eastern horizon there is a jagged break, as though Nature's artist, when making a sweeping outline, had caught his pencil-point. Here, oozing from mossy recesses among the roots of "a brotherhood of venerable trees," the waters afar off, in that pleasant valley, seek the light through many channels—now rippling over golden sands, now bubbling over snow-white pebbles, and at last uniting to form a sparkling meadow-brook.

Wooing the waters from a thousand springs, nearer and nearer flows the growing stream, again and again checked by a dam, but straightway leaving it behind, as unruffled as in the ages when men were not; and now as a goodly stream—one worthy of a name—it reaches the last hinderance, and with unchecked flow leisurely seeks the river.

The hum of machinery, the splash of the water-wheel, the roar of the tumbling waters, as in a solid, silvery sheet they pour over the dam—all these prosaic reminders that civilization was near at hand were quickly out of sight and hearing as my boat rounded an abrupt bend of the creek and entered a little forest of linden, hickory, and hornbeam. A few scattered trees of other kinds are also to be seen, but those I have named so far predominate that if each crook in the creek's channel must have a name, then we will call this one Linden Bend; and here, at sunrise, July 29, 1885, I commenced these studies of Mechen-tschiholenssipu (Big Bird Creek).

The dense foliage of the stately lindens and hickories, and the filling-in of every interspace by the hornbeams, throws so dark a shadow as to give to the spot a gloomy aspect; yet it is very attractive. Where the channel narrows, so that the branches of the trees upon its banks are closely interlocked, the sunlight is excluded during summer and early autumn, often for considerable distances. Flowers are wanting, except when the rank May-apple is in bloom, and later the honey-sweet blossoms of the linden scent the air and draw millions of bees from all the country round. The humming of these creatures, as they are busy in the branches overhead, drowns all other sound, dulling even the clear whistling of the crested tit, and by its monotony adds, in early summer, to the gloom of Linden Bend.

I have said there were no flowers: the scattered dogwoods must not be overlooked. Early or late in April, as the weather permits, these sturdy growths fling their torn, milk-white banners to the breeze. They are not always, however, signals that the warfare of the seasons is over. Too often these symbols of peace are lost in the drifts of an April snow-storm. Many very large dog-woods are growing in a near-by swamp, and now, late in July, are sombre, unsuggestive trees, their size, shape, and sparse foliage alike rendering them quite inconspicuous. It is true, they prove convenient perches for the song-thrushes, and I judge are favorite trees with these birds; but once out of bloom, they count for nothing with the rambler, and would never be missed did the farmer cut them all down. Not so in early spring; then they are richer in blossoms than in leaves, and, for a time, the most conspicuous feature of many a sprout-land and of the creek's shore here.

There are several large shrubs the white bloom of which, in April and later, compete with the dog-wood in floral display; and particularly true is this of certain reaches of the creek's bank, beyond the bend. A pretty arrow-wood blooms profusely early in May, and often, at its side, a vigorous thorn quite eclipses its more modest neighbor.

A curious growth is the crooked hornbeam. Even the youngest sapling has a jaded, care-worn look. Many of them have more the appearance of mossy elk-horn than of wood. It may be said to grow without a plan, and for general uncertainty outranks the average white man. It springs from the ground, closely to the water's edge, and leans over it. That is about the only law of its growth. Often, where the main stem meets with that of another tree, or a projecting branch, it will twine about it as closely as a vine, and so, before reaching any considerable size except length, has probably turned many angles of every degree. Another peculiar feature is the uniformity of the diameter of the trunk for an unusual length; in this respect resembling the grape-vine or poison ivy. An hexagonal stem of one of these trees which I was tempted to measure is uniformly ten inches in circumference for twenty feet. It bends sharply at two points, and makes a shapely letter Z, slightly tilted upward, and so far resembles the "N maple" on Poaetquissings Creek, some miles away.

The English hornbeam, which is also called "yoke-elm," like the American form, has the trunk "usually flattened and twisted, as though composed of several stems united."

Pulling my boat ashore, I counted fifty of these trees, and all had the trunks, for a space of a foot or more from the ground, either quadrangular or pentagonal. Usually, they were distinctly diamond-shaped, in section, then approaching a true square, and from this becoming hexagonal, and so approaching a truly cylindrical form; but this is seldom perfectly acquired except by a few of the terminal twigs.

From many of these hornbeams branches could have been cut bearing a marked resemblance to a deer's antlers, and so would be of use for hat-racks where the genuine article could not be obtained.

While lingering in the shade of these dwarfed trees, and of the upreaching lindens about and beyond them, I was struck with the painful silence brooding, at the time, over all. Do such localities usually have a depressing influence over animal life, particularly birdlife? I floated with the tide for a long distance, yet neither heard nor saw a single bird. To be sure, it is July, a comparatively birdless month, so far as singing goes; but I doubt if another stretch of creek valley in the county is so completely deserted—cannot at least boast of a crested tit or a song-sparrow.

It is not always so. Come on a bright May morning when the leaves are half grown, and see the northward-bound warblers. I can vividly recall one sunny May day, twenty years ago, when I floated by Linden Bend for the first time. The preceding days of bright sunshine, followed by moonlit nights, had brought the warblers, and never since have I seen so many congregated in a limited spot as there were then among the lindens and sloping branches of the crooked hornbeams.

Among them, conspicuous for their numbers, size, and splendid singing, were water-thrushes. They were the southern large-billed species, and, in New Jersey, the least abundant of the three kinds. Evidently a number of them had been migrating in company, but whether still on the move, or purposing to remain, I did not determine. As I have seen a few individuals about the creek every summer since then, it is probable that the greater number remained during the summer of '65. Certainly the sweetness of their songs and general air of content suggested that they had chosen this secluded nook of the creek valley for their summer home. There is, indeed, nothing remarkable in the occasional great abundance, here in central New Jersey, of southern birds, usually rare, or, at least, not common. Such instances I have noted three times since 1860, and can only make bare mention of the fact that beyond their numbers they offered nothing of special interest to the observer.

To return to these water-thrushes — true warblers, bear in mind—at Linden Bend. The incessant see-saw of their tails, as they walked along the sloping, muddy shore, or tripped the whole length of some horizontal branch of hornbeam, told me at once what birds they were, and but for one curious habit they might have passed unnoticed among the hundreds of brilliantly colored warblers that threaded every tangle of intermingled branches. Possibly because these more active species, or, shall I say, better tree-climbers, monopolized the choicer feeding-grounds, the water-thrushes, or wagtails, took to the water, and with swallow-like dexterity and grace snapped up the "skaters," those quick-motioned spiders, until scarcely one was to be seen. And then, at intervals of ten or fifteen minutes, these birds would rise to the very tops of the tall lindens and sing a few bars of wellnigh matchless melody. Perhaps I am extravagant in sounding its praises, but it was music that grew sweeter with each repetition, and caused the songs of other birds to seem commonplace in comparison, and this, I take it, is a test of its exceeding merit.

Hard by I once had a curious adventure with a cousin of this water-thrush, our common oven-bird. The day before, I lost overboard a number of trout-flies, tied together with a bit of fine copper wire. The buoyancy of the feathers was not sufficient to keep them afloat, and, as it was high tide at the time, they sunk beyond my reach. I revisited the spot the following morning, when the tide was out, hoping to recover them. As I approached I saw an oven-bird fluttering on the very edge of the water. Its efforts to escape became more violent as I drew near, and it was very evident that the bird was a prisoner. Reaching the spot, a curious spectacle presented itself. A large shiner had evidently swallowed one of the trout-flies as they sunk. How far the fish wandered after this I could not tell, but by strange good luck it had finally returned to the place where the hooks had fallen, and caused several of them to become firmly fixed in a slightly projecting tree-root. One hook was yet free, and this the oven-bird had mistaken for an insect, and seizing it, was itself securely held. The advancing tide would have caused a double tragedy, and I was glad to prevent the certain drowning of the poor bird. Releasing it, I hoped to be successful in retaining it as a cage-bird, but it proved impracticable. It chirped complainingly all that day and through the night, and died at sunrise on the following morning.

Perhaps I am venturing on the dangerous ground of generalizations, but I believe it is true that warblers cannot be tamed, as can the majority of finches and thrushes. I have tried, time and again, to rear summer warblers, redstarts, and others of the family, but never have been successful. They need the active life of the woods as much as an enormous supply of living insects. Those that I attempted to rear were sufficiently well fed, but the curtailment of their liberty became at once depressing after they were fully fledged, and death resulted from violently beating against the wires of the cage in their efforts to acquire freedom.

To return to the creek. Curiously enough, rare as the Connecticut warbler appears to be in so many places, yet here, in October, it is sure to be found. Perhaps earlier, sometimes even later; for the southward flight of warblers is notoriously irregular. Here, too, it sings. It is said to be a sad and silent species, but finds melody in its heart while tarrying at Linden Bend.

Though not loud, it has a fully expressed song, something similar to that of our common yellow warbler, but with more notes; and occasionally, when concealed in a tangle of smilax, or poison ivy, often utters a shrill chirp suggestive of a larger bird.

Certainly, during their autumnal migrations, birds are not much given to singing, but if their southward progress is checked, and they tarry for more than a day, one will often hear the songs of the past nesting season repeated. In the chinkapin woods, not two miles away, I have heard, in October, migrating warblers sing as merrily as ever they sung in early June. Particularly is this true of the beautiful black-and-yellow warbler, and of the sprightly green black-capped fly-catcher. But of all our migratory birds no one is so uncertain in this respect as the wagtail. I have often watched one half a day, and heard nothing but an occasional chirp; yet at other times, when nutting in these same woods, I have been charmed with its song, that seemed to derive additional sweetness from the bracing frostiness of early autumn.

Here, at Linden Bend, it was, but under another generation of trees, that Natty Fairthorne had a strange wild-goose chase. It was in November, 1791. Natty had been all day looking for ducks, and found none. An hour before sundown, keenly disappointed and somewhat unsteady, he sculled up this part of the creek, near which he lived. When at Watson's Ford, half a mile below, it began to snow, and before he reached the lindens "the air was thick." At length, above the moaning of the wind in the old trees, Natty thought he heard the "honking" of bewildered geese. At once he was a new man, and on the alert. The supposed cries of the geese were incessant, and surely came from the bend at the linden woods. Sculling with all his strength in that direction, he peered into the outer darkness, and finally felt sure that he saw the geese. A long, dark line, close to the water, was moving steadily up the creek, and above the roar of the wind could be heard their wild "honking." Natty steadied his boat, took deliberate aim, and fired. Luckily the powder flashed in the pan. Immediately the voices of several men rang through the air, and a belated surveying party, some of whom had seen the flash, demanded who dared attack them.

The truth was soon known, and Natty promised never again to shoot at geese in a snow-storm. The surveyors' singing had deceived him, and he always insisted, when twitted about his goose-chase, that men "who couldn't sing better than they did deserved to run a risk."

I have searched the scanty records, but in vain. Although the north bank of the creek is very steep, and often fifty feet high, yet nowhere does it boast of a "lover's leap." Score this to the credit of the Quakers.

1*

If long ages before them the Indians living along the bold north shore had a tradition of such silliness on the part of one of their maidens, they kept it carefully to themselves, for all which we may be devoutly thankful.

It is vaguely hinted in one old record that here there was once a battle fought between Indians and Indians. This fact seems to have so slightly impressed the primitive chronicler that we must rest content with so bare a statement as that Linden Bend has had its tragedy; but as to every particular, "lost is lost; gone is gone forever."

While yet overshadowed by the towering lindens, my course was suddenly checked by some unseen obstacle that took firm hold of my little boat. I had run upon a sunken tree, the boat being wedged between two outreaching, arm-like roots. There were yet hours of daylight, so I did not worry, and every vestige of annoyance passed away when a song-thrush, perched upon an overhanging bough, sung those sweet strains of which one never tires.

Perhaps nowhere else in this long valley could a thrush sing to better advantage than here. The steep bluff upon one side, and wall-like setting of tall trees upon the other, resulted in its song being distinctly repeated once, and a second fainter echo gave back the louder notes. This, too, late in July, weeks after the care of nest and young are over. The bird was singing solely for its own pleasure, and enjoyed, I am sure, the delightful echoing and re-echoing of its notes, that filled the valley. Indeed, the bird often stopped suddenly, and turning its head to one side, seemed anxious to catch the entire repetition of some few strains of peculiar beauty or emphasis which it had just uttered.

In all my wanderings this was the first time that I had heard a bird's song under such circumstances, the nearest approach to it being when the whippoorwill sat upon my grandfather's wood-pile and sung the livelong night. Its monotonous song was indistinctly echoed—but that was nearly forty years ago.

I was willing, if need be, to wait until the incoming tide released me, should the thrush remain singing. This was not to be. I was, as usual, fated to have some unwelcome intruder break the charm. A noisy kingfisher came hurrying down the creek, and his rattling cry not only drowned the thrush's voice, but drove him, in disgust, to the near-by woods. The new-comer's harsh notes were echoed to perfection, and as it flew on a depressing silence brooded over the creek. Linden Bend, for the time, was desolate, until my splashing and rocking of the boat, in earnest efforts to release it, caused the creek to renew its usual animation. These movements promptly brought in part the hidden life to the front, to see what might be the cause of so great a commotion. An enormous bull-frog popped his wondering eyes above the water, a beautiful snake crawled from the creek to the muddy shore, and knowing it was safe, stared back at me with all the impudence born of mock courage; fishes leaped into the air, and myriads of coal-black scuttle-bugs crowded into the little waves, as if to enjoy the novelty of rocking in troubled waters.

This is not an uncommon experience. Curiosity is

well developed in all animals, and when experience has not taught the necessity of extreme caution, any occurrence outside the routine of their methodical lives very generally induces them to come forward and determine its nature.

A capital opportunity to determine the number and species of birds in a given area is offered whenever a quarrel occurs, particularly among nesting thrushes, and this is quite often. Once the trouble begins, every bird of every kind will hasten thither. More than once, probably because English sparrows put in an appearance, I have known such quarrels to end in a general riot. I once saw a house-wren become so excited that for fully a minute it was dumb. It must have seemed eternity to that bird.

I was soon again afloat, and quietly moving onward, when the place of the thrush was taken by a pretty redstart; but it did not stay. Once, a few notes were quickly whistled, and the bird was gone. I made no effort to follow its erratic passage through the tree-tops. It requires sharper eyes and a more nimble body than I now possess to do this satisfactorily.

Redstarts, which are usually abundant from spring until late in autumn, are excellent songsters, and, quite unlike the average warbler, are as merry-hearted in August as in May. Strangely enough, very few people appear to know them. I took one, not long ago, from the clutches of a cat, and carried it all day, showing it to every person whom I met. In every case, but one, I was asked what bird it was. The exception declared it to be a barn-swallow.

In May they build the daintiest of nests, using only choice materials; fixing them among forked branches of small trees, seldom at a greater height than six or seven feet. The supports of their nests are always wrapped with an abundance of thread-like fibres, such as require the very sharpest eyes to find. Of all the many nests that I have found, none have been so far distant from water that the sitting bird could not look out upon it. One nest was in a button-bush, that fairly trembled upon the brink of a mill-dam, nearly thirty feet in height. At times, the wind carried back great clouds of spray, that for the moment enveloped the bush; but the birds were never discouraged, and the brood was successfully reared. Proximity to the water does not hold good of redstarts' nests the country over; but as far as my own observation goes, the birds themselves are essentially "water warblers." They constantly visit my door-yard, it is true; but they seem to live by the creek-side. It is the relative abundance of insect life that decides the question with them, and is not this, as a rule, near ponds and ditches rather than upland fields—the creek and river rather than the forest? At all events, since the first of their kind, at the opening of the warbler era, gave chase to a fly, their appetites have never been satisfied.

It is said of these birds that they will chase insects while you are very near their nests, but their love of a tidbit will sometimes carry them still farther. I once saw one drop a beakful of fluffy nesting material to chase a fly. As it did so, a summer warbler seized the falling bit and made off. The redstart caught the fly, pursued the warbler, secured the nesting stuff as it fell, and carried it in triumph to its unfinished nest.

As we have seen, the little redstart, unlike the interrupted thrush, could not sit still, and so it is always. I can only think of them as twisting, turning, and running, creeper-like, around the branches, varying these movements continually with sudden sallies into the air, yet never so far absorbed in insect-hunting as not to find time to utter a few clear notes, worthy to be called a song.

Probably no one of the warblers captures, daily, so many insects as does this species. I tried once to count the clickings of a redstart's beak, and so estimate the number of flies that it caught, in a given time; but it proved a hopeless task. The bird's beak snapped with all the regularity and nearly the rapidity of the ticking of my watch. It was making a most unsubstantial meal from a cloud of May-flies. What warbler, besides this, can gracefully turn a somersault, and often does so, either for convenience or fun? It is the erratic flight of the pursued insects that has taught the redstart to perform this remarkable aerial manœuvre; and yet it is difficult to see how this circular course could be of use. Often, I believe, it is a mere matter of play, for the thoughts of the redstart do not run exclusively in the one prosy groove of eating.

Often, in early summer particularly, I have seen the bird fly directly out from an outreaching branch, then close its wings and dive downward and backward, and reopen its wings as it mounted upward again. The course of the flight was an elongated oval, and the bird regained its proper position within a few inches of the point where its downward course commenced.

The redstart gave place to a much rarer and no less interesting little bird—the yellow-bellied fly-catcher. It came, scolded, sulked, and was about to depart, when it was joined by another, possibly its mate, if so be it, like some birds, they remain mated from season to season. These were silent, so far as true singing goes, yet were sufficiently lively to recall another pair I saw in June, to which I was attracted by their loud chattering. On a near approach, I found them bobbing their heads, fluttering their wings, and impatiently dancing in a manner that gave unmistakable evidence of a very far from amicable dispute. Their noise, indeed, brought other birds to the scene, and soon a number of summer warblers, song-sparrows, titmice, and cat-birds, were hopping about the trees and underbrush, intent upon learning all the particulars, or pretending to know them. It most vividly recalled the apparently instant appearance of every woman in the village when my horse ran away and landed me in the duck-pond on the common. Had I not resisted, my escape from the waters of the pond would have been promptly followed by drowning in a deluge of household liniments, camphor, balsam-apple, and hartshorn.

Among the many birds I have mentioned, curiosity cropped out, just as it did among lower animals, not an hour ago.

At last, the fly-catchers' quarrel came to an end. One of them remained comparatively quiet, while the other, as if rejoicing over a victory, sung, in his own quaint manner, " Chesapeake, O Chesapeake!"

Then, as now, afloat, I very slowly urged my boat forward, and was soon directly beneath the songster. This he did not like, and flew down the creek, but not so far away that I could not hear him above the cawing of crows and chatter of blackbirds in the marsh, singing, without an alteration of any note, "Chesapeake, O Chesapeake!"

Rowing but a few rods farther, the limits of the leafy Linden Bend were passed and I entered an open meadow. The change was as abrupt as painful. But the grassy banks were on a level with my eyes, and I looked upward and onward, seeing only the cloud-flecked sky and distant, shadowy woods. Stay! there was one tree, a tall, dead tulip. Saved for the shade it cast, for long years it was the shelter of the cows when summer showers passed, their noontide retreat from fierce midsummer suns. For a decade it has stood, leafless, and more shattered by each winter's storm, until now it is but the merest ghost of its former self. Such trees do not mar a landscape. They are not disgusting. They turn to dust in a becoming manner, offending neither eye nor nostril. The dignity that encompassed them as aged trees clings to them still, though bared of every branch. The many mysteries of years gone by—where fled the squirrels that I saw but as swift shadows—where hid the woodpeckers whose tapping I heard, yet failed to see them at work—from what nook issued the complaining owl—where fled the honey-laden bees—all these sources of wonderment, that filled the hours of many a ramble, are now revealed. The holes and hollows of the dead, decaying tree are no longer hidden retreats of mammal, bird, or bee. The prying sunshine gives up their secret. Here, then, it was that many a creature looked out at me and laughed, while I stood wondering where they might be hidden.

To be sure, a dead tree is an uncanny prophet. It bids me look to the future; but, surrounded by the sights and sounds of untamed nature, my pulses shall beat no less firmly because they cannot beat forever. I can gather buttercups and chase butterflies in a graveyard without stopping to read *hic jacet* upon every tombstone. This world is too full of offerings to quit work and wonder if the next is even fuller. I once gathered a fern, a sprouted acorn, and a bluet from Thoreau's grave, without wondering, at the time, if he were then gathering greener growths on the pleasant hill-sides of another world.

Wherever I chance to be, give me living, stately trees—trees that peeped through the sod and saw the sunrise of an earlier century. Among them, and among them only, can I be alone; man's handiwork, here, has marred all other scenes; and the ocean and the prairie are beyond my reach.

This weedy, bush-grown, long-neglected pasture, which gave evidence of nothing but a most prosaic history, still contains the evidences of stirring scenes enacted here less than a century ago; and long ages prior to that, this same lonely pasture was the site of an Indian village.

The only victims, among the residents of this valley, of the yellow-fever epidemic of 1793, died in a small farm-house, still standing some distance back from the creek—a house with a history, of which more hereafter.

In the pasture between it and the creek, a number of Philadelphians, in '93, encamped for a time, while the scourge was raging in the city. Some years after, the circumstance having been forgotten, Charles Lucien Bonaparte, having noticed a number of diminutive earthworks, had a careful examination made of the spot, under the impression that an Indian village site had been discovered. Very soon a few arrow-heads were found, and much burnt earth and charcoal. The prince was delighted, and arranged for an exhaustive search over the entire area; and soon after, an abundance of glass and glazed pottery was brought to light. The enthusiasm of the prince became disgust, and subsequently his attention was given wholly to zoology.

After all, he was right. Although the circular ridges and one low mound were the work of the Philadelphians, the meadow was an Indian village site. Recently, one portion was badly gullied by a freshet, and immediately afterwards I found abundant traces of the dusky savages. Recalling this, I landed here and walked for half an hour over every spot where the sod was broken. Relics of Indians were as abundant as ever, but not a trace of the Philadelphians.

Returning to the boat, I pushed out from these suggestive shores, and passing a dense cluster of arrow-wood, startled a lonely chat, perhaps the last of the season. I waited long, in hopes that it would sing, but it would not. Approaching cautiously, I obtained a better view of the bird, and was much interested in its strange actions. At irregular intervals it threw back its head, and with its beak pointing directly upward, uttered a peculiar and rather faint *cluck!* that recalled the cry of a night-heron when a long way off. Had I not seen the bird, I should never have imagined the sound was uttered within a boat's-length of me. Ventriloquism, however, is not confined to the yellow-breasted chat.

Chats were unusually abundant two months ago, along the hill-side, and, indeed, wherever blackberry canes were densely clustered. Their singing, if one may call it that, was amusing, but became tiresome at last, and fairly annoying at times, when the strains of the thrush and rose-breasted grosbeak were marred by it.

One of these chats selected a branch of a small locust in the garden as his perch, and with all the regularity of clock-work, amused his nesting mate, throughout the gloaming, by his endless series of strange utterances and curious antics. His ventriloquial power was remarkable. It suggested the following:

> A mournful cry from the thicket here,
> A scream from the fields afar;
> The chirp of a summer warbler near,
> Of a spring-tide song a bar;
> Then rattle and rasp,
> A groan, a laugh,
> Till we fail to grasp
> These sounds, by half,
> That come from the throat of the ghostly chat,
> An imp, if there is one, be sure of that.
>
> Aloft in the sunny air he springs;
> To his timid mate he calls;

> With dangling legs and fluttering wings,
> On the tangled smilax falls;
>   He mutters, he shrieks—
>   A hopeless cry;
>   You think that he seeks,
>   In peace, to die,
> But pity him not; 'tis the ghostly chat,
> An imp, if there is one, rest sure of that.
>
> Afar in the gloomy swamp, where flits
>   The Will-o'-the-wisp by night;
> This elf, a-dreaming, restless sits,
>   And mutters his strange delight,
>   In quavers and sharps,
>   And flute-like note,
>   With the twang of harps;
>   That swell the throat
> Of the mystical, weird, uncanny chat,
> In league with foul spirits, I'm sure of that.

The sun was now sinking behind the tall wild-rice of the distant marshes; the linden-shaded reach of the creek behind me was an abode of darkness; the day was done.

Turning my boat to the convenient shelter of an overhanging elm, I wended my way homeward, over many a dusty field, pleasing myself with the thought that no spot could prove more satisfying than these bird-beloved windings of Mechen-tschiholens-sipu.

CHAPTER II.
BUZZARD'S REST.

THE blackness of night hung over the east, when—to please me, at least—it should have been brilliant with the sun's cheery rays. "Would it rain?" I asked myself at every step, and scores of times paused to see if Nature did not somewhere throw out to me a hint. "A gray east *is* a dry day," my neighbors persist in saying, but could I be sure of this? Then there was the rhyme about "Evening red and morning gray," and all that; but here was a blue-black east, and a generally smoke-colored outlook, and I knew not what it meant.

There are, I think, weather sayings enough still current in this neighborhood to make a portly volume, and accepted by my neighbors as of greater reliability than the daily reports in the morning papers. I could, however, recall none that fitted this peculiar August morning, and wished I had Miles Overfield's opinion, not so much for its intrinsic value as a matter of curiosity. "I do not see," Miles once remarked, "that this newspaper weather business amounts to much. The old-fashioned almanacs had it down for a whole year, and in handier shape."

"But not quite so reliable," I suggested.

"It was as near right as you get it now," he replied, with great earnestness. "Of course, once in a while you had to kind o' twist the words about to make it fit."

"I should think so," I replied.

"But not much more than nowadays," he continued. "I'm not goin' back on father's old almanacs and the moon. I've nothin' agin book-learnin', but somehow it comes back to me you stayed home once in October, and I got the quails, and stayed home not long ago, and I caught the big bass;" and Miles looked happy when he finished his little speech.

It was all true enough, but I subsequently tested his ability as a weather prophet, and summing up the matter at the end of six months, found that just thirty-five per cent. of his predictions were correct.

I told him this, and he was by no means discomfited. "One-third right!" he exclaimed. "Well, if I size up one-third right at the final reckonin' I guess the Lord will accept t'other two-thirds."

I recalled this as I walked towards the creek, and the time passed so pleasantly that I forgot the weather of the moment, and the fact that as I left the house the old mercury barometer was "falling" and the wind south-west. The grass was dry, too—another bad sign; but perhaps the clouds were but the edge of a storm that had spent its fury over other regions. Although every indication favored rain, yet there was a chance that it might not, and these "chances" prove so often to be delightful days that I always take them. In the course of a year, I gain far more outings than I get soakings. Let it be borne in mind, too, that a rainy day in the woods is better than a fretful one in the house.

And here let me say something concerning the animal weather-lore current in this neighborhood.

Happily there still remain a few of those great, cavernous, open fireplaces, flanked by high-backed settles, whereon the young people love to lounge while their elders, resting from the day's labors, talk drowsily of old times, recount the adventures of their youth, and repeat the tales of their grandfathers. As one of such young people, I have passed many long winter evenings, listening eagerly to what the septuagenarians might relate, and occasionally venturing a question or two, that more light might be thrown upon obscure portions of remarks made at the time. Then, particularly, are we likely to hear much of that very curious animal weather-lore that for the past two centuries has been handed down from father to son. Time and again, as the weather chanced to be discussed, I have heard some uncouth rhyme repeated, usually prefaced with the remark, " You know the old saying."

That all animals are more or less affected by coming atmospheric changes is unquestionable. This simple fact has been recognized the world over, but, unlike many other simple facts, has not resulted in leading to any important discoveries. It has, however, given rise to the innumerable sayings to which I have referred.

Inasmuch as the animal weather-lore current in England and Sweden dates far prior to the settlement of this country by the Swedes and English, it would seem probable that such sayings as now are or recently were current in south and central New Jersey are merely adaptations of English and Swedish weather-lore to our fauna, just as the European names of the commoner birds found there were applied to those American species most closely resembling them; and so, any rhyme or brief saying referring to them would be applied to the analogous bird found here. This is eminently reasonable, for, if the given habit, voice, or other peculiarity of a European bird did, or was supposed to, indicate a given meteorological condition, the same rule should hold good in America. As a matter of fact, however, I can find no similarity between the English and Swedish and the American weather-lore, except such as applies to domestic animals; nor do I find any common English sayings in use.

That which I have heard, and have recorded from time to time, appears to have originated where it now is, or lately was, in use. To a great extent, I believe it to be original with the descendants of the immigrants that settled central New Jersey and the country generally about Philadelphia; but a portion of it, very possibly, was derived from the Indians.

At present, a portion of this weather-lore is repeated as nursery rhymes, and it is due to this that it has been preserved to the present time; and, so far as I have been able to determine, not one of the rhymes or sayings has ever been published. That among the earliest papers and almanacs of the country there may be found some of them, or slightly different versions of the same, is probable, but my searchings therefor, in the larger libraries, have not resulted in any such discoveries.

The main interest, however, in connection with weather-lore is to determine whether they do or do not correctly represent the relationship of the animals mentioned to the given condition of the weather. In other words, is the zoology of the weather-lore misrepresented or not? I am forced to declare that, as a rule, those who by virtue of their ingenuity framed these rhymes and brief sayings did not correctly interpret Nature.

Very many of the early English settlers were, no doubt, excellent observers; but they appear, at times, to have more desired to be looked upon as weather prophets than as naturalists, and strove to have glib nonsense sayings pass current as evidence of their wisdom instead of taking pains to correctly interpret the course of Nature and determine the relation of animal life to its environment.

Often, during my rambles in the neighborhood, I have questioned the few remaining descendants of the original settlers concerning the local weather proverbs, and I find the impression is still prevalent that the purport of all these sayings is substantially correct, and therefore, to a great degree, that my neighbors are laboring under erroneous impressions. "Is there not wisdom in a multitude of counsellors?" they ask; and I, standing alone, am voted the fool, while they pose as sages.

Let us consider this weather-lore, bit by bit, as I have gathered it from time to time, and discuss its merits, if it possess any, and also its absurdities.

Of such sayings as refer to our domestic animals, the following are the most noteworthy. Of the cow, I have heard it said:

"When a cow tries to scratch its ear,
It means a shower is very near;"

and again—

> "When it thumps its ribs with its tail,
> Look out for thunder, lightning, hail."

As is now pretty well known, a short time before a shower in summer there is often a highly electrical condition of the atmosphere, which makes all animals more or less uneasy. Therefore, the lashing of the tail, if not merely to brush away flies, may refer to this uneasiness, and so, too, the ears may be more sensitive than the general surface of the body. This is a probable explanation, but, after all, it is not proved that the cow at such a time suffers as much from it as is supposed; nor is it easy to see how the flagellation of a very insignificant part of the body can ease a painful sensation common to the entire surface. On the other hand, it is certain that flies and other troublesome insects are sensitive to atmospheric changes, even a slight lowering of the temperature, such as no mammal would appreciate; and for an hour or two before a shower, for this reason, they congregate in extraordinary numbers about animals—horses and cows particularly. I have thought that they seek the cows for warmth when the air suddenly cools; and is it not more than probable that the nervousness on the part of the animal, shown by frantic efforts to scratch its ears with its hind-feet and the lashing of its tail, has to do with the excess of irritation caused by innumerable flies, and not with any unusual electrical titillation? If so, the cow's action is still indicative of an approaching change in the weather, and so far may be claimed as a sign of such change; but the connection of the two facts is not such a one as is usually given. It is an indirect, not direct, indication of the prophesied rain-storm. But bearing heavily on the subject is the unquestionable fact that an unusual number of flies often suddenly make their appearance, and torment cattle almost beyond endurance, during the four or six weeks of drought which in summer, early or late, we are so sure to have. In such cases the signs fail. I have asked many a farmer how this could be, and the one reply that I have received in every case is that "there was a shower in the neighborhood." It usually happened, however, that the neighborhood was as parched as we were, and, seeing the signs fail with them, they were covetous of the shower they supposed that we had had. Perhaps it is with such indications of changes in the weather as it has been said of autumnal proofs of the character of the approaching winter. Miles Overfield once remarked, "When the signs get to failin' 'long in the fall, there'll be no tellin' about the winter."

Of pigs I have heard it said, very frequently,

> "When swine carry sticks,
> The clouds will play tricks;"

but that—

> "When they lie in the mud,
> No fears of a flood."

The first of these couplets is of twofold interest. I have watched them for years, to see what purport this carrying of sticks and bunches of grass might have, and have only learned that it has nothing whatever to do with the weather, or at least with coming rain-storms. The drought of summer is so far a convenience as to throw light upon this habit, as it did upon the uneasy cows. Pigs carry sticks as frequently then as during wet weather, or just preceding a shower. Furthermore, these gathered twigs are not brought together as though to make a nest, but are scattered about in a perfectly aimless manner. From some cause, the animal is uneasy, and takes this curious method of relieving itself. The probabilities are that it is a survival of some habit common to swine in their feral condition, just as we see a dog turn about half a dozen times before lying down.

In an interesting paper on local weather-lore, read by Mr. Amos W. Butler before the American Association for the Advancement of Science, during the Philadelphia meeting of 1884, the author has another version of this saying: "When hogs gather up sticks and carry them about, expect cold weather." This is wholly at variance with what I have observed, for my memoranda record this habit almost wholly during the hot weather, and this must necessarily be the rule with New Jersey swine, or the local weather prophets would not have coined the verse as I have given it.

As to the other couplet, it is about as near meaningless as any saying can well be. Some rustic rhymer, a century ago, may have added it as a piece of fun, but it has stuck most persistently. As it stands now, it has stood for quite one hundred years.

In reference to the dog, I have heard the following more pretentious stanza, which has now taken its place among our nursery rhymes, where, indeed, it is best fitted to remain:

> "When drowsy dogs start from their sleep,
> And bark at empty space,
> 'Tis not a dream that prompts them to,
> But showers come on apace."

Here we have essentially the same inference as in that of the rhyme about cows, but it is not to be explained away so readily. Such acts, as described, cannot be attributed to annoyance by flies, for they, too, often emerge from dark quarters, where they have been unmolested; but the all-important fact must not be overlooked that such acts are not confined to summer. If they were, the electrical theory might be advanced with some confidence. From what I have noticed in such dogs as I have owned, the habit of dreaming, which in the rhyme is denied to be the explanation, is probably the key to the mystery. Again, statistics show that the correspondence between such habits and sudden showers is only what we should expect in the way of coincidences. Dogs certainly are not to be considered as reliable barometers.

The same may be said of the domestic cat. Its movements have all been carefully noted, and the yawning, stretching, scratching, and waving of the tail appear to have been accredited with some special meteorological significance. Careful observation has not confirmed any of these impressions. Table-legs are scratched time and again by Tom or Tabby, and no rain falls for twenty-four or forty-eight hours. They stretch themselves after a nap, lick their sides and wash their faces, with the same regularity in midwinter as in midsummer, yet it is only showers, and not snow-storms, which these actions are supposed to predict.

When in summer the signs fail, my country friends conveniently forget the remark they have made; but, if the day does prove showery, my non-combative neighbors take much delight in repeating over and over again, "I told thee so," with a suggestive emphasis, showing how much, like other people, they love to gain a victory if open warfare can be avoided.

The only weather rhyme referring to a cat that I have heard, and which is essentially the same as that about dogs, runs thus:

> "When Tabby claws the table-legs,
> She for a summer shower begs."

That is, begs it will hurry, with no doubt in her mind of its possibly disappointing her.

The weather-lore of the commoner wild animals is of much more general interest. Weather sayings referring to animals do not appear to have been so numerous as are those referring to birds. I have been able to learn of but three examples. In reference to minks and weasels, I have heard it said—and possibly others may be familiar with this mystic rhyme—

> "When storm-winds blow and night is black,
> The farmer may a pullet lack;
> But if the moon is shining clear,
> No mink or weasel dares come near."

This involves an interesting phase of the life history of these animals; for while they probably can see a little when it is quite dark, and are safely guided by the sense of smell, nevertheless, the experience of trappers about home proves that they do wander about during moonlight nights. Indeed, on careful inquiry, it seems that the trapper generally anticipates better success during the moonlit nights than when it is very dark. I strongly suspect that the truth lies in the fact that when it is dark and stormy the watchful house-dog is not on the alert, and thus the cunning weasel or mink is free to raid upon the poultry-house and feast upon the pullet that it seizes. How my neighbors will take to this explanation I can only surmise. Like other people, they fight vigorously for the opinions they have cherished through life. The musk-rat and gray squirrels have given rise to many trite sayings, and have long been looked upon as weather prophets, but that they are nothing of the sort I have elsewhere * endeavored to show.

The following may or may not be a local saying:

"When flying-squirrels run on ground,
The clouds 'll pass you by, be bound."

What this may mean has been a question with me for a long time. It is a common remark, either in this or a simpler form, and many who have little faith in pigs or dogs as weather prophets build largely upon the habits of the flying-squirrel. The saying itself implies that a drought exists at the time that these animals frequent the ground rather than the trees, coming, of course,

---

* "Rambles about Home," p. 73. New York: D. Appleton & Co., 1884.

thereto, in order to find food. If the saying be true, the summer food of the flying-squirrel must be more plentiful on the ground than in the tops of the tallest trees. What that food is exactly, I am not aware; nor have I had any opportunity to verify the statement that flying-squirrels frequent the ground during "dry spells." Those that I have seen near home are so strictly crepuscular that only the initial movements of their nocturnal journeys are readily traced; but, whenever I have seen them sally from their retreats, it was to take a tree-top route for several rods and then to be lost to sight. Take the year through, it is probable that they seldom come to the ground to forage. When they do so, is it an evidence of continued dry weather? I can neither contradict nor affirm; but are not the probabilities against such being the case?

Speaking of the opossum, it is said that if found in autumn in hollow trees rather than occupying a burrow in the ground, the winter will be milder.

This seems to be very reasonable, and would pass admirably as a weather sign, but for one unfortunate circumstance. While you may find one or more in a tree, your neighbor may find as many in the ground. I have known this to be the case more than once. Under these circumstances, meet your neighbor at the line-fence and compare notes. What about the winter?

From their greater abundance and never-failing presence, it might be thought that the weather-lore of birds would be much more elaborate than that referring to other classes of animals; but my observations do not confirm this. There is simply a greater number of sayings current, and fully one-half are too trivial to repeat. It would seem as if a weather-lore possibly of Indian origin and referring to birds then abundant, but now wholly wanting, was current more than a century ago. These sayings were subsequently applied to other species, nearly or more remotely allied, and whatever meaning they may originally have had has been lost; but the apparent absurdity of such "proverbs," as now used, seems never to have occurred to those who repeat them.

That the dusting of chickens, cackling of geese, and the "pot-racking" of Guinea-hens have not given rise to an elaborate series of weather proverbs is, I think, surprising. The only familiar reference to the chicken heard about home is that the rooster, crowing at night, says, "Christmas—coming—on!" It does appear that the midnight crowing of cocks is more frequently heard in December than in June; but, so far as the meaning is concerned, it unfortunately happens that the nocturnal crowing is as often heard in January as in December. Calling attention to this, I was once gravely assured that the cocks crew differently then, and said, "Christmas—come—and—gone!" I accepted the explanation. This is not a weather matter, but is not irrelevant, as it shows how very common it once was to couple any unusual occurrence with something sooner or later to happen, and therefore, in the matter of weather especially, to claim it as prophetic of that event.

Of the examples of weather-lore of birds, the following are not uncommonly heard in Central New

2*

Jersey. Of the cardinal-grosbeak, or winter redbird, it is said:

> "The redbird lies, without regret:
> However dry, it whistles 'wet!'"

That is, the bird is credited with knowing it will not rain, and teases the farmer by singing "wet" in his ears all day. Others put another meaning on the redbird's note, and claim it to be a sure sign of rain. This is more like the ordinary sayings commonly heard, and let us give it a moment's consideration. At present, the time of year when the cardinal-birds sing least is during the hot summer months. Not that they are absolutely mute for even a few days at a time, but relatively so as compared with their joyous strains through autumn and winter; and again, early in summer, when they are nesting, these birds, like robins, are more apt to sing directly after a shower than at any other time.

So much for the gay cardinal as a weather prophet. The rare summer redbird—a tanager—which also utters a whistling note, well described by the syllable "wet," shortly and sharply expressed, is likewise said to prophesy rain. The probabilities are that the note of the redbird, cardinal and summer, suggesting the word "wet," has given rise to the belief that their utterance was a sign of a coming shower or storm. It is often by such illogical methods that these sayings have become established. After a few repetitions they become fixed in the mind and their origin forgotten; they are invested with an importance not their due, and not attributed to them by their originators. Ultimately they are incorporated in the weather-lore of the country.

Of the innumerable swallows, it is said, with as little show of reason,

> "No rain e'er poured upon the earth
> That damped the twittering swallow's mirth."

No? Well, of late, the whole host takes refuge from storms — the barn-swallows in the hay-mow, the cliff-swallows under the eaves, the sand-martins in their burrows, and the chimney-swifts in their sooty homes in the chimneys. Why this change of habit? For a wonderful change must have taken place, if the couplet quoted was ever true. I do admit that swallows and swifts appear to be noisier before and during a shower; but does not this arise from the fact that at such a time they collect in great numbers near their nests, to take refuge, if the storm should increase in violence? And again, the silence of other birds makes the twittering swallow a more prominent bird than under other circumstances; but nothing of this warrants the extravagant assertion that no storm ever put a quietus upon them.

The larger hawks, too, are supposed to give warning of a coming shower when they utter their peculiar cat-like scream. Among our old people the following may sometimes be heard repeated:

> "The hen-hawk's scream, at hot, high noon,
> Foretells a coming shower soon."

This couplet is of some interest, as, at present, it is not applicable to our larger hawks and buzzards. Indeed, the only one of them that is prone to cry out while circling overhead is the red-tailed buzzard or hen-hawk, and this bird is very seldom seen in midsummer, and now certainly is only heard in autumn, winter, or early spring. The saying implies that formerly these birds were abundant at all times of the year, and during the summer would cry out in their peculiar fashion. The settlement of the country and general deforesting of such a large portion of it have driven these hawks to more retired parts during the nesting season, and there, throughout summer, their cry may indicate that it will soon rain; but, if so, why does not the same cry in autumn have some reference to the weather?

It is scarcely necessary to continue the list. Other birds than those mentioned — reptiles, batrachians, and fishes — have all given rise to certain current sayings, but of no more value than those I have given, and all, I think, based upon illogical inferences. Snakes are claimed as excellent barometers; but the habits upon which the belief rests are those that characterize every day of the creature's life. Toads and frogs are largely depended upon, but a careful record for a single season will show how little they are to be trusted; and even the fishes cannot disport themselves in summer, but straightway the clouds must open upon us, a tornado visit us, or premature frosts balk the calculations of the farmer.

Curiously enough, I do not find that insect-life has entered to any important extent into the weather-lore of this neighborhood. Contradictory remarks are often made as to ant-hills: thus, when they are very high, it will be a dry day; others insist that it is evidence that it will soon rain. Spiders' webs, also, are variously held as of barometric value; but a careful record of several summers contradicts this emphatically. The positions of the paper-hornets' nests, which in autumn are often prominent objects in the country, after the foliage drops, are variously asserted to be indicative of a "hard" or "open" winter, as they chance to be placed in the upper or lower branches of a tree. My scepticism as to the value of this sign arises from the fact that there is, as might be expected, no uniformity in the positions of any half-dozen such nests.

It may be rash to say that meteorological science can gain nothing from scientific observation of animal life; but the character of the weather-lore that has been handed down from father to son for the past two centuries plainly indicates that the observations which gave rise to them were anything but scientific in character. Mankind now, as formerly, may be close observers of Nature, but this does not imply that they are accurate observers. They assume as correct the appearance, but it is no unusual circumstance for an animal to be doing the very opposite of what might naturally be supposed was the case. The simple and sad fact derived from a study of local animal weather-lore is that, in the days of our grandfathers, painstaking naturalists were few and far between.

Reaching my boat, in which musk-rats had been carousing during the night, I pushed it very cautiously from the shore, desiring to disturb no creature that might be lingering on the bank of the creek.

I had gone but a little way, and seeing some new bird at every boat-length, I could not but go slowly, when I came to an abrupt bend of the stream, and extending eastward through a little forest was Doctor's Creek, as my neighbors have it, but known in the past century, as it should be still, as Buzzard's Rest.

Venerable birches and towering hickories, as if jealous of the stream that flows at their feet, bend lovingly over it, and combat every summer sunbeam that seeks to gild the sluggish waters.

As I turned the boat's prow from the main creek and entered the Rest, the silence was profound. The name, as in days of old, proved, to-day, to be aptly chosen. A score of gorged and listless vultures were sitting in the upper branches of the trees.

The most prominent object at the mouth of this tributary creek is a magnificent birch, measuring something more than two feet in diameter. It leans over the water at about an angle of forty-five degrees. The largest of its branches are strangely angular, and at once attract attention. In this feature of angularity they recall the crooked hornbeams of Linden Bend.

Beyond this tree, but still distinctly in view, are other equally large birches, one of which, now dead, leans over the water in a nearly horizontal position. One fancies these trees, collectively, the rafters of an enormous roof, that once shut in the valley.

Buzzard's Rest is a favorite haunt of the kingfishers, and seldom a half-hour passes without their harsh cries disturbing the quiet of this secluded corner.

This bird is considered strictly migratory, and possibly, a century or more ago, came and went with the regularity of our summer songsters; but since I have known them, a few are sure to be found wintering in every little valley through which a fish-stream runs. When the brooks are frozen, the bird is cunning enough to search for air-holes, and if the opening in the ice be a yard in width, will plunge into it, secure its prey, and emerge in safety. Occasionally, the kingfisher would sadly miscalculate its bearings, and coming up under the ice be drowned. This was the fate of one that lived throughout the winter in the shed covering an old-fashioned water-wheel. This bird in some way learned that the fish collected in a deep pool behind the waters of the dam, and continually passed through the broad sheet of falling water when foraging there. After passing a pleasant winter, it forsook the dam for the mill-pond, and was caught under a cake of floating ice, that covered but a small portion of the pond's surface.

The miller told me that this kingfisher soon became quite tame, after winter set in, and delighted to sit on the sill of a south window of the wheel-shed. When the wheel was stopped, the kingfisher often sat close to the edge of the pool beneath, watching the minnows, but was not able to capture any, as the depth of the water was not sufficient to allow the bird to dive. Several times the miller caught a number of the fish and placed them in very conspicuous places, but the kingfisher did not appear even to notice them; and the miller was very positive that none were eaten.

Another and very different bird that constantly frequents these overhanging birches, is the little green heron. When this lively little wader thoughtfully promenades the broad branches, and at times stops to gaze intently at the water beneath, a charm is lent to this romantic spot. Other species of this family of birds are usually found here, the night-herons particularly; and years ago, as certain old records show, the banks and shallows of the creek were "spotted gray and white with birds like unto storks." Then, as now, these conspicuous birds found the proximity of the forest to their feeding grounds conducive to their safety.

It is natural for those inexperienced in observing birds, to suppose that the branches and foliage of a tree would afford but little if any protection to a bird as large as a night-heron, standing as it does fully two feet in height, and having a bulky, conspicuously colored body. As a matter of fact, when it is perched in a tall tree, it seems to study the effect of light and shade, and remaining quite motionless, is difficult to detect. I believe my eyesight is better than that of most people, and yet I have more than once spent fully half an hour in determining the precise position of a cunning heron that so "mingled" with the branches and leaves of a beech, that it seemed a part of the tree in which it stood.

After a few weeks of field observation, it will be readily admitted by all, that the majority of birds have a well defined color sense. Of course it will not be apparent if the birds are not disturbed, but it becomes evident when they are pursued, unless they seek to escape by a protracted flight. Often I have known small birds, that from some cause, such as nesting, were averse to leaving a particular spot, to drop to the ground and barely escape being trodden upon, while I was craning my neck and scanning every twig of the tree or bush upon which I supposed them to be sitting. This is a trick of species haunting shrubbery that took me several years to discover.

While it so happened that no kingfisher or heron rested on any of the trees, there was a host of smaller birds, yellow warblers and mottled tree-creepers being noticeably abundant. I was much struck with the indifference of these birds to the proximity of the vultures. They hunted for insects on the very branches whereon the latter were sitting, and often were within a dozen feet of them. They had evidently learned to discriminate between them and birds of prey. Their fearlessness brought to mind the young poultry that I carefully observed some months previously. Under the pines in my yard, clucking hens had been guiding to the best scratchings their broods of quarter-grown chicks, while above them the busy grakles had been passing two and fro all day long. Never for a moment did the chickens regard them. Their shadows darted, like swallows, across the sunlit sward, yet never a chick started as this trick of light and shade crossed and recrossed its path.

Once, while watching them, a sly sparrow-hawk darted from tree to tree, and its shadow at once caused every chick to cower, even before the mother-hen uttered her warning cluck. I am convinced these chickens saw a difference in that shadow, and caught no glimpse of the bird.

I suppose the difference between harmless species and birds of prey is taught their young by the parent birds, and argues well for the mental capabilities of the former, that so early in life they can discriminate between the shadows of hawks and grakles, as is certainly true of them.

Among wild birds, an interesting instance of this is that all birds at once recognize the fish-hawk. Chickens do not, at first, but after a week or two appear also to recognize the difference between this bird and the true falcons. The fact that small birds of many species often nest in the immediate vicinity of the fish-hawk's home-tree clearly proves this fact. The vast quantities of insects attracted by the remains of fish scattered about a fish-hawk's nest make the spot attractive to fly-catchers of many kinds, and there they are pretty sure to congregate.

When my boat was directly beneath the turkey-buzzards, as these true vultures are generally called—a position that is quite undesirable, let it be known—they lazily flapped their enormous wings, and after something of a struggle were fairly afloat upon the upper air. They gave, I think, about twenty quick strokes of the wings before they were as many feet above the tree-tops. Then, one that I noticed particularly, with apparently unmoved wings soared steadily upward at an angle of forty-five degrees against the wind, which was very gentle at the time. The others gradually arose to a great height by circling, or rather by describing a broad spiral course.

The common impression prevailing in this neighborhood is, that turkey-buzzards will eat, in fact are fond of, decayed cabbages. It is true, apparently, that tho odor arising from a field planted with this vegetable, when once they have commenced to wilt, attracts these filthy feeders; but that they really do more than visit the locality is improbable. Nevertheless, I do not subscribe to the view that these birds are guided by an acute sense of smell to their unsavory food. Whenever opportunity has offered, I have sought for information on this point, and the result has invariably been to lead me to conclude that sight, not smell, was the guiding sense. In no instance has the result of any of my observations or experiments been susceptible of any other explanation than that of acute vision, and not astonishingly acute either. It is a significant fact that in midwinter, when far less odor arises from dead animals than in summer, and none at all for much of the time, the few buzzards that remain with us find their food quite as readily as in July and August. In one instance, a carcass of a sheep, uncovered by the drifting of snow, was quickly discovered by them, because the body lay in full relief against a nearly black background; but another carcass, equally uncovered, but lying upon snow, was not seen, although the buzzards passed directly over it, and but a few rods distant.

It is hard to believe that one of these vultures can see a sheep at a distance of a mile or more, as is undoubtedly true; but this is easier than to accept the statement that they can smell it even at half that distance. If they depend upon their sense of smell, it is only during seven or eight months in the year. In winter their sense of sight must practically do the whole work. If equal to the task for a part of the year, why not for all time?

A marked feature of this beautiful spot, and one that to-day affected the sense of smell no less decidedly than that of sight, was the tangle of grape-vines that cover even the underbrush, and no less often reach to the very tops of the tallest trees. This vigorous vine and the Virginia-creeper strive for every available space to which to cling, and often both intwine the main stem of a towering oak and encumber half its branches. The poor tree has a hard time of it, and often becomes but a mere prop for these rank growths. My attention was particularly called to one enormous grape-vine, not only by its remarkable girth, but by the abundance of its fruit, for the penetrating heat of August sunshine distilled the aromatic essence from the ripening grapes and caused the air to be heavy laden with a sickening sweet.

I wonder that grape-vines have not given rise to "fish-stories," and I sincerely trust my reference to the vine near Buzzard's Rest will not induce others to bring about such a practice. This vine, it may be briefly stated, is a foot in circumference at the ground and for some distance beyond, and is something more than one hundred yards long.

This vine extends directly upward but five feet, when it turns at a right angle for the same distance, and then reaches upward, backward, and downward, "to the place of beginning," as they say in deeds. Then it grows directly upward to the very highest branches of a swamp white-oak, a distance of forty feet from the ground. Having secured itself there, the vine returns for a dozen feet or so, and then crosses a clear space of thirteen yards and climbs about another oak still taller than the first. Then seeking the largest trees, it threads its way on and on through the little woods, until its ultimate fibres are lost among the countless twigs of twenty tree-tops. I have said it is one hundred yards long. I do not mean that this is its actual length. I could measure this much with approximate accuracy, and there was yet more, hopelessly beyond my reach.

Imagine some great flood that stranded a rope-walk here, and you can conceive how such a grape-vine looks among the trees. How it crossed from tree to tree and cleared open spaces where nothing but low shrubbery has grown, since the vine started on its erratic wanderings, I leave the reader to conjecture.

Leaving it, finally, in all its tangled glory, I hunted long for birds'-nests of the past summer, but found none; and only by chance, as I was withdrawing from the "Rest," did I see a nest of the yellow-throated vireo, thirty or more feet above the water.

This fine songster always builds quite out of reach, so far as the egg-hunting small boy is concerned, and is disposed to return to the same situation, summer after summer, to rear its brood. In a maple-tree in the lane, at home, the same individuals have for four summers built their nest. It is not the same nest, repaired year after year, but a new structure on the same or an adjacent limb. I say purposely the same individuals, for I am convinced that very many of our birds remain mated longer than a single season. This is a matter worthy of most careful study, and I was glad to find a correspondent of a scientific periodical remarking that, while "it is generally taken for granted that our song-birds and migrants are in the habit of seeking mates every season, and not keeping to the same mate year after year," he believes "that almost if not quite all birds are fairly constant in their attachments."

To determine whether most or even a proportion of our birds are permanently mated or but for a season, requires so great an amount of patient observation that it is not surprising the subject has been practically neglected. A chance occurrence, years ago, called my attention to this subject, and I commenced, at that time, a series of observations, which have been repeated during each of the succeeding summers. While by no means what I wished, I have, probably, gathered sufficient material to, at least, warrant calling attention to the subject, especially as the remarks in "Science Gossip," quoted above, are likely to bring the subject prominently before active, out-door ornithologists.

The birds that I have studied, in hopes of reaching a satisfactory conclusion, were all land birds; and these may be separated, for convenience of study, into two classes, Resident species and Summer migrants.

Of sixteen resident species of birds, my observations show that during the whole year the sexes remain together; and of these sixteen only three—the crow, purple grakle, and cedar-bird—are gregarious. Of course, in the latter case, it is impossible to determine whether the mated pairs of the early summer remain together or not, associated as they are with other pairs; but certainly there is no more reason why permanently mated birds should not form flocks than that individuals or unmated birds should do so. It is, furthermore, highly improbable that any antagonism should arise between the sexes after the nesting season. There is certainly no confliction of interests. If there existed such anatomical differences as made one sex decidedly weaker than the other, then post-nuptual habits acquired by the stronger sex might draw them away from the others, and an absolute separation, for a time, result; but this is not the case in any one of the sixteen birds I have had under observation.

In the case of crows, I believe I have never found a strictly isolated nest. There have always been others quite near, and usually five to ten pairs build in such proximity that each pair is more or less associated with all the others. When the young leave the nest, they remain with their parents and neighbors, and the little colony, now perhaps treble the original number, remain associated until October, when they are lost in the large flocks formed by the uniting of scores of small colonies. During the nesting season, each bird could distinguish his or her mate from a dozen or more individuals; so why not from a thousand? And when the nesting season returned, why should not the mated birds of a past year renew the labors of nest-building and the rearing of their young? The old sites are revisited, and every action is indicative of familiarity with the locality. To say, each spring, these are not the crows of last year, is merely to assume it, and that often against evidence to the contrary.

It must be borne in mind, too, that it is the female bird that decides upon the locality for the nest. She it is who returns to her home of the past summer; and her mate is sure to be found attending upon her. If, after hundreds of miles of winter wanderings, the female crow can unerringly return to her abandoned nest, or to the tree upon which it rested, which is unquestionably true, what improbability is there in her being joined by her mate, even though for months they have been separated; a circumstance, indeed, that probably but rarely occurs.

A word here concerning the English rook. Richard Jefferies, in one of his charming essays, remarks: " The general idea is that they pair in February, but there are some reasons for thinking that the rooks, in fact, choose their mates at the end of the preceding summer. They are then in large flocks, and if only casually glanced at, appear mixed together without any order or arrangement. They move on the ground and fly in the air so close, one beside the other, that at the first glance or so you cannot distinguish them apart. Yet if you should be lingering along the by-ways of the fields as the acorns fall, and the leaves come rustling down in the warm, sunny, autumn afternoons, and keep an observant eye upon the rooks in the trees, or on the fresh-turned furrows, they will be seen to act in couples. On the ground couples alight near each other, on the trees they perch near each other, and in the air fly side by side. . . . After the nest time is over they flock together, and each family of three or four flies in concert. Later on they apparently choose their own particular friends, *that is, the young birds do so.* All through the winter, after, say October, *these pairs keep together*, though lost in the general mass to the passing spectator." The same can truthfully be said, I think, of our purple grakle, a bird that in many ways resembles the rook.

Until birds are marked, it may not be possible to prove them permanently mated, but I venture to assert that the general impression of such as will take the trouble to study particularly our resident birds for several years, will coincide with my own, that courtship and marriage are not repeated, year after year, with the regularity of the coming and going of the seasons.

The same may be said of the common cedar-bird. This species is peculiar in that it is permanently gregarious. During the breeding season, which is often as late as July and August, the several pairs forming each flock breed at the same time, and with the nests quite near each other. In one instance, I found two nests upon one tree, and on each of five trees, but a rod or two distant, a single nest. This sociability is maintained during the five or six weeks that they are held in one locality by the care of their offspring; and when the latter are ready to leave the nest, they remain with their parents.

If such small flocks, of not more than twenty or thirty, were not permanently mated, there would be quarrelling continually among them, unless it always happened that in every one of them there were an equal number of each sex. If the flocks were made up in any hap-hazard manner, as is probably the case with the enormous gatherings of red-winged blackbirds, an excess of one sex over the other would probably result, and a general breaking up of all such gatherings, late in the winter or in early spring, would necessarily result; but the smaller flocks of cedar-birds, that have kept so closely together from November to May, do not disperse, and a general stampede for wives and husbands takes place. All contention upon this point is among themselves, and the small proportion of unmated birds, common to gregarious or non-gregarious species, either remain in single blessedness for a season, or join other communities where mates are to be had.

In this case, as in that of crows, it is necessarily a matter of probabilities, not demonstrable facts; but when we come to consider the following non-gregarious species, we are treading upon firmer ground.

It is a somewhat significant fact that birds are very seldom seen alone; and if we do chance to come across a single individual of one species, it is pretty sure to be in the company of other kinds of birds. To meet with a bird that is strictly alone, even in the late autumn or winter, when birds have no thoughts of nesting, is the very rarest occurrence I have noted during many years of rambling.

Prominent among our resident birds is the familiar bluebird. Since 1874 I have recorded them thirty four hundred times, and when not in loose flocks, there was always at least a pair, and flying in such close company it was evident that they had mutual interests, whether it happened to be December or May. Of their nests I have examined seventy-three, and fifty-five of them were built, year after year, in six different localities. One hole in an apple-tree was certainly occupied by the same pair for five successive summers. The male bird was readily recognized by a peculiarity in the plumage.

As both he and his mate remained during the year, and in stormy weather often took shelter in the old nest, it is simply absurd to suppose these bluebirds separated at any time of the year, and the male formed a new connection. Indeed, there was never more than a week passed that the pair were not seen together.

The common thistle-finch, or yellow-bird, is always found in pairs, or more generally in small companies. They are as gregarious in summer as in winter, and their nests are often near together. Even if it cannot be shown that they remain mated, there is certainly no dissociation of the sexes at any time.

The equally abundant bay-winged sparrow (the vesper-bird) is a peculiarly resident species. They do not appear to wander at any time from the limited quarters of some field of a few acres. Where they nest they live; and whether in June or January, it matters not, the pair are ever in close companionship.

. The more social song-sparrows apparently remained paired. Scores of couples, that were found breeding, have been subsequently observed from week to week, and the relief from the care of their offspring did not result in the parents parting company.

The crested titmouse proved a much more difficult bird to study, because of its wandering tendencies. During eight months of the year they are very abundant, and, I think, always in the company of their own kind. During nidification, and through July and August, these birds are seemingly much less abundant, but the fact is, they are unnoticed, because quite silent, as compared with the same birds in autumn and winter.

"A noisy tit is Jack Frost's trumpeter," and there is a grain of truth in this weather proverb. Like bluebirds they build their nests in holes in trees, and the same locality is occupied several summers in succession. The association of the sexes during the winter is adduced as plausible evidence that no divorcement and re-mating occur. I have positive knowledge that, as in the case of bluebirds, the locality where nesting occurred was frequently revisited during the year, and occupied as a shelter from severe snow-storms in midwinter.

Since the above concerning crested titmice was written, I have had an opportunity of closely observing a pair of these birds while constructing a nest. Barely ten paces from my study-windows stands an aged locust, with a great cavernous hollow in its trunk some six feet from the ground. On the 18th of April, 1886, I saw a pair of tits flitting to and fro among the branches of the tree, and occasionally entering the hollow trunk. The weather was very warm and spring-like. These birds remained much of the time about the tree until the 24th, but did not commence building a nest until that day. I could not positively determine the matter, but think the male only carried the materials from the adjacent hill-side and garden to the tree, and the female arranged them. While the male bird was thus employed he sang incessantly. This work of gathering materials for a nest continued, with some irregularity, until May 2d, when the birds disappeared. Ten days later, the tits were again about the tree, and remained until evening; since when I have seen nothing of them.

They were not disturbed, but left the neighborhood, after so much labor, voluntarily. I mention this instance, and it is not an unusual one, to show that for weeks before they finally settle down to rear a family these birds are mated, and if for weeks prior to nidification, why not for a much longer period?

I am quite sure that during the winter they were seen in pairs as frequently as singly; and their predilection for hollow trees, at all times, suggests that like pigeon-woodpeckers, they often prepare nesting places which, before completion or directly after, are permanently abandoned.

It is impossible to believe that such a sentiment as Platonic friendship ever entered the mind of any species of bird.

The Carolina wren affords a most striking instance of birds remaining mated from one year to another. I have had a pair of these birds under almost daily observation for two years, and it matters not what the season may be, there was never more than a week passed that the pair were not seen together. They commence nesting in April and raise four broods.

A pair of cardinal-grosbeaks were found nesting, June, 1883, and the female was readily distinguished by a peculiarity in the coloring of her wings. The pair remained in the locality during the succeeding winter, nested in the old site in 1884, and in 1885 chose a new position in a thicket of smilax a few yards distant. This pair of redbirds were always associated during the two winters that I had them under observation.

Meadow-larks, if not in loose flocks, as though two or

three broods were united, are always in pairs, and there is every appearance of their close companionship during the winter. I have hundreds of references, in my note-books, to single pairs frequenting certain fields the year through.

I can speak less positively of blue-jays, as my opportunities for close observation have been fewer; but the important fact is known that, when they are no longer nesting, they often remain associated in pairs, and jointly occupy some cunningly chosen roosting-place in a hollow tree or barn; and further, that occasionally they have a brood as early as March is at least presumptive evidence that some of these birds are mated for a longer period than a single summer.

The flicker or pigeon-woodpecker offers an interesting example of permanent mating among birds. They are usually found in pairs or small flocks; and it is not uncommon for a pair to jointly peck a deep, commodious nest in a tree late in autumn or in midwinter. These nests are never used, that I am aware of; but as they are the result of joint labors of a pair, it is quite impossible that a few weeks later they should separate and form new ties.

The two owls—the little red and the barnowl—are found to occupy their nests in hollow trees long after the young have sought homes of their own; and in the case of the barnowls, so strongly attached do they become to a chosen tree, that when either bird is captured or killed the widower or widow will soon find another companion, and continue in the old home, indifferent to the fact of its being associated in the mind of the bird with its partner's death. Indeed, I am sorry to conclude, that grief at the loss of a mate is of very short duration usually, notwithstanding there is so much evidence of their faithfulness to marriage vows during their lives.

The familiar little sparrow-hawk finally offers a striking instance of permanent bird-marriage. A pair of these pretty falcons have for five years nested near the residence of a neighbor, and when the labor of rearing their young was ended, they retired to the shelter afforded by the projecting eaves of my neighbor's house, and there remained until the following spring. These birds were quite as affectionate and mutually considerate in winter, as when they had the common interest of offspring to keep them together.

Dr. Brewer says of the winter falcon, "These hawks remain mated throughout the year, and their affectionate treatment of each other is in striking contrast with the selfish indifference of the Red-tail species when their breeding season is ended."

In the case of our game birds and others that are subject to great persecution, the chances are, of course, against both parents surviving until the following breeding season. It is quite possible that such a state of constant change results in blunting the affections, and the association of the sexes becomes a mere matter of temporary gratification, something akin to, but not so gross as the habits of the cowpen-bird, which is never mated, and for several months in the year deposits fertile eggs in the nests of other birds, and sometimes in empty nests, long after the birds who built them had reared their broods and departed.

Polygamy among certain of our birds is unquestionable. I have positive knowledge of this among quails, and, probably, purple grakles; and it is well known to be true of that introduced pest, the European sparrow. This much married condition, whatever the cause that has given rise to it, continues from year to year, when occurring among crows, as I have proved by patient observation extending over several years. I cannot speak positively with reference to the quails; but it is certainly true of the sparrow mentioned.

When we come to consider the summer visitors, or such species as, wintering in the south, appear in New Jersey late in April or in May and remain until autumn, there is abundant evidence that a considerable proportion of them are permanently mated. Details of many long series of observations are scarcely necessary. Suffice it to say, that I have very carefully studied songthrushes, brown thrushes, cat-birds, chats, house-wrens, indigo-birds, vireos of three species, and others, and that the same individuals reappeared from year to year, in one instance for eight years, I am fully convinced. It is, indeed, hard to realize that many of these birds should remain together for so long a time, when but a small part of each year is spent in the rearing of the brood. It is quite possible that they do not retire to other portions of our country in company; but it does appear that they part with a mutual understanding to meet again when separations do take place. It is not simply the same male bird or the same female that reappears spring after spring, but the same pair of birds.

In conclusion, let me call attention to a few points

bearing upon this subject. All who have been accustomed to study birds in their native haunts have noticed the many marked individual characteristics of each species. One soon becomes not only familiar with wrens as wrens and cat-birds as cat-birds, but he recognizes individuals among them, and the wren that nests in a box near by, erected for his accommodation, very soon learns the difference between the occupants of a house who never disturb him or his, and a stranger of whom he will at first be distrustful. I do not think I am putting this matter too strongly.

Remembering the individuality of a pair of wrens or cat-birds, we can be pretty sure whether or not they are the same pairs, from year to year, that come to our bird-boxes or the thicket.

Again, marked peculiarities in the construction of nests, if repeated year after year, as is sometimes the case, suggests, to say the least, that the builders of such nests are the same individuals.

Another consideration is the remarkably prompt appearance of migratory birds at their former nesting sites. Not merely in the same neighborhood, but near the same tree, bush, or hollow in the ground; and a marked disposition to remain there, and particularly to roost there until nesting begins. This is especially true of the Baltimore oriole, which I have often found, at dawn of the day of his arrival, examining the remains of last year's nest, and have seen him commence repairs that same day when the structure permitted it. His mate is usually but a few hours later, contrary statements notwithstanding; and the arrival of Madam Oriole was not celebrated by any billing and cooing. They were plainly "old married folks" before they came.

Of course, in the lives of young birds, there comes a time when the mingled joys and sorrows of courtship must be undergone, and curious scenes are yearly to be witnessed. These frantic efforts to secure the smiles of some fair one have been elaborately detailed by many ornithologists, and it has been inferred that the same ordeal must yearly be repeated; but in very many more instances than has been supposed, I believe the very opposite of this to be true.

Having brought my boat again to the main creek, I did not find departure from the "Rest" as easy as expected. By brute force, of course, I could have torn myself away; but there proved to be too much yet to see to warrant my obstinate withdrawal, for now that I was in a more favorable position to do so, I made a critical examination of the banks of the creek, wholly with reference to details. I knew it as a whole: what of the component parts? Now, for the first, I noticed numbers of those beautiful crimson lilies, which are worthy of a better name than "Turk's-cap."

Towering above the rank underbrush, determined to catch the kisses of every struggling sunbeam, were the stout and stately stems of this queen of flowers, six, seven, and one eleven feet in height, each with many fully expanded red, yellow, and black blossoms. When I first saw them, they were reflected in the still, dark water beneath, till a sportive zephyr broke the glass and scattered innumerable gems that mocked the queen-lily's dignity.

Not only the lily, but sweetly-scented, white-spiked clethra flowers bloomed, half-hidden, close to the water's edge, its snowy blossoms in marked contrast to the brilliancy of the scarlet lobelia growing near; and close to my boat, and over all the shallows, rank pickerel-weed and coarser splatter-dock, tinted the waters with the blue and gold of their bloom.

I will not admit that I soon tired of flowers, but whenever afloat I am never unmindful of the fishes. At the mouth of this tributary creek, where my boat was now at anchor, the water was very clear and the sand and pebbles at the bottom plainly in view. Scarcely a fish was to be seen for several minutes, when suddenly a pair of lithe and active stone-catfish came directly beneath me. They interested me very much by overturning flat pebbles gracefully with their wedge-like snouts. Occasionally a stone would prove a little heavier than anticipated, when the fish's whole body would be rapidly curved, straightened and recurved, as if to squeeze into its nose all the strength that it possessed. At last, over the heavy pebble would go, and with a quick, nibbling motion of the mouth, the newly exposed surface would be rifled of everything acceptable to a catfish's palate.

Although these two fishes were constantly near together, they did not co-operate in any of the stone-turning. Nevertheless, their association was not accidental, for I frequently startled them by thrusting down a stick into the sand, which caused them immediately to dart away at the same instant; but they invariably swam in the same direction and returned, swimming side by side. They evidently derived some advantage, or, shall I say, comfort, in being thus intimately associated, but the why and wherefore of it all I failed to determine, or even to get so much of a clew as would warrant a guess.

It was but a few days ago that I was shown a fine adult specimen of one of these catfish, then in an aquarium, and was seriously informed that it was a hybrid "between an eel and a common catfish." As this would be a cross between fishes of different families, and one, too, a marine species, so far as its breeding is concerned, it would have been a novelty indeed had it been the case. Here is an example of current ignorance worthy of note. This species of catfish is not very abundant, it is true, but because a little eel-like in its shape, ignorance suggests so remarkable a solution of the problem. "What is it?" Did it never occur to the namby-pamby, *cui bono* folks, who affect to decry natural history studies, that the universal curiosity of mankind, as demonstrated by the certainty that the question, "What is it?" will be asked, whenever any strange creature is exhibited, is a curiosity worthy of satisfaction? Can these would-be worthy people justify themselves in endeavoring to quench a desire for such important knowledge— a desire implanted in the breast of nearly every child by that Creator whom they suppose they are reverencing, but are really insulting?

The tall trees in the distant meadows shut out the last rays of the setting sun, and the dim light that now prevailed made the "Rest" unutterably gloomy. Its larger trees, a half-mile distant, were wrapped in haze; the outlines of those near by were but dimly traced against the leaden eastern sky. Every flower had faded from view. Nothing invited. All repelled. Yet I felt urged by some unrecognized influence to remain. The influence was unmistakable. It compelled a course of action wholly at variance with my plans for the day. I certainly had no desire to float idly at this point until nightfall or even later. I was hungry and supperless, yet I found it next to impossible to leave. Thrice my hand reached forward to the anchor-chain; thrice I let the chain fall back into the water and waited, I knew not for what.

One by one the birds in the thickets ceased their chirping; the titmice no longer whistled; the last marsh-wren of the day sang a hurried roundelay and sought its nest in the reeds; the scattered hylas peeped complainingly, and a single fretful cat-bird was my sole companion. He soon grew tiresome, and I longed for an owl to hoot or bittern to boom, but neither uttered a sound. There was an almost noiseless interim of half an hour, and then the katydids were ready to begin their night-long concert. Surely I had not waited for them! And half angry with myself for remaining, turned once more to the anchor, when I marked a mere speck against the dull red of the sunset sky, and then another and another. These shapeless dots grew steadily in bulk and soon assumed definite outlines. They were gradually coming nearer and nearer to where I waited, and each quickly grew to a bird of great size, as it passed over and alighted on the birch-trees beyond. The buzzards had returned.

Quickly shipping my anchor, I sculled as closely as possible, without being seen by them, and watched, as best I might, in the uncertain and rapidly decreasing light. My efforts were rewarded by the acquisition of one fact. The buzzards murmured to themselves as they settled down to rest. It was a curious sound. Not harshly guttural, as might be imagined, but a fairly smooth and soothing utterance. I had not waited for nothing. For the first time, I had heard a turkey-buzzard sing! The sounds soon ceased, and when all was quiet, save the ceaseless racket of the katydids, I shouted loudly, when, with a pig-like grunt, each buzzard stood alert, with half-open wings. I shouted again. Again the answering grunt, but not one left its perch. I remained quiet for a few minutes, and gradually they sunk again to more easy positions, and were soon, I hope, asleep.

For the third time I withdrew to the main creek, and as I turned my boat's bow homeward, the rising moon flooded with silvery, uncertain light the deep recesses of the leafy "Rest," and there, silent as the eternal hills, and sharply limned against the eastern sky, were the weird forms of twenty slumbering vultures. It was an uncanny sight.

CHAPTER III.

WATSON'S CROSSING.

A FORETASTE of October, in the early morning of hot August days, is not infrequently the experience of him who is astir at dawn. Recklessly plunging through a fog-enveloped wilderness of weeds, I chanced upon the bank of a winsome little brook, as it hurried to the hidden meadows beyond. The world was yet at rest. Beyond the rippling of the water, not a sound was heard save the muffled crowing of a distant cock, and at longer intervals the drowsy barking of a dog.

I watched the steady flow of the brimming stream for many minutes, and at last the chatter of the squirrel, the cry of the flicker, and querulous plaint of the nuthatch floated from the hidden trees, and with them swept by a chilly breeze, bringing a crimson leaf to where I sat. Every sound suggested autumn, and the leaf forecasted the painted forest.

As the fog rose, the shapely gum-tree, from which had come the pretty leaf, came into view, and half its foliage was as ruddy as the waif that I held in my hand. There are gum-trees on the hill-side that drop scores of these "autumn" leaves in August, as surely as the month rolls round, yet my neighbors never fail, as they pick them up, to wave them before you as an infallible sign of an "early fall." Dropping, as they do, in August, I admit they prove an early fall, but for themselves only.

But I am on my way to the boat, and propose to go " 'cross lots," if so be it the meadows will afford a footing. It is not wise to do, except at this time of year, so treacherous is many a grassy spot when the springs are full. And after a mile or more of tramping over soft ground, how one longs for a solid rock to stand upon! An uncertain footing is a source of weariness not only to the flesh but to the mind. Try poetizing over some gorgeous meadow bloom while your feet sink deeper and deeper in mud of unknown depth, and tell me then whether I am right or wrong. There is a curious page in my note-book where half the lines rhyme with one four-lettered, vigorous exclamation that custom taboos; but a soothing word, under some circumstances, nevertheless.

The nearest rock in place, from where I stand, is some hundreds or thousands of feet beneath the meadow mud; the next is that at the head of tide-water, where a flinty-hard ledge crops out and ripples the broad and shallow waters of the Delaware.

But if there are no bed-rocks here, we can boast of the next best thing, an occasional bowlder. What a marvellous history have these transported fragments of some distant mountain ridge, yet how few are willing to listen while their story is being told. The great ice age, when glaciers and floods were mightiest, is to most a myth; and poor palæolithic man is denied recognition, in spite of the many traces he has left of his sojourn in the river's valley.

I know of two fine bowlders in the meadows, but I use them only for stepping-stones—never as texts. My last public talk about them was disastrous. "There's the stones, as you say," remarked one of my audience, "and the lunertic 'sylum, a big pile of stone, is four miles up the river." I made no reply, and to this day that graybeard passes in and out as a Solon, and I am the crank.

One of these bowlders is milky-white and very hard, and so much of its surface as is exposed is very smooth. I formerly thought that if it had been lying in a higher and drier meadow, the Indians would have made use of it, and perhaps have carved some curious image upon it, and I was right, after all. Recently, the low stage of water gave me the chance to examine it closely, and upon one side there are shallow depressions, where celts were sharpened. Such marks are unmistakable. Not fifty rods away there is a knoll that the highest freshets only partly cover, and the ashes of the Indians' camp-fires are there exposed whenever the sod is broken. And there, when it was last ploughed, I found a dozen celts, perhaps every one shaped and sharpened on this very bowlder in the marsh.

The higher banks of the meadow ditches are still densely green, and as the eye glances along the leafy wall it is seldom that it catches a bit of color. It was not so to-day. As I skirted the south side of Faxon's Brook I found a great cluster of rosy centaury. It was backed by ferns and bitter-sweet, the latter laden with its orange berries. Nothing to equal it have I seen this summer. Centaury is to be looked for in high and dry localities, according to the text-books; but I know of no other spot where it grows in such luxuriance as here. Has some recent freshet brought the seed from a distant point? And from this spot onward, until I reached my boat, there was color everywhere. I anticipated a red-letter day in consequence.

For no half-mile of the creek's course is it so astonishingly crooked as where we approach its next point of interest, Watson's Crossing; for thus it was known in colonial days, and by this name only shall I hereafter mention it. The railroad crosses the creek at this point, and the farmers unmindful of the earlier and better history of the place, or else ignorant of it, call this twist of the stream "High Bridge." Fortunately, the railroad passes over a trestle sixty feet in the air, and is, moreover, so shut in by trees that it does not materially affect the absolute wildness of the spot.

While beautiful at all times, Watson's Crossing is charming now. Lusty button-bushes crowd its banks, and jut out, as small peninsulas, at every turn. They are now at their best, heavy with perfect globes of delicate white bloom. Creeping over many is the venturesome Rutland beauty. So lithe a growth, so fair a face, Rutland may well be proud of her charms; and it is not to be wondered at that she blooms only where the waters beneath afford her a mirror, in which, while the day lasts, she can gaze admiringly.

Nestling about the roots of the button-bushes, and indeed wherever it is permanently shady, grows the inconspicuous ground-nut, now in full bloom. The flowers are small, sweetly scented, darkly purple and brown, and their shape recalls to me those gloomy drab bonnets such as every strict Quakeress wore, or still wears, for aught I know. It is an appropriate blossom for these Quaker grounds.

The Indians held this plant in high esteem. Peter Kalm, the Swedish naturalist, found it abundantly in southern Jersey, and remarks concerning it: "Hopniss or Hapniss was the Indian name of a wild plant, which they ate at that time. The Swedes still call it by that name, and it grows in the meadows in a good soil. The roots resemble small potatoes, and were boiled by the Indians, who eat them instead of bread. Some of the Swedes at that time likewise ate this root for want of bread. Some of the English still eat them instead of potatoes. Mr. Bartram told me that the Indians who live farther in the country do not only eat these roots, which are equal in goodness to potatoes, but likewise take the pease which ly in the pods of this plant, and prepare them like common pease."

As my boat floated slowly down the creek, just clearing the bushes, I was struck with the vast numbers of primroses. The flower-stalks stood far above the surrounding grass and weeds, and every blossom fully blown, they made a magnificent display. In color a light or greenish yellow, they contrasted strongly with the frequent clusters of dark, almost orange, Rudbeckias, six and seven feet in height. These were here the most conspicuous flowers, and dwarfed to utter insignificance another yellow bloom, a St. John's-wort, growing in the grass, and quite hidden, except for the profusion of its small, golden-tinted flowers. I looked in vain for other colors. All, like the Assyrian's cohorts, were gleaming with purple and gold. But if not flowers of other hues, there were stately trees in abundance, and here the lindens and hornbeams gave place to sycamores, willows, swamp white-oaks, birch, sumac, locust, butternut, and hickory. A greater contrast in foliage could not well be imagined than these trees afforded.

Passing through a small forest of the trees mentioned, I came to the scanty remaining traces of a once busy place. Two hundred and one years ago Matthew Watson, having spent two years in the village of Burlington, after his arrival from England, came to the south bank of the creek and finding it a "goodly spot, well worthy of settlement and cultivation," did purchase the same forthwith; built a "most comfortable and generous house," and put under cultivation "rich acres on every side, excepte where the Creek runneth, on my northbounds, and here have I builded of stout oaken logs a most commodious and well appointed wharf; and from it, there is dispatched each weeke a shallop of 40 tons burthen, also builded of oaken timber, cutte from my timber tract." So runs the record, and in 1703, when Matthew died, there was no busier site on this same creek. But prior to this the spot had not been a forsaken wilderness. An Indian trail from the Delaware, across the State to the sea, crossed the creek quite near, and the narrow path was marked at the top of the "bold north shore" by an enormous tulip-tree, which reaching far above the surrounding forest growths, was a landmark to be seen for many miles. The bluff here was less steep than usual, and for an acre or more was covered with walnut, butternut, and hickory trees, supposed to have been planted by the Indians.

A century ago the spot was known as "Gun-slip," and only recently has this meaningless name been correctly explained. It is a corruption of "Oconio's leap," and the story of two centuries ago ran that a Unami Indian of that name once climbed nearly to the top of the tree to rob an eagle's nest, when the eagles attacked him. Seeing that his safety lay in sudden flight only, he gave a mighty leap, hoping to alight unharmed among the thick-set branches of the trees beneath; but that the old she-eagle caught him as he jumped, and *let him down gently to the ground.* A beautiful example of a nursery tale told by *matter-of-fact* Quakers.

It was here, just a year ago, that I stopped to talk with a neighbor, and he told me a strange story. He had been mowing, some weeks before, a rank growth of weeds, and while thus engaged, noticed a few paces before him a clump of elders about which a pair of little yellow warblers were constantly flying, as though in trouble. Suddenly one of them flew directly in his face, snapping its bill and chirping excitedly. Not stopping his work, the mower was again and again saluted in the same manner, and he saw that the bird's actions meant unmistakably a protest against his farther progress. He quit mowing, and the bird flew back to the bushes. He cut another swath, and brought the bird back almost at the same moment. The mower's curiosity was now thoroughly aroused. He walked ahead to the bushes and found a nest containing young birds. Weeks after, I went to the place, and found the cluster of elders as he left them. The nest now was, of course, empty.

I see no reason why this should be doubted. I have knowledge of many incidents quite similar to the above, and were dogs or even cats the heroes, such anecdotes, when narrated, would create but little surprise.

There seems to be a very general impression that intelligence among animals increases as they ascend the scale of anatomical structure. I cannot think so. Years of familiarity with a multitude of varied forms of life, lower than mammals or than birds even, have led me to conclude that in the more simply organized brains may be localized intelligences that outrank those of structurally higher animals. The element of danger in a creature's environment is one great stimulus to a development of mother-wit, and those that, in spite of a multiplicity of enemies, continue to hold their own, exhibit far more frequent evidence of effective brain-power than do such as by brute force, or exceptional facility in escaping attack, maintain their places among us.

I should not expect to find marked evidence of forethought among opossums or even squirrels, but that a comparatively helpless little warbler should display such wisdom does not surprise me, although the danger threatened its young and not itself.

My neighbor's story of the little warblers recalled the fate of a brood of king-rails in my mucky meadow. The tangled white-joint grass was being cut, and steadily over the marshy stretch the mower forced his way. Not a bird there but must have heard the meaning "swish" of the deadly blade, if it did not divine what the sound meant. The blackbirds hovered overhead and protested at the invasion of their weedy haunts, although their young had been long upon the wing. The liquid notes of the swamp-sparrow trickled from the hedge-row, mourning, I thought, that the protecting grass should be no more; and all unmoved upon its nest sat a king-rail, which, deprived of its earlier brood, was patiently rearing another. There it sat, and another sweep of the scythe would pass closely over it, if not, indeed, through the poor bird's body. The mower drew nearer, with arms drawn back, when, quick as a flash of light, the bird fled from the swift stroke of the shining blade, and, with a wild cry, forsook her nest. An armful of grass was piled about it, and the mower passed on. Towards evening the poor bird returned, but only to find her young dead from neglect or exposure.

Again and again, in the gloaming, I heard the wild cries of the bereaved king-rail, as it seemed to utter curses on those who would not leave unmolested even that little tract of waste land.

As I tarried a moment to examine the curiously twisted branches of an overhanging maple, I noticed a broad hemlock slab floating towards the boat, and when quite near, discovered that it was burdened with a living freight. Coiled upon a mat of dead leaves that had lodged or been placed upon the slab, was an enormous water-snake. While it was yet at its ease, and I at mine, I examined the couch of the sleepy, if not sleeping, serpent as best I could from a distance. It appeared to have no coarse material in it, but made up of just such stuffs as were suited for a comfortable bed. I am disposed to believe that water-snakes gather these bunches of dead grass and leaves, rather than trust to finding a suitable hap-hazard accumulation. It is true, I never surprised one of them while at work, but base my suggestion primarily upon the fact of the uniformity of the materials. Drifted rubbish, I take it, would be of a more mixed character.

Again, I have had for some weeks an exquisite little green snake in a Wardian case. It has chosen one corner for its resting-place, and has arranged the mosses in such a neat fashion that nest-building in a primitive way seems to be a practice with some serpents. My little green snake had hard work to remove one obstacle, but by dint of pushing and prying finally succeeded, and worked more ingeniously than if it had carried materials in its mouth, as a water-snake would have to do. So much for a snake's bed: does its occupant ever think? What transpires in its brain, as it stares you so boldly in the face? I wish the problem could be solved. If not intelligence, what can it be that gives such a meaning expression to its glistening eyes?

The snake's raft and my boat came slowly together. Reclining at full length, I leaned over the bow, and in a few seconds was within reach. Very deliberately I moved my hand over the gunwale and reached outward. The snake was watching my hand rather than me. It did not dart its pretty tongue, but stared. I reached to within six inches of its body, and was about to clasp my fingers over one of its coils, when with a lightning-like snap it bit my thumb severely, released its hold, and was gone. I could not but laugh immoderately at the precipitancy of its retreat after nipping my thumb. The snake was really an arrant coward. But to return to the question: if the snake was not thinking, and as predetermined to bite as I was to touch, what was the creature's brain doing during those anxious moments? Can we imagine any other than a mental activity such as is known to be possessed by man? What intelligence or mind may be, I have not the most remote conception, beyond its intimate connection with the brain; but after a lifetime spent in studying our familiar wild animals, I have utterly failed to find other mental differences between them and mankind than those of degree.

It has been suggested that enthusiasm on the part of the observer may "saturate its object . . . with thoughts, ideas, and emotions foreign to its intrinsic nature." Is not this an admission that "thoughts, ideas, and emotions," not foreign, may be generated by a snake's brain? If so, I have erred only in misinterpreting, quite insignificantly, their mental powers.

When this same snake is speeding through the water, or creeping cautiously through the meadow-grass, in pursuit of prey, it knows that speed is necessary to capture a fish, and caution required to secure a mouse; and during the act, what thought but that a given plan, learned by experience, must be followed out? How does man differ from all this? Does not the hunter, in pursuit of game, follow much the same rules, and, so far as his proper business is concerned, think practically the same thoughts?

To return to the irate serpent of the raft: it had no

4

intention of leaving its comfortable quarters permanently, and before my boat had drifted half its length, had reappeared and was resting its head and neck upon the slab. As I made no offensive motion, it soon crawled again to its old place, but never, for a second, lost sight of me. The snake in returning so promptly, after showing itself a coward not five minutes before, was thoroughly contradictory, and I could only think that here again we have a mental characteristic that is remarkably well developed in man.

Next to the mooted point, the maximum length of a water-snake, or of any species of serpent, is that of the creature's age. My neighbors seem to believe that death only comes through violence. While I have been altogether unsuccessful in my efforts to determine these points, I have found that the common water-snake grows more and more slowly each year, and when the supposed maximum size is reached—about six feet—a considerable length of years is yet before the creature, if no ill-luck crosses its path. A snake of this species, and of about the length mentioned, lived under a stone wall in Laurie's mill-pond for seventeen years.

Judging from his dingy colors, his sluggish movements when in the water, and apparent love of quiet, the snake I saw to-day had probably weathered a quarter of a century, and long may he continue to flourish!

It is an interesting fact that wherever the early settlers chose a site for a village or laid out a highway, they found that the Indians had preceded them. Probably every road, two centuries ago, was the route of an Indian trail, and the sites of every community, whether of Dutch, Swedes, or English, were those of Indian villages. It was the case here, at Watson's wharf. The Indian path crossed the creek, a few rods down the stream, and where the wharf was, stood, long years before, a group of wigwams. Here is a positive statement, yet never a white man saw them, nor did Indian ever point out the spot as the former home of some of his people. Since that distant day, when the red men abandoned it, until now, it has never been known. It is my own good-fortune to bring it into the light of the present. By a mere chance, I became a discoverer. It is a pleasant experience, and as trace after trace of the former occupants were brought to view, I pictured to myself every phase of their quiet lives while dwelling here.

The last rain had gullied the terrace and uprooted a small tree, and on the newly exposed soil I found many fragments of pottery. It was this that led me to explore the spot more completely, and bring to light whatever else it might contain. The earth itself was deeply discolored by minute fragments of charcoal and the direct action of fire, while the circle of large white stones that defined a hearth were still in place. Within the enclosure there was one of those curious slabs of slaty rock, with a number of circular pits on one side, that are reasonably supposed to have been used as lapstones, and that when the Indian cracked nuts, he placed them in the pits to prevent their slipping from under the hammer. It is a curious fact that these pitted stones are more common where nut-trees are abundant than elsewhere.

A cylindrical pebble, nearly two feet in length and made perfectly symmetrical by pecking away every inequality, brought to mind the early cornfields of the neighborhood; for the cultivation of maize is indissolubly connected with the history of the Indian. These pestles were used in crushing the corn in wooden mortars, usually made of the wood of our sour gum, which the Delawares called by the short and euphonious name, *tachquachcaniminschi.*

The omnipresent axe and arrow-heads were likewise buried in the earth and ashes, and just beyond the hearth-circle was a dozen or more flat pebbles, notched on two sides, which were once the weights of a fish-net.

Continuing the search, I found a fragment of clay tobacco-pipe, and finally, deepest down of all, a bear's claw, a perforated fossil shark-tooth, and a carved steatite trinket. Could I but have found a trace of the old hunter's canoe, there would have been no chapter wanting of his life's history.

The discovery of such wigwam sites is not an unusual occurrence, and but one mystery hangs over them. Why, when they were abandoned, was not the personal property of the occupants carried away? The axe, the pestle, the pitted slab, the arrow-heads, the several ornaments were perfect, yet here they were, lying in the blackened earth, as though intentionally thrown into the fire. Did the Unamis, the Delawares of the Crosswicks valley, burn the house, with all that it contained, when one of their people died? The appearance of this "find" was certainly suggestive of such a custom. Yet it was one that did not always hold good, for they are known to have had extensive cemeteries, where very different but no less elaborate funeral rites were observed.

It is useless to conjecture just when this Indian had his "wattled hut" at this place. That it was many centuries ago is probable; the absence of articles of European manufacture is indicative of this; but the fact that it might have been less than five hundred years ago does not warrant the popular notion that the Indians are but recent comers to these parts. When all the evidences of their antiquity are duly considered, it must be admitted that the final migration of the Delaware Indians to New Jersey occurred centuries prior to the Christian era.

Startling though the assertion may be, it is safe to affirm that the Indian was preceded by an even ruder people. Sift the meadow mud through your fingers, and then search the underlying gravels; for not until this is done will you have read the story of the races, backward, to the beginning. The occupancy by man of the valley of the Delaware, and of this creek, is divisible into three distinct periods—the Indian, whom all know; the Eskimo, whom few have suspected; and farthest back the scarcely recognized palæolithic man, who "was no more capable of making a stone arrow-head than he was of building a pyramid."

Writes a celebrated archæologist in the *North American Review:*

"Who were the earliest inhabitants of America, and when did they live? are questions which have generally been approached solely from the point of view offered by discoveries in the United States.... In the following essay I propose to deal with them as portions of one great problem common to the Old and New Worlds, and to show that the first traces of man, as yet discovered, prove him to have lived in the same low stage of culture on both sides of the Atlantic, at a time when the hands of the geological clock pointed to the same hour over the greater part of the world. The story of early man in America is a part of the greater story of the first appearance of man on the earth, so far as he has yet been revealed by modern discovery."

So I am not alone in the advocacy of very ancient American man; but ask me for no particulars concerning the important questions of origin or antiquity. Of the latter only will I say, it is a matter of "time relative" and not of "time absolute."

Having gathered up my treasures and returned to the boat, I quickly forgot the Indians when again afloat, and a few yards' progress brought in view the most gorgeous display of yellow bloom I had yet seen. It was the yellow Gerardia, and although abundant up and down the creek, is nowhere else so luxuriant. I gathered an armful of the rank flower-stalks, and while returning to the boat, was forced to stand a moment and admire a fruit as yellow as the bloom I carried. It was the climbing Celastrus, but in this case was a bush rather than a vine. The crop of berries that it bore was simply enormous. Again, at the very water's edge, was a yellow hawkweed, and it was with unfeigned pleasure that, half a rod distant, I could bury my boat in a wilderness of clematis, now in the very height of its blooming.

While I lingered here, a pretty butterfly, the red admiral, alighted upon my knee as I was writing, and seemed wholly at ease in this unusual position. Something upon my clothes was attractive to it, and the graceful movements of its proboscis, and occasional down-dipping of one antenna and then the other was amusing. I noticed that the right and left wing moved separately down and up, as though to retain the creature's balance, which the wind threatened, and at each such movement of the wings the corresponding antennæ likewise dipped. This butterfly occasionally flew to the bushes near by, but never to remain long away, and sooner or later returned and was my companion for a great part of the day.

An acre or two of neglected meadow reaches to the creek's shore, a half mile distant, and now it is brow-deep in boneset. It was scarcely penetrable, and a paradise for butterflies and bees. Many of the latter, indeed, took my intrusion rather ill-naturedly, buzzing and staring me in the face, but none stung me. The common milk-weed butterfly was remarkably abundant, and made good the remarks of Scudder concerning them: " Having multiplied to excess, vast swarms are found together; together they mount in the air to lofty heights, as no other butterfly appears to do, and play about in ceaseless gyrations; and sometimes they crowd so thickly upon a tree or bush as by their color to change its whole appearance." This they did to-day, and a small sassafras sapling was so covered that they appeared to outnumber the leaves, and gave the tree a permaturely frost-bitten appearance. I cautiously drew near, and counted one hundred and seven of them, and there were almost as many more. Then giving the tree a vigorous shaking, they all took flight, and made a distinct rustling noise as they did so. They did not mount the air to any height, but scattered over the snowy boneset blossoms, and reminded me of an October shower of painted leaves.

A migration of what was unquestionably this species of butterfly took place near by, in September of 1881. They flew at a height of probably two hundred yards only, and moved in a long, narrow body, that took an hour to pass a given point. The migration is known to have extended twenty-five miles, and if the direction was not changed, or the journey ended, a few hours would have brought them to the sea. It is rather curious that several such migrations occurred at about this time in the New England and Middle States. Since then I have not seen it repeated.

Associated with the bees and butterflies that sucked endless sweets from the fragrant boneset were hundreds of beautiful dragon-flies. These darted everywhere in the most erratic manner, but did not seem to molest any other creature. I counted five distinct species, some of which were brilliantly colored. These insects also migrate in countless thousands; and often the air is filled with them, flying at a considerable elevation, all in the same direction, and taking hours and even days to pass a given point.

While the bloom above was crowded with busy life, the ground beneath appeared to harbor no creature of any kind. I looked in vain for a frog, snake, toad, or turtle; but no sooner had I passed the meadow's boundary than I found all four of them. A water-snake was hurrying creekward with a toad in its jaws, and a frog sat near, as though contemplating the toad's fate, and perhaps wondering if its turn would come next. I released the toad, which hopped away gleefully and quite unhurt, and the snake savagely bit at my hand for dispossessing it of its lawful prey. The bite was but a pin-prick, scarcely bringing the blood, although the snake was a large one.

Every creek, I suppose, has its monsters; usually of serpentine shape, although not always. The older fishermen about here still insist upon a wonderful water-snake, sometimes captured but never killed. There is one curious feature about these stories. They all refer to adventures in the lives of older men, now dead. No one living has ever caught the Crosswicks sea-serpent; but as soon as an old man dies, it is suddenly remembered that he did have such an experience. Comment is unnecessary. Nevertheless, there are big snakes, large turtles, and many overgrown fishes in the creek, and an occasional *bona fide* specimen is exhibited at the cross-roads tavern, and subsequently is heralded in the local paper. Every ensuing year the history of the monster is repeated, and a pound in weight or a foot in length is added. It is really strange that many a large catfish caught by our grandfathers has not grown to a whale by this time.

4*

Again afloat, I took a long, last look, and while the beauty of the bloom upon its shores, and the crowded, branch-locked towering trees above were being scrutinized, in hopes of some novelty I had failed to see, the cars came rumbling over the high bridge. It was a strange combination of the natural and artificial, which on the whole was far from pleasing, yet was not barren of fruit for the contemplative rambler. The cars disturbed a number of swallows, which had been resting on the timbers of the trestle, and until now had made no sound, and been quite unsuspected. Certainly for two hours a hundred swallows of two species had been sitting still, neither flying at short intervals nor twittering above a whisper. I have seen something akin to this, later in the month, when telegraph-wires would be lined with these birds, but then they were more or less restless and twittered continually. I could not but think how unsafe it is to declare such and such a creature wanting in any locality, where it rightfully belongs, because we do not happen to see it.

The day was drawing to a close as I left Watson's Crossing fairly behind me and floated leisurely with the tide for half a mile, until timber-land was again reached. The intervening open tract is all a pasture meadow, well in grass, but not to the exclusion of many flowers. Purple and yellow, of course; it is almost in vain to look for other colors. Here where cows were grazing grew rank vervain, with its tapering purple spires, that imparted a Tyrian hue over all the landscape; and it was a positive relief to reach a drooping willow—although an exotic—a broad-leaved catalpa, or tropical sumac.

The latter, with its velvety bloom of richest red seems always out of place among our plainer trees. Indeed, one spot where stood a thrifty sumac in full bloom, with wild-rice, cat's-tail and purple cock's-comb grass growing immediately about it, was a little tropic, that needed but a few humming-birds to make complete. There were few birds of any kind in the neighborhood, but while I lingered at the sumac a silent, morose cuckoo flew from the opposite shore and clucked in his peculiar way when once hid in the thickest cluster of the tree's foliage. It was the first of these birds that I had seen for many days, so I followed his movements as best I could, with as much interest as though a novelty. To me, in truth, for years past, it has been a most entertaining bird. His talents certainly do not lie in a musical direction; yet the broken, gutteral cluck that he so frequently utters is not discordant; and further, it does not appear to have been noticed by ornithologists that these birds neither all cluck alike nor is this clucking their only utterance. They occasionally give a more birdlike cry, something like the first syllable of a wood-pee-wee's song. Like all young birds, the brood peep quite shrilly when handled. As to the ordinary clucking of adult birds, it accords well with the surroundings, and when accompanied by the "z-ing" of the harvest-fly, completes the essential features of an August afternoon.

I am much surprised to find these birds recorded as such devoted creatures, both to their mates and to their young. The mother bird, it is true, looks well after her offspring, but as childless lovers, earlier in the summer, they are, it always appeared to me, exceedingly prosaic. I have never been so fortunate as to witness these evidences of conjugal affection so graphically described by Alexander Wilson. They seem rather to live on the plan of every one for himself, and consider their own comfort to the entire exclusion of that even of their mates. However it may be with other birds, it is highly improbable that the cuckoo cares a jot whether he renews his acquaintance with his last year's wife or consorts with a stranger. The cuckoo in the sumac persisted in remaining characteristically prosaic, uttering no sound after he first announced his presence, and not deigning to go through those beautiful evolutions among the branches in which he sometimes indulges when insect hunting. I have occasionally seen a cuckoo, with apparently closed wings, encircle a large limb of a tree without touching it; as though in some mysterious manner it gave the necessary impulse to its body, and determined the direction by the curvature of the tail. Their flight is easy and deliberate when passing from tree to tree, giving one the impression of a lazy bird; but often when in a tree their movements are the climax of graceful locomotion.

I have been referring to the commoner yellow-billed species. There is another, the black-billed, which has essentially the same habits. Both, I have ever found, are partial to the proximity of running water, and they often remain so closely to the overhanging branches, that while often heard, they will seldom be seen, unless one is afloat and observes them then. The cuckoo in the sumac remained quite closely to the water's edge for some time, and then by short flights, from bush to bush and tree to tree, kept a creekward course until out of sight. Had I been on shore, I would never have suspected that a cuckoo was near—unless, indeed, I heard it clucking.

As I proceeded, the meadows became more marshy and shrubs were scattered along the creek's bank; but soon, standing alone, was found a thrifty plum-tree, and a black haw so near by that their branches intertwined. The fruit of the wild plum was about half ripe, and either pale yellow or orange and red. It was far too beautiful to leave behind, and I gathered all that was within easy reach. With this fruit I felt that my cargo was completed, and the scanty remnant of daylight remaining demanded a hurried passage to my next anchorage for the night, and this was yet to be found, at or near the great swamp white-oaks whose towering tops were still plainly visible against the dull crimson of the sunset sky.

The mysterious impulse that bade me remain after sundown and until well into the night, was not brought to bear upon me this evening. A suitable place to hide my boat was now my only thought, and while a few last rays of sunshine glinted through the tree-tops, I found the desired haven in a cluster of button-bushes, near the big oaks; and crushing the beautiful white alisma's bloom, as I drew the boat upon the shore, was about to start, with my many treasures, when two vines commanded my attention. A climbing pea, with purple bloom, was on my right, and a clambering mikania on my left. I gathered a long piece of each, that neither should feel slighted, and brushing through the tall club-rush, rich with nutty-brown bloom, was soon fairly homeward bound, with not a wish for further novelty.

But it was not to be. As I came to my neighbor's pasture meadow, I found the spot anything but quiet, as I expected. Hundreds of excited birds filled the air, which but a glance needed to identify as night-hawks. Graceful and erratic as swallows in their flight, they remained remarkably near the ground, and seemed scarcely to rise above the level of my head. For a moment I stood perfectly still, and felt the wind from their wings as they rushed by; but all the while I heard no vocal utterance. Each was too busy with the myriads of small flies, which I could not see, but felt were in the air, to sing or even twitter to a passing fellow. My curiosity was, of course, roused to know what insects these were, that kept the night-hawks abroad at so unusual an hour; and resting my burden at the foot of a large elm, I prepared to investigate the matter. This was easily done. Striking a light, I found that from the foot of the elm there had issued and was issuing a brood of winged ants, which the night-hawks discovering, had chased while the sunlight lasted and continued in pursuit long after they were able to see the insects. This was not surprising, for they had but to fly with their beaks widely opened to take as many as they desired. Usually, the night-hawk flies only during the subdued light, shortly before sunset and for a brief period afterwards, if the sky is clear; but exceptions to this are so far common, that it is a question if they cannot successfully pursue their prey, guided by some other sense than that of sight. Ornithologists differ as to this. Dr. Brewer, in the "History of North American Birds," says: "It has, strictly speaking, no claim to its common name, as indicating it to be a bird of the night, which it is not. It is crepuscular, rather than nocturnal, and even this habit is more due to the flight of the insects upon which it feeds at morning and at evening than to any organization of the bird rendering it necessary." This is probably too emphatic an assertion. It seems so, certainly, when I recall my own observations in past years; and I find a writer in the "American Naturalist," Vol. VII., stating it to be "both diurnal and nocturnal in its habits, but more properly the latter." This more fully accords with my own conclusions, except that the term "crepuscular" is preferable to nocturnal. The writer just quoted further remarks, "It is in the dusk of the evening that they may be seen in the greatest numbers; when, in certain localities and at certain seasons of the year (especially in the fall), thousands may be seen darting around in their rapid and necessarily irregular flight. As darkness approaches, they descend to the earth and skim along the surface, snatching up any ill-fated bug that may have failed to find shelter."

This is true of them, as I have noticed for years, when they gather over the meadows. At times they fly at so great an elevation that it is difficult to distinguish them from the ever-present swallows; but as the air cools and sunset draws near, lower and lower is the plane of their flight until they barely skim the tall weeds of the marshes.

The comments, during haying and harvest, of some of

my farmer-neighbors upon this bird, in its relation to the weather, are very funny. If by chance night-hawks are seen early in the afternoon, the farmer will smilingly rub the palms of his hands together and exclaim, "fine weather, fine weather;" but if too busy to observe them until evening, then the lower flight of the birds is marked with a troubled countenance, and it is peevishly announced that it will soon rain. A more worthless barometer than a night-hawk it is difficult to imagine; yet two centuries of experience with them has not lessened the faith of the illogical farmers.

The flying ants soon proved more troublesome than mosquitoes, as they covered my hat and shoulders, and commenced crawling over me in a most annoying manner. I hurried away, and recklessly brushed them from me with my bundle of botanical specimens, to the ruination of the latter, and, I was glad to find, destruction of the former. Once free, I walked with great haste towards home, fearing further delays, and recalled an exodus of winged ants I had observed with some care years ago.

Late in the afternoon of October 6, 1872, my attention was called to a great multitude of large-sized insects that filled the air, and appeared to be some unusual form of insect life, judging of them from a distance. Closer inspection showed them to be a brood of red ants that had just emerged from their underground home and were now for the first time using their delicate wings. The sky at the time was wholly overcast; the wind strong south-east; thermometer 66° Fahr. Taking a favorable position, I noticed, as they slowly crawled from the ground up the blades of grass and stems of clover and small weeds, that they seemed dazed, without any method in their movements, save an ill-defined impression that they must go somewhere. Again, nearly every one was pushed forward by those coming after it, which seemed to add to its confusion. Every action plainly indicated that they were wholly ill at ease.

Once at the tip of a blade of grass, they seemed more than ever puzzled as to what to do. If not followed by a fellow-ant, they would invariably crawl down again to the earth, and sometimes repeat this movement until a new-comer followed in the ascent, when the bewildered individual would be forced to use his wings. This flight would be inaugurated by a very rapid buzzing of the wings, as though to dry them, or prove their owner's power over them. After a second's rest the violent movement of the wings would recommence, and finally losing fear, as it were, the ant would let go its hold upon the blade of grass and rise slowly upward. It could, in fact, scarcely be called flight. The steady vibration of the wings simply bore them upward, ten, twenty, or thirty feet, until they were caught by a breeze, or by the steadier wind that was moving at an elevation equal to the height of the surrounding pine and spruce trees. So far as I was able to discover, their wings were of the same use to them in transporting them from their former home that the "wings" of many seeds are in scattering them, both being wholly at the mercy of the winds.

Mr. Bates, in describing the habits of the Saüba ants, says: "The successful debut of the winged males and females depends likewise upon the workers. It is amusing to see the activity and excitement which reign in an ant's nest when the exodus of the winged individuals is taking place. The workers clear the roads of exit, and show the most lively interest in their departure, although it is highly improbable that any of them will return to the same colony. The swarming or exodus of the winged males and females of the Saüba ant takes place in January and February, that is, at the commencement of the rainy season. They come out in the evening in vast numbers, causing quite a commotion in the streets and lanes." This quotation from our author's fascinating "Naturalist on the Amazons" is of especial interest, because of the great similarity and dissimilarity in the movements of the two species at this period of their existence. Remembering, at the time, the above remarks concerning the South American species, I looked carefully for the workers in this instance, and failed to discover more than a dozen wingless ants above-ground, and these were plodding about, very indifferent, as it appeared to me, to the fate or welfare of their winged brethren. On digging down a few inches, I could find but comparatively few individuals in the nest, and could detect no movements on their parts that referred to the exodus of winged individuals then going on.

On the other hand, the time of day agrees with the remarks of Mr. Bates. When I first noticed them, about 4 P.M., they had probably just commenced their flight. It continued until nearly 7 o'clock P.M., or for a considerable time after sunset. The next morning there was not an individual, winged or wingless, to be seen above-ground; the nest itself was comparatively empty; and what few occupants there were seemed to be in a semi-torpid condition.

It was not possible for me to calculate what proportion of the winged ants were carried by the wind too far to return to their old home; but certainly a large proportion were caught by the surrounding trees; and I found, on search, some of these ants crawling down the trunks of trees, with their wings in a damaged condition. How near the trees must be for the ants to reach their old home I should like to determine, and further, what tells them which road to take. Dr. Duncan, in his volume on the "Transformations of Insects," states, " It was formerly supposed that the females which alighted at a great distance from their old nests returned again; but Huber, having great doubts upon this subject, found that some of them, after having left the males, fell on to the ground in out-of-the-way places, whence they could not possibly return to the original nest." In the instance I have described, it seems impossible that more than a very small percentage could have returned, and indeed, if they did so, it was forty-eight hours after their departure, for during two days I continued to revisit the old nest.

Speaking of the little yellow ants, abundant in paths and about houses, Dr. Packard, in his "Guide to the Study of Insects," remarks: "The females, after their marriage flight in the air, may then be seen entering the ground to lay their eggs for new colonies, or, as Westwood states, they are often seized by the workers and retained in the old colonies." This latter occurrence was not the fate of any considerable number of the ants I observed. Dr. Packard further says that these flying ants, "having no more use for their wings, pluck them off, and may be seen running about wingless."

Had I spent an idle day, the injunction "Go to the ant, thou sluggard, consider her ways and be wise," might have been applicable; but soon after reaching my home I found the tables turned; the ants were considering my ways, were exploring every pocket, and prospecting even deeper, perhaps hopeful of establishing a new formicary. It is needless to add, that I entered an effective protest.

CHAPTER IV.
SWAMP WHITE-OAK BEND.

An angry Carolina wren is a capital alarm-clock. This morning the bird was astir before dawn, and roused me promptly at 4.30.

Once out-of-doors, I tarried longer in the yard than I intended, as the antics of the bird piqued my curiosity. Strange to say, the creature was more excited than usual, and noisier than ever before. Probably a prowling rat had come too near, and yet I saw no evidence of damage to the nest. The five young birds were taking an enviably comfortable nap. Still, the parent—I saw but one—was far from satisfied. Mounting a little weather-vane, it rattled its peculiar pr-r-r-r; then dashing into the elm, it screamed *jim-mée;* then from the roof of the ice-house called *zu-réi-ka*, and so on, until its vocabulary was exhausted. I lost fully an hour following the bird from point to point, hoping to learn the cause of its trouble.

I never knew this wren to mingle its many so-called songs. The one that it utters at the outset is sure to be repeated so long as the bird remains on a particular perch. When it changes its position, even if it be but for a few yards, its new song will be of a wholly different character. For years I have been trying to determine if these notes, which are so extraordinarily varied, bore any reference to the circumstances of their utterance. In this I have failed. They are apparently meaningless, and uttered at random; mere series of exclamations, as it were, and not always loudest or most elaborate when the excitement is intense.

It is noteworthy that at times, when all is serene, many of these same wild cries are sweetly sung, and would not be recognized if the bird were out of sight. And, too, it must be borne in mind that this same wren is greatly given to low chirpings and twitterings when two or more are in company.

I know of no species that more fully bears me out in the distinctions I long ago drew between the singing proper of birds and what may reasonably be called their conversation.

As late as August 29th I found a nest of this bird in a novel position, in a miniature cave on the hill-side. The whole interior was beautifully lined with interwoven grass and twigs. The nest was perfectly dry, and safe from flooding during ordinary summer showers. This was a discovery in local ornithology, for I find no record of a like occurrence. I thought at the time that possibly some unusual circumstance led to the spot being chosen, and that I would never find another such nest; but it really is a habit of the species to build in such localities.

To-day, on the same hill-side, down which I was hurrying, I found another of these "cave dwellings." It was, I am positive, an artificial excavation, and the same care had been exercised to make the walls secure. The entrance was covered with rough twigs and bits of lichen, and proved simply perfect as a blind. The coincidence of the bird's leaving the nest, just as I passed in front of it, alone led to my discovering it. I doubt if, an hour later, I could readily have found it again.

The occupant of this earth-retreat, like my erratic friend in the yard, was far from pleased at my inquisitiveness, and when I was far over the dew-drenched meadows, I could still hear its shrill scolding, though the sound was softened almost to a song, through the kindly office of the fog-thick air.

As I listened, I recalled another and unfortunate wren of my acquaintance. In a hollow oak that stood alone on the edge of a marshy meadow, a Carolina wren made his home during the past winter and devoted his time to singing and spider hunting, when not obliged to defend his castle from besieging blue-jays, prying owls, or prowling mammals. I made his acquaintance early in December, and many were the curious adventures of the bird that I chanced to witness. These culminated at the close of the winter.

During a blustering snow-storm, an opossum wandered to the tree and climbed to the very roosting-place of my wren. The tracks in the snow showed that he had entered but a short time before I happened on the spot. I am not positive, and can never determine the truth, but it is my firm conviction that the wren, which appeared to know me well and was quite tame, intended to relate his troubles. Fluttering near my head, he chirped, twittered, and scolded in an excited yet earnest manner.

I surmised the difficulty, but was not so well satisfied

that assistance could be rendered. My hesitation was evidently painful to the impatient wren. He swooped down and snapped his beak, and chirped close to my face, and looking at me with eyes that glistened with intelligence; then impatience controlling him, he would again dart at me and command, as though fearful that coaxing would not prove effective.

From me the wren constantly flew to the tree, and, resting a moment at the entrance to its hollow, chirped so energetically that he fairly lifted himself from his feet. Then back to me he would come, never alighting upon me, but hovering just above my head, and always sufficiently in front for me to see him.

Every movement of this distressed bird was eloquence itself, and impressed me with the fact of the great intelligence of birds, beyond any other occurrence in my experience.

I finally endeavored to dislodge the opossum by smoking it out, a process that very naturally increased the excitement of the wren. In due time I was successful, and was gratified to see the creature appear at the upper entrance to the hollow of the old oak. It stared about with characteristic stupidity, quite indifferent to my presence, and to that of the exultant wren, which darted at its face as fiercely as any hornet.

I soon brought the opossum to the ground, and the wren was again in possession, singing exultantly as I withdrew, perhaps intending to thank me for my services. But, alas! my efforts in behalf of the bird were far less successful than I supposed. The little fire that I had placed at the foot of the tree was fanned by a passing breeze to a lively flame, and my efforts to dislodge it proved unavailing. The wren's home, so long a landmark, soon disappeared, and with it the hermit of the hollow oak.

Again standing upon the creek's bank, I was glad to push my little boat from its moorings, and once more float with the tide, or leisurely pull against it, as the case might be. This morning I could have dropped anchor in mid-stream, so attractive was every feature of my surroundings; and what music is sweeter than the lapping of waves under the boat's bow? I divided my attention between this and the far-off whistling of a cardinal-redbird, the first I had heard for several weeks. It sang but its own song now, though I have recently learned that this beautiful songster may, after all, be called a "mocking-bird." Early one morning, not long ago, I heard one distinctly and exactly repeat the trisyllabic cry of the whippoorwill, and then conclude the utterance, each time, with its own well-known whistling. To most people it would have appeared that a whippoorwill and cardinal were singing at nearly the same time, the latter commencing before the other had finished. The question arises, why should this one cardinal imitate another bird, when others quite near by did not do so? My investigation of this rather forbidding problem proved successful. The redbird's home was in a vine-clad birch, and directly beneath lay a mossy, prostrate log, whereon a whippoorwill sat, both day and night, and during the latter season, of course, serenaded the cardinal with a monotonous repetition of the command to castigate unfortunate William. I do not wonder that the redbird learned to repeat the notes of his down-stairs neighbor when they rung in his ears nightly for several weeks.

I have intimated that the other cardinals about here were not given to mocking their neighbors. Do I know this? May not many a short song of some unseen bird have been the utterance of a cardinal? The acutest ear could not have detected the difference had the bird ceased singing with the syllable "will;" but this it did not do, and I made the discovery partly from this fact, and that the whippoorwill does not sing hours after sunrise.

It is never wise to be positive in the matter of birds. I have insisted that the cardinal-redbird is not a mocker. I take it all back.

Perhaps the creek was never at a lower stage than now. Above tide-water the river is but a valley of wet rocks, and here, where the tide creeps meadowward twice daily, is the stream, as usual, but so shrunken that many a low-lying meadow-tract offers a firm footing to the rambler. In numerous little sink-holes, from which the water has evaporated or soaked away, I find the skeletons of small fishes, neatly wrapped in the scale-armor of their shrunken skins. They are curious objects, and no length of soaking restores their former graceful outlines. As I pick them from the mud, the imprint of their shrivelled forms is left—fossil impressions for the naturalists of ten thousand years to come. This is possible, of course, so I wrote on the smooth surface from which I lifted a minnow, *Fundulus multifasciatus.* Will it not startle the paleontologist of the indefinite future to chisel from a rock an already labelled fossil? I trust that he will not go mad.

I was soon within the shadows of the great swamp white-oaks. Here the creek curves gently to the north, and upon its left bank grows a number of these magnificent trees. Like all the oaks, they are beautiful at all times, even when bared of every leaf. Like all large trees, they attract birds of many kinds; but, strangely enough, they were apparently deserted as I rowed beneath their overhanging branches.

It makes a vast difference in our impressions of a locality, whether it is silent or noisy, as we draw near. If the former, we are apt to consider it abandoned, and jumping at the conclusion that

"something ails it now,
The spot is curst,"

we hurry by. On the other hand, if the song of a bird, the splash of a turtle, or warning bark of a squirrel is heard, we are assured that it is a pleasant place, and prepare to tarry.

To-day it was none of these, but the wake of a musk-rat as it crossed the creek, or nearly crossed; when, as though it had forgotten something, it returned to the point from which it started. This may seem too trivial an incident to record, and indeed, a single trip would have been; but why did the musk-rat return so promptly? This was what piqued my curiosity, and caused me to check my progress down stream. Had I seen the animal take something over the creek or bring something back, all would have been plain enough, but this was not the case. That swim of fifty yards each way was apparently without an object, and so was a proper subject for a naturalist's consideration. I felt convinced that there was something behind the scenes. Why should not the musk-rat's brain be as active as its body? The creature doubtless had plans and purposes of its own; and it was my desire, if not my business, to determine what they were.

When the musk-rat returned to the north shore it looked after me, as I very slowly withdrew, and when the distance between us was doubled, rose upon its hind-legs and uttered a shrill squeak; then it plunged into the water. I saw that it was again crossing the creek, and quickly urged my boat forward. Instantly the musk-rat dived, and I saw nothing more of it, until detected in creeping very slowly from the creek and then skulking behind the clustered stems of crowded Nuphar. I held my boat back and waited. The musk-rat sat watching me. Tired at last I slowly withdrew, and when I could no longer see the cunning creature, it evidently became satisfied that all danger was past, and again commenced swimming to the opposite shore, and this time not alone. A series of wakes told the story, the brood of the cunning musk-rat followed their parent.

It must not be supposed that this mammal is everywhere abundant. It has always been subject to constant persecution; and considering the numbers trapped during the winter months, it speaks volumes for their cunning that they have escaped extermination. But whether abundant or rare, one need not expect to see them frequently during the day. They are essentially nocturnal, or rather crepuscular, and glory in still moonlit nights, when often a dozen can be seen at one time.

At intervals this creature looms up in zoological literature in a curious way. That musk-rats are fond of mussels, every boy upon a farm well knows; but it is the disposition of some, who profess to have dived a little more deeply into this remarkable matter, to invest this whim of the animal with a deal of mystery. The latest screed upon this subject is the most utterly absurd of all; and alas! is trumpeted forth by a school-master.

It was bad enough to have impossible gymnastics ascribed to the musk-rat; to assert that it deftly forced its toe-nails between the slightly open valves, without irritating the sensitive "foot" so that it would be withdrawn, and that with its fore-legs thus encumbered the musk-rat sought the shore—vainly sought it I imagine. All this vagary from a hopeful (?) pupil; and now comes the further elucidation of the problem from the teacher. He has been wandering along the river shore, ay, and picked up mussels. Better yet, he has surprised them with their "feet" out and pinched them until the whole body was paralyzed. Here is the real secret of the musk-rat, then; they have learned the pedagogic squeeze!

To go back a step. These lovers of mystery assume, at the outset, that the shells of mussels are seldom or never injured by the musk-rat. This, of itself, is not true. Thoreau, in "Early Spring," remarks: "I find ... several have one valve quite broken in two in the rat's effort to wrench them open. . . . *All the rest show the marks of their teeth at one end or the other.* You can see distinctly also the marks of their teeth where, with a scraping cut, they have scraped off the tough muscle which fastens the fish to its shell; also, sometimes all along the nacre next the edge."

Again in "Science," No. 107, Mr. Beecher says: "I have *often* seen the posterior margins of the valves slightly notched, and the epidermis scratched, from the efforts of the musk-rat to open the shell." This author does not believe that the hinge of the shell is successfully attacked by the musk-rat, but adds, "*this portion is sometimes injured.*"

So much concerning the "never mutilated" shells.

The pedagogue declares that he can squeeze mussels until they are paralyzed. It is a gift confined to few, to say the least; and he argues that his accomplishments are not beyond the capabilities of a musk-rat.

Of course the latter, having no opposable thumb, must use both fore-feet, in lieu of the powerful hand of a pedagogue, and squeeze until the mussel cries "enough." As soon as the valves are opened enough to give this agonized utterance, pop! in goes the paw of the rat and the coveted morsel is secure.

But in our southern and western waters the shells of these mollusks are vastly thicker than are those of the Delaware River species, and the musk-rat eats of them as freely as of those that are thin-shelled. This matters not. It is the magic of the squeeze and not brute force that accomplishes the desired object. Even when the shell is not only thick, but ribbed and prickly with testaceous spines, it is the same; let the creature but feel the thrill of a pedagogic squeeze and it is doomed.

Ay! but when did the musk-rat learn the secret and secure the transference of the magic that lurks in the hand of a school-master?

Again afloat, but not much more than floating. While I had tarried to watch the musk-rat, the outgoing tide had not tarried with me, and now had nearly run its long appointed course. The trees cast so inviting a shade that I concluded to land again, and having passed the last of the group of swamp white-oaks, beached my boat upon the muddy shore, where towering forest-trees were thickly clustered. They grew so closely to the water's edge, that only at low tide was there any space between their trunks and the creek. Birch, linden, button-wood, maple, and willow were about equally represented in numbers, but varying as much in size as in the patterns of their leaves. With the miscellaneous undergrowth, the locality possessed plant life of every shade of green; and this it is that prevents the painful monotony characteristic of some forest tracts. It is scarcely less objectionable to be in a forest exclusively of pine or oak than in a gaudy flower-garden. The sameness of the one wearies as readily as the other pains by its excess of color. In the association of widely different species of trees there is a grateful variety without painful contrast.

What few birds I saw seemed partial to certain trees.

Not a redstart was seen except on the willows, and the titmice and creepers singled out the scattered buttonwoods. This was not for the moment only, but held good for the while I tarried in the shade of these growths. As they were all evidently busy insect-hunting, each found food, I suppose, peculiarly attractive to itself, in the trees they frequented.

I was somewhat surprised at the variety and volume of bird-music to be heard. The red-eyed vireo's throat and wings were well-matched, and to decide wherein was the greater activity would have been a difficult matter. If the bird flew unusually fast, its notes were always proportionately louder and more rapidly uttered. The song is not melodious; yet when heard afar off, with the bird hidden among the upper branches of the trees, it is a pleasant sound, to say the least, and one sure to lead us deeper and deeper into the woods; for the desire to see the birds that we chance to hear is well-nigh irresistible.

To-day there were hosts of summer warblers, active as the trembling leaves, in their search for insects, but save an occasional faint chirp, all were silent. On the other hand, the Maryland yellow-throats and crested tits were singing constantly. It is strange that so much difference should obtain, in this respect, among our song birds. Now that nesting is over, many find next to nothing to sing about. Can it be that their existence is less joyful for the ten months of freedom than during the two of their married life? Possibly we may get from them a clew as to which birds are mated for life, and which for a season. Is the fact that some birds sing at all times of the year an indication of their life-long happiness? As I write, I hear the song-sparrows, the swamp-finches, and a cat-bird, all in full song; the latter, perhaps, singing more briefly than in June. I know that there is much evidence to be brought forward that both the song-sparrow and cat-bird are permanently mated.

A sudden, violent agitation of the surface of the water caused me quickly to cease thinking of birds, and regard the strange commotion in the creek. It was evidently not due to a passing breeze, and peering into the depths—very shallow just then—I saw countless hundreds of young shad. It was a little late for these fish. Usually they reach tide-water, coming from the upper portions of the river, by August 1st; but herein Nature's methods have been somewhat disturbed of late, and many thousands of artificially hatched shad are now set at liberty at such times as the Fish Commission see fit. These, perhaps, have just arrived from some hatchery, and are later than their wild brethren. Be that as it may, when once full-grown no difference is detected, and no questions need be asked, when the baked shad comes to the table. Still, it must be confessed that the interest centring in these fish is much lessened since their artificial propagation. It places them among fishes where chickens are among birds—very useful, but not suggestive of untamed nature.

The thousands of young shad that crowded about my boat were not only very tame but very stupid; at least gave every evidence of being quite at the mercy of the tides. I carefully lifted several from the water, and although every precaution was taken not to injure them, they quickly succumbed. The mere act of lifting them from the water and immediately returning them proved a shock, and twenty seconds exposure to the atmosphere was fatal.

The kingfishers for many a mile seemed to know of this school of fish, and they followed it as closely as gulls do the moss-bunkers along our sea-coast. Again and again these voracious birds would dart into the midst of the young shad, and swallowed them usually without preliminary butchering.

I followed these fish a short distance, when, as though the tide had turned, they very suddenly reversed their positions and moved slowly towards the river. Considering their helplessness, it is a marvel that any of their number should ever reach the ocean. Not simply for the reason that the kingfishers followed them so closely, but because they were also attended by numbers of pike, perch, water-snakes, and had even to run the gantlet of scores of hungry turtles. This in the creek where I saw them. What their experiences in the river were to be can be imagined.

Nevertheless, centuries ago, the cunning Indian fishermen, at this very bend of the creek, captured thousands of shad by methods of their own—perhaps beneath the larger of the oaks still standing here.

Loskiel records, "There is a particular manner of fishing which is undertaken in parties, as many hands are wanted, in the following manner: when the *shad-fish* (*Alosa clupea*) come up the rivers, the Indians run a dam of stones across the stream, where its depth will admit of it, not in a straight line, but in two parts, verging towards each other in an angle. An opening is left in the middle for the water to run off. At this opening they place a large box, the bottom of which is full of holes. Then they make a rope of the twigs of the wild vine, reaching across the stream, upon which boughs of about six feet in length are fastened at the distance of about two fathoms from each other. A party is detached about a mile above the dam with this rope and its appendages, who begin to move gently down the current, some guiding one, some the opposite end, while others keep the branches from sinking by supporting the rope in the middle with wooden forks. Thus they proceed, frightening the fishes into the opening left in the middle of the dam, where a number of Indians are placed on each side, who, standing upon the two legs of the angles, drive the fishes with poles and a hideous noise, through the opening into the above-mentioned box or chest. Here they lie, the water running off through the holes in the bottom, and other Indians, stationed on each side of the chest, take them out, kill them, and fill their canoes. By this contrivance they sometimes catch above a thousand shad and other fish in half a day."

It was at this bend of the creek that the Indians had one of their fish-dams, and a century afterwards traces of it were plainly to be seen at low tide. The few Indians that lingered about the settlements of the whites still used it, and fished at times in company with their pale-faced neighbors. It is due to this fact that references to such fishing sites and methods of capturing shad have been recorded in several old commonplace books, some of which I have seen. The best of these is in a letter of Mahlon Stacy, who wrote "From the Falls of Delaware, in West New Jersey, the 26th of the 4th month, 1680." He says: "Fish, in their season, are very plenteous. My cousin Revell and I, with some of my men, went last third month into the river to catch herrings; for at that time they come in great shoals into the shallows. We had neither rod nor net, but, after the Indian fashion, made a round pinfold, about two yards over and a foot high, but left a gap for the fish to go in at; and made a bush to lay in the gap to keep the fish in; and when that was done, we took two long birches and tied their tops together, and went about a stone's cast above our said pinfold: then hauling these birch boughs down the stream, where we drove thousands before us, but so many got into our trap as it would hold. And then we began to haul them on shore as fast as three or four of us could, by two or three at a time; and after this manner, in half an hour, we could have filled a three-bushel sack of as good and large herrings as ever I saw. . . . And though I speak of herrings only, lest any should think we have little other sorts, we have great plenty of most sorts of fish that ever I saw in England, besides several other sorts that are not known there—as rocks, catfish, *shads*, sheep's-heads, sturgeons."

As my boat rested upon the steadily widening cushion of untracked mud, I looked carefully for any signs of life peculiar to such an environment. There seemed to be nothing except minute forms that would need a microscope to identify. But if wanting in readily visible animal life, it was full of sound. The steady draining off of the water caused a constant sibilant snapping as the surface cracked and bubbled.

With not a spider even darting over the mud, and no subterranean creature peeping above it, it would have been monotonous waiting for the tide to turn, had not a cat-bird kindly entertained me the while. He seemed strangely out of place. Why he should have left the briers on the hill-side and wandered thither is hard to imagine, for the relative abundance of food in the two localities cannot vary materially. At all events, here he was, and with the agility of a marsh-wren clung to the stems of pickerel-weed and wild-rice, and then venturing upon the drier edge of the mud flat, hopped with that teetering of the tail that is a feature of sandpipers and water-thrushes. Do all birds that come here from the uplands walk in such a manner, as though they caught the trick from the incessant seesaw of the rippling waters? I was perfectly quiet, and presently the cat-bird flew to the bow of the boat, and sitting there chirped vigorously as he watched me, lying full length in the bottom of the boat. That chirp was a call to his mate, I took it, and presently she came—at least another cat-bird came—and she too eyed me for a moment intently. I could not be more sure of her meaning had I perfect knowledge of a cat-bird's language. She told her mate that I might prove dangerous, and advised his quickly retreating. He was not so easily persuaded, and even dared hop a few paces nearer, she scolding vigorously all the while. I remained motionless. He came a little nearer and twittered "See here, see here!" She was by no means convinced, and remained at a safe distance. Her mate, growing still braver, flew almost to my feet and perched upon the stern of the boat. Then I waved my arms vigorously above my head and the poor bird flew shrieking with terror to the woods, followed by his more cautious mate. A half-hour afterwards she was still scolding, and I doubt not gloried over his mishap. When the months roll by, and a new nest is to be built, if any dispute arises, she will be twittering "Remember the man in the boat." Like all of her sex, whether in feathers or smooth skin, they never omit an opportunity to tease, or forget the few times in their lives when they really have the best of an argument.

The creek here, as in many portions of its channel, has greatly altered since Indian times. It was then much deeper, somewhat narrower, and its waters clearer. This better condition, in fact, continued until the beginning of this century, when the general deforesting of the hill-side was commenced, and in the past eighty-five years the rains have gullied the bluff in many places, and carried to the creek's channel countless tons of sand and gravel, which the current has never been powerful enough to remove; and often for hundreds of rods there is a broad and shallow flow, where formerly it was deep and narrow.

These great changes, deplorable as they may be, have not robbed the creek of all its beauty. After the catbirds had departed, and I had sought in vain for some substantial traces of the old Indian fishing-dam, I worked

SWAMP WHITE-OAK BEND. 111

the boat back to the water, and proceeded a few rods down the stream, when I came to a stretch of weedy, open meadow, aglow with brilliant color. Here

> The golden dodder's tangled net,
> With waxen blossoms thickly set,
> Enwraps the vervain's purple spire;
> O'erspreads the rose with thread-like fire;
> And like a gilded serpent twines
> The mazy host of tangled vines.

One large thicket of impenetrable growths was a cluster of blackberry canes ; and here, too, was a grand display of color. The canes were nearly leafless, but still covered with a generous yield of fruit. This was but half ripe and bright crimson, with here and there at pleasing intervals a twig with coal-black berries.

When absence of contrast has long prevailed, how heartily is the crimson and black, the purple and gold, the cardinal-flower among sedges, greeted. For weeks the upland fields have been glowing with rich yellow, in itself a pleasing color, but how tiresome to live amid acres of blooming partridge-pea, to the exclusion of even an occasional blade of grass.

This pretty meadow — weedy, my farmer neighbors call it — is bounded by a few large trees; and as I approached them I heard a gentle tapping high overhead, which I attributed to a woodpecker. While seated in the boat, I looked into every tree as best I could, but caught no glimpse of the bird. I looked skyward until my neck ached, but in vain. Then, very naturally, I "got mad." The tapping was remarkably constant, yet the bird was playing bopeep very successfully. It must never happen that a naturalist gives up the chase. Believing the bird was doing its best to avoid me, I determined to out-wit it. I turned the boat's bow inshore, and was on the point of stepping out, when there was the busy woodpecker almost at my feet. But it was not a bird. A curiously bent twig was caught and released by each passing ripple, and by its motion made the tapping sound. I assumed at the outset that the noise was made by a bird, and so looked for it among the branches of the tall trees. How unsafe it is to be positive; yet had I gone away without seeing a woodpecker, or learning the cause of the tapping, I could never have been convinced that the bird was not where I supposed it to be.

Here, months earlier, however, I did see a beautiful red-bellied woodpecker that came near out-witting me. It was *in* a hollow tree, instead of *upon* it, and judging from the length of time it remained concealed, must have found the cavernous hollow an excellent feeding ground.

This rare woodpecker has been slighted by ornithologists, or is a most prosaic, unentertaining bird. Wilson states that it is not partial to fences, but loves tall trees. Audubon says that it prefers the forest to open country. These facts will apply to nearly all of the family.

Unlike many birds, this woodpecker shows no disposition to suit itself to circumstances, and just as steadily as our large trees are felled do they decrease in numbers. In this they resemble the red-headed woodpecker. I have never found their nests; but once, in midwinter, discovered a pair industriously pecking a hole in a chestnut oak. Like their cousins, the flickers, these also probably make more holes for nests in one year than they can occupy in a dozen. In this they prove a blessing to others, as the bluebirds and great crested flycatchers use them, unless ousted, as is too apt to be the case, by the gray squirrels.

I am free to confess that woodpeckers, as a family of birds, have failed to interest me. There is little if any mystery about them, and several species being resident, they are every-day features of an out-door ramble. You may see one or many in June or January, and they are always the same: agile climbers over the upright branches of trees, picking, pecking, hammering as they go. No birds so seldom induce me to pause, when passing through the woods; yet once I had a pleasant surprise, due to the cunning of a pair of woodpeckers. During a violent snow-squall I took shelter behind an old walnut-tree, nearly four feet in diameter; and while standing there, partly shielded from the storm, a pair of beautiful redheaded woodpeckers suddenly appeared immediately above my head, having, like me, taken refuge from the cutting north wind and driving snow. The moment they were at rest they saw me, and with a shrill chirp again took wing, but as suddenly reconsidered the matter, and eying me very closely, concluded to risk whatever danger there might be in my presence, rather than face such a snow-storm. I could only assure them by remaining perfectly quiet, and for a quarter of an hour I stood like a statue, and they sat near by, in a painfully alert attitude, ready to face the storm if I moved. As rapidly as the snowing commenced it stopped, and

I moved my arms slightly when the sunlight broke through the clouds. Instantly the birds were on the wing and out of sight.

To a student of animal psychology this is no trivial incident. There was a deliberate exercise of choice; a consultation between the birds, and a decision reached and acted upon; and all transpiring in less than one minute. If not an exercise of true reasoning powers, what shall we call it? Certainly no mythical "instinct" can be called up to explain such facts.

The last bird that I saw to-day, and the least, was probably the happiest; for it evidently combined pleasure with business. I watched for a full hour a dainty little flycatcher, that when not busy was singing. Ché-pink—Che-piṅk! it warbled with a pretty toss of the head, and then deftly sailed out for an insect. Not always out, but rather down; for it often dived into a thicket twenty feet below, and the sharp snap of its beak told the story of an insect's capture. Then with an easy, upward flight it regained its perch, and whistled these two syllables, peculiarly its own, Ché-pink —Che-piṅk! It was Traill's flycatcher; a bird that comes and goes with the migratory hosts that summer farther north; but it likewise stays every summer and haunts the tree-clad reaches of the Crosswicks valley.

It is a common practice among those who delight in studying our song birds, as they find them in their chosen haunts, to class a very large number as "minor songsters," giving them credit for good intentions rather than meritorious performance. I confess to an entire want of sympathy with those who draw such distinctions, and rejoice in being able to derive as much pleasure from a simple ditty as from the most varied, eloquent, and artistic effort. The surroundings make the song. Is not the wild scream of the hawk, as it hovers on the edge of a storm-cloud, answering the rattling thunder with its defiant cry, akin to music? The whistle of the cardinal, in crystal-clear midwinter days; the hopeful warble of the bluebird, as it hints of spring; the cheery call of the crested tit; the faint lisping of restless cedar-birds; simple sounds that we hear at intervals, months after the grosbeak, the orioles, and the warblers have departed; are they not as delightful to the ear, as soothing and suggestive as any summer song of nesting thrushes?

It is the homely " air " that we habitually hum, when in a meditative mood, that is dearest to our hearts; some simple song, first heard in infancy, it may be, that we never forget, and always prize far beyond the intricate maze of scientific opera. So the unpretending efforts of the song-sparrow, the grass-finch, and all the host of " minor songsters," afford, I believe, at least as much pleasure as the wonderful performances of the masters of melody.

A glorious sunset closed the day. The feathery clouds that for hours had been floating westward crowded the sun's path, as though they would dispute his progress. Now he turns upon them, and breaking a passage through their deep-closed ranks, reillumines the darkened reaches of the creek, while the blushing clouds retire.

CHAPTER V.
DEAD WILLOW BEND.

In an August day there is nothing particularly august, even if it ends in a gust. This may prove more inconvenient than grand, as when my house was struck by lightning. One good thing, however, may be said of the month; its sultriness does not reach the shady recesses along the creek; and as all the indications were those of a tropical day upon the uplands, I made haste, as usual, on this my fifth outing, to be again afloat.

Not a creature crossed my path as I hurried along, following wherever the grass had been well cropped by the cows; for every twig and leaf was dripping with dew.

My neighbors speak of dew as something very different from water, saying that it will saturate one's clothing far more quickly. I am half disposed to believe it. I have never found a leather shoe that was proof against it.

How little is required to raise the commonplace to the dignity of grandeur! Every object, however homely, was at sunrise to-day made as beautiful as it was prominent by the magic of this daintily-defining dew. Every blade of grass bore aloft its brilliant crystal; every leaf sparkled with its clustered gems; every airy highway of Arachne was a wondrous structure, built of stolen moonbeams.

Two tracts of meadow that I passed over this morning, had it not been for the dew, would have proved strangely monotonous, considering what a wealth of bloom overspread them but a few weeks ago. In that one nearest my home Flora was certainly prodigal with her favors, even so early as April. Along each hedge the dog-wood fluttered its snowy raggedness; and beneath, violets, blue, purple, ashen, and white, bloomed in profusion. Spring beauty, wherever the ground was dry, shyly peeped through the relics of departed years. Wind-flowers, though trembling in every breeze, showed a bolder front, and vied with adder's-tongue and bellwort in courting recognition. With azure snow the distant knolls were dusted, and I knew that the wee Houstonia was again in bloom.

Later, when standing in the midst of them, I could not but recall the curse of familiarity. How true it is that many of the most beautiful objects in nature are the most abundant, and yet they are systematically overlooked and neglected. The bluets prove this. Why one should exclaim over a rare flower of no special merit, and yet be indifferent to the azalea, kalmia, or iris, is incomprehensible to me. If a plant has no particular attraction, it is proper that it should seldom loom up in one's pathway; and I am thankful, for one, that so many of the choicest wild-flowers are so extraordinarily abundant. Think of the bluets! They grow so closely sixteen are found to the square inch, or more than twenty thousand to the square yard—more than a million to the acre! I have stood in the midst of many acres of them. Must they be snubbed because of their abundance?

The banks of the little brook that skirted both these meadow tracts and the stream itself were no less brilliant with spring-tide blossoms. From the shallower waters there arose a leafy growth of spear-like equisetum, and the spotted frogs crouching at their roots seemed less a terror-stricken host than an alert army bearing its weapons aloft, ready to battle with the hovering, hungry-eyed herons. Hard by the beautiful orontium was clustered, but not a frog was near to wield their golden clubs.

Flora was clearly averse to have any nook or corner slighted, and the very mud of the creek's bank was hidden, even to the water's edge, with a marigold that had no rival among the yellow blossoms of its day.

Golden ragwort, worthy of a better name, a month later overtopped all other bloom, and its fiery blossoms set these meadows in a blaze.

And yet later the very grass was hidden by golden Cynthia, that paled the more ambitious evening primrose growing with it; nor yet content with her prodigality, had scattered blue iris by every pool, and clustered its yellow sisters at the creek.

Almost the first bird I saw this morning, as I floated out into the stream, was one of those melanistic house-wrens which frequent the darkest and most inaccessible nooks of our woods. In years gone by, I knew it as the "wood-wren," and it was as well defined a species in plumage, habits, and peculiarities as any of the wren family. We are told now that the wood-wren, of which Audubon wrote so pleasantly, was nothing but a house-wren soiled with charcoal dust! All the professionals agree to this; and yet I cannot but think it a little strange that every house-wren that wanders to the remote woods, and lives a life strikingly different from its kind that tenant the boxes in our door-yards, should show decided melanism. Do abnormally dark feathers cause them to retire to the quiet retreats of gloomy woods? It would appear so, yet this of course is utterly absurd. Whether house-wren or wood-wren, it matters not; but here, delighting to clamber over prostrate and mossy tree-trunks; to thread its way among the tangled stems of dwarfed kalmias, and to skim along the water's surface, picking up "skaters" as it goes, these wrens in nothing recall their noisy brothers, that sing and scold, the livelong day, about our houses. Nor are they noisy and fretful, like the typical "*œdon.*" Like all active birds, they chirp frequently, and often pausing in their insect-hunting, sing the song of the wren at home; the same notes, but yet more tuneful; freer of the harsh, rasping rattle that too often converts the song to mere noise.

These wild wrens, too, nest in a different manner. Choosing a hollow in some decayed tree, they place the nest quite out of reach, often six or eight feet from the opening that leads to it, or build on the ground among the roots of a large tree, where they are exposed to the attacks of small mammals.

That Audubon's wood-wren was a charcoal-dusted house-wren is, of course, not impossible; but that a darker-plumaged variety or race of the *Troglodytes œdon* has taken itself to the woods, is not unlikely to be true. Like all birds that continually haunt the banks of streams, this wren had the trick of jerking its tail quite like the spotted sand-piper or golden-crowned thrush. Is it necessary in consequence of the yielding of the soft mud over which it hopped? I went ashore to see if so small a bird left any tracks, and found that they were quite deep; as well defined as sparrow tracks made on new-fallen snow. Returning to the boat, I saw the wren again a few rods farther down the stream, and I wished for those of my friends who believe in the power of snakes to charm birds. On a mat of dead grass, close to the water's edge, was coiled a huge water-snake, and the wren was evidently, by a torrent of abuse and vehement scolding, endeavoring to drive the creature away. It flew at it, and snapped its beak so sharply that I could plainly hear it; but the snake was quite indifferent to the turmoil about, and only left its bed as I came opposite to it. But the wren claimed all the credit, and sang exultantly as I passed by.

Passing rank growths of aquatic weeds which to-day seemed quite deserted, I reached that charming portion of the creek, Dead Willow Bend. Perhaps of all our forest-trees a dead willow is the least expressive; far less so, surely, than the decaying oak or elm that for centuries has been a landmark, once to the Indian and since to ourselves; but such dead willows are nevertheless suggestive. Their short and bulky trunks are pretty sure to be hollow, and the rambler naturally looks for animals lurking in their roomy interiors. Perhaps it is for this very reason that our mammals generally are careful not to occupy them. I give the coon, skunk, and mink credit for too much common-sense. They seem to know, quite as well as I do, that the average hollow willow is a target for every idle loafer that passes by, and its crumbling trunk becomes as well known as the dusty highway. Sometimes it happens that clustering shrubbery about such trees hides every vestige of the trunk, and then a safer hiding-place is afforded by it. This is true of our great dead willow here—the tree has a history.

A year ago I happened here, and found on the creek-bank, near by, a fragment of a man tied up in rags. It was not, as one might suppose, a ghastly sight, and I felt no need to report the remains to the coroner. I slowly approached the spot, making almost no noise, but the crackling of twigs was sufficient to reach the ears of this fragmentary man. He roused in an instant, and in all his incompleteness stood before me.

Rubbing his eyes, he drawled out, "I believe I've been asleep," and then looking up at the sun, added, "Hang me if 'tain't to-morrer."

"It is to-day, and early in the morning," I replied.

"The last I knowed, it was moonlight, and I begun to get tired, and laid down my fishin'-tackle, but I didn't know I'd been asleep. You look sort o' puzzled," this dilapidated fisherman continued, "as tho' you didn't expect to find any one here, let alone me. Well, you see, I do make out to get round, if there is a lot o' me gone ;" and the fellow glanced at the stump of his right arm and then at his wooden leg, with the one eye that remained to him. "You're a stranger about here, I take it," was my reply to his remarks concerning himself.

The fact is, I was too much surprised to see so apparently helpless a man so far from any house or even public highway.

"Stranger about here?" he repeated; "not exactly, for I was here some five years ago, and had a bit of a lark in that dead willer yonder. You see, I don't foller the land, but the water," and he pointed to a neat cedar boat, with one oar resting at the stern. "That's my home eight months of the year, and I can go from the falls to the sea-shore when o' mind to."

"But what about this dead willow?" I asked.

"It come round this way. 'Long late in October I drifted in here, gettin' stuff for a drug store, fishin' and the like, when up there come the biggest sort of a rain, all of a sudden. I'd no notion of gettin' wet, so I looked round, and seein' the willer was big and hollow—it wa'n't kivered with weeds then—thought I'd creep in and wait for the rain to stop. 'Twan't no easy job fur me, but I made it out and sort o' chuckled to myself as I heerd the rain a pitter-patter agin' the tree, and felt the wind shakin' it clean to the roots. But 'tisn't a red apple that's always the sweetest, you know. The rain sort o' gathered overhead and poured a stream down my back. That riled a swarm o' black ants, and they took refuge in my coat and tickled worse than a flea's bite. Then the blowin' came on in airnest. One puff opened a big crack in the willer and my wooden leg slipped through, and was held like a rat in a steel trap. There I was, and gettin' desprit, I tell you, when luck turned a little, and a puff o' wind opened the crack agin and let me go. I got out, spite o' the dark, and left fur hum."

I drew a long breath, and stared at the garrulous cripple in silence.

"Don't you b'lieve it?" he asked, with some irritation in his voice; "if you don't, we'll stay strangers one to t'other, that's all;" and he hobbled to his boat.

I watched him embark, and as he sculled down the creek I wondered who he was. To this day he remains a stranger, both to me and to my neighbors.

The willow is a test tree with those who anxiously await the coming of spring, and by its leaf-buds one is apt to swear when aiming to be weatherwise. They were held by the early Swedes who settled here to be governed by the sun's movement more than by the actual conditions of the weather. By mere chance, it occurred to me to test it as the winter of '85 drew to a close.

My almanac, under date of March 20th, states, "10 A.M. spring commences." Opens her engagement for the season, I presume is meant, and so to be present at the rising of the curtain I hurried to the meadows. I have read upon play-bills, "Curtain rises promptly at 7.45 P.M.;" but it happened otherwise. 10 A.M. came and went, and not an intimation was there of the grand acts about to be performed. The torn and tattered hangings of the late tragedy, winter, was all that I found. But I am not given to despair, and the next day, and the next, and all that week, I walked over the crisp meadows to a distant hedge of willows. Though still the curtain did not rise, it was not in vain that I went. The orchestra did all they could to keep peace with the audience, and they succeeded. Why, then, complain that I found no green thing save where, nestling at the wrinkled feet of gnarly oaks, the tufted mats of emerald moss, keeping a brilliant summer to themselves, shone fitfully through the whirling clouds of wind-tossed leaves? The shores of the little brook were lifeless as I approached them. The long, gaunt limbs of the hornbeams, stretching aimlessly into chilly space, were the only objects that the shuddering waters reflected, and typified a comfortless March day. Comfortless? How rashly do we use the Queen's English, if there be not perfection in our surroundings. Comfortless, indeed! In spite of the March wind, a dainty frog, clinging to trembling blades of grass, piped merrily; even undaunted when the gusts dashed icy spray in his face. Surely, fur-wrapped and stoutly booted, I need not complain. I pressed forward to the willows, and was greeted by the birds. Scattered over every bush, hovering over last year's nests, and bending topmost twigs of every tree, were the crimson-shouldered starlings whose united voices flooded the meadows with melody.

As I listened, I gathered catkins from the clustered alders, but found no green thing. They seemed plump golden caterpillars, shivering and squirming in the gusty puffing of the petulant wind; but being flowers, how eagerly we clutch at them, gather and toy with them. Why not feel the same towards caterpillars themselves? They are as a rule quite as harmless, and many are far more beautiful than any flower.

The army of frogs in the marsh was not so brave as the little soldier in the brook. Every blast of the March winds quickly silenced them for a time. From many a hundred cosey nooks, flooded with sunshine and cheery with the promised warmth of spring, exultant frogs had for days been rejoicing over the lessening gripe of winter. It was a clear, full-voiced expression of mingled joy and content, and in nowise, as it is often called, a croak, or melancholy plaint. Still, when a sudden blast from the north blows the brown rushes, above the roar of its fell swoop can be heard an unmistakable tone of sadness, a cry translatable, "We weep! we weep!" Indeed they have cause to do so. I too turned for shelter to an oak near by, but before I could reach the hollow in its trunk the meadows were again at rest, and over the out-stretched acres of the marsh came again the hopeful voices of that faithful legion, the burden of whose song was "Keep up, keep up, keep!"

And so passed another day, without any green thing; but the meadows were fruitful of promises, and putting faith in the birds and frogs, I was persuaded to go again and again, and promised to keep up. Twice it rained. Once it was a conscious shower, that, knowing it was unwelcome, was very gentle while it stayed, and hurried off as soon as practicable. The next was an ill-tempered dash, that allowed no drop to fall quietly to the earth, but forced it rudely into every nook, and made disconsolate all unsheltered creatures.

It is a matter of surprise that our rains of a year have not been captured by the professional essayist and made the matter of a thoughtful book. They are readily classified, for each has features peculiarly its own. Let some lover of out-of-doors con this matter over, and give these fogs, sprinkles, showers, gusts, nor'-easters, equinoctials, snows, and hail-storms, that attention which they deserve. Each one is rich in rare suggestiveness.

Even the last rain, ill-tempered as it was, put no quietus on the patient frogs. They sung the louder, so I thought, as the rain came rattling on their upturned faces and turned the dripping grass-blades on their backs. "Keep up! keep!" they shouted as I passed; and though it rained, I walked the length of that long willow hedge, finding no green thing. Nor did the rain keep back the early birds; great blue herons sailed among the clouds and then came trooping to the tall trees by the marsh. Advance-guard of the coming host, my pulses quickened as I marked their coming. But these were not the only birds to arrive from the south; there were small birds in abundance. All the world knows when the geese go north; it is a fact sure to be recorded in village papers. The eyes that detect the geese, even when mere dots against the sky, fail to see the twittering hosts in the shrubbery. It is, nevertheless, an excellent indication of milder weather when the Arctic birds, that have wintered south of us, come in great flocks, and enliven for a day or two our woods and meadows. To-day the meadow copses were thronged with white-throated sparrows, and each sung in a subdued tone a few contemplative notes, as though intended for no ears but the singer's. These were not the birds of the past winter months. Many of these passed northward a week ago, but are the winter sojourners of some more southern valley. They come in advance of our summer birds, and foretell mild weather with moderate certainty; but sometimes, let it be borne in mind, they sadly blunder. A cold storm catches them, bewilders and disheartens them, and as if afraid to make another effort, they tarry until almost summer weather.

These pretty finches gave me confidence, and I hurried to the willows. No, the leaf-buds were still brown, but swollen; and I found no green thing.

But the past was in another month, and what of to-day?—this breezy, frosty, threatening April 1st?

The east was but faintly streaked with rosy light as I sought the meadows; but the robins were before me, and each in his post, from the mist-wrapped, leafless trees, sung his morning hymn. Anon the clouds parted as the sun slowly rose; the fog, as a curtain, rolled upward and away; a flood of light spread over all the scene; spring, at last, with a sweet smile, came upon the stage—the willows were a-greening.

Waste-land, as my neighbors call it, is always an eyesore to them, and many who have passed Dead Willow Bend almost daily for years have failed to discover its beauties. But no contemplative rambler would fail to be held by them, at least on such a day as this, when the waters chanced to be without a ripple, the sky without a cloud. Not a leaf trembled on any twig; not a bird broke the silence. Above and beneath a fathomless depth of unstained blue—on either side, a wilderness of green.

Guiding, but not propelling my boat, I slowly and silently moved forward, wondering that nothing should appear. At last, from some distant meadow, a broad-winged bird came flying towards me. Nearer and nearer it came, and not alarmed by my presence, settled in the tall grass not twenty yards away. It was a bittern.

Turnbull, in his "Birds of East Pennsylvania," says of the bitterns, they are "plentiful from the middle of April to October." This word "plentiful" is a convenient term when one desires to speak in very general and non-committal terms, but it certainly does not give any very definite idea of the numbers of this or that bird likely to be met with during a summer. If the one in question were a pest, one-tenth their actual numbers would be considered more than plenty. As it is, the bittern being strictly inoffensive, and at times exceedingly entertaining, there are never enough of them to suit the rambler's taste, and I for one cannot agree with Dr. Turnbull that they are "plentiful." Speaking in exact terms, and solely with reference to the valley of this creek, they are moderately common, never abundant.

When any bird betakes itself to haunts not usually frequented by its nearest kin, it becomes invested with peculiar interest; the more so in proportion as its habits differ from those of the family of birds to which it belongs. In the case of the bittern, its singularity consists in two features: it is a hermit, and the possessor of a very un-heron-like voice. Upon these peculiarities rests its fame. I have for years been accustomed to improve every opportunity to study the habits of the bittern, and although more summers than I care to recall have passed since I first saw them, I do not feel that we are thoroughly acquainted. There are certainly great individual differences among them, and some are far more shy and difficult of approach than others. Possibly this is due to past unpleasant experiences with mankind.

All others of our many herons, even the least bittern, love one another's company. They are always more or less associated when they arrive in April—a few of several species remain all winter—and for weeks continue to feed in companies. Indeed, this continuance of association is more or less noticeable after the breeding season commences. They have often favorite trees in which they roost, and become so partial to them that, if not molested, they will return to them year after year. In the *American Naturalist* for 1878, Dr. Lockwood has given a most entertaining account of a heronry believed to have been at least fifty years old. Here they not only roosted but nested. It is somewhat different here. Night-herons, the blue, great blue, and little green, all associate in clustered elms and maples, and remain apparently upon the best of terms. Perhaps these roosting-places are the combined remnants of separate heronries, in existence before the general destruction of the forests in this valley. Being the largest of our birds, and still the most prominent feature of our avi-fauna, may not heronries along its banks have given rise to the Indian name of the stream, Mechentschiholens-sipu (Big Bird Creek)?

But naught of this applies to the bittern. When the dog-toothed violet begins to bloom in the sheltered nooks and corners of the meadows, then the bitterns appear singly, here and there, and before the first of May, if the air be not too frosty, you may hear from sundown until midnight their weird call from the marshes, *puck-la-grŏŏk—puck-la-grŏŏk*. I have not much patience with any effort to describe the voices of birds by coining syllables that when pronounced are supposed to imitate the utterances of this or that bird. In this case, however, there is more chance because of the very unbirdlike character of the sound. I find many descriptions of the bittern's voice, and add the above to the series because I noted it down under very favorable circumstances. Some months ago, while I was watching minnows in a meadow brook, and at the time wholly concealed by the surrounding reeds, a bittern alighted within ten paces, and soon after, it being near sundown, uttered its strange cry. Immediately I put the sound into words while they were yet ringing in my ears, and had an opportunity of comparing and correcting them before the bird saw me and flew away. For this reason, I submit them as better than most of the published descriptions of this bird's cry.

The so-called "booming" is not, I think, wholly a vocal sound. In this case, the bird's beak, when it uttered the cry, was not quite withdrawn from the water, and its voice, therefore, was materially modified by this fact. Indeed, the sound is not unlike, in some respects, that caused by the sudden withdrawal of a stout stick from tenacious mud, except that it is a series of three such sounds, instead of a single report.

My experience in listening to bitterns also leads me to conclude that the individual variation in their utterances is very marked, and most authors who have attempted to describe them have given their impressions of the sound as heard at a distance. If I correctly understand what is meant by " booming," a term constantly applied to the bittern, then I have never heard this bird "boom" when within twenty yards or less of it; but if a quarter of a mile distant, then the sound may be described by that term. Thoreau, in "Summer," speaks of the "bittern pumping in the fens." This, in five words, covers the whole ground more completely than all the essays on "booming bitterns" ever published.

I have never found that this bird was particularly partial to our meadows. Certainly all the other herons are, and this may be the reason why he, a regular hermit, so often shuns them. Early in the spring, while his cousins are coming, he wanders along the creek shore and willow hedges, but before the middle of May he leaves the lowland marshes and becomes, for the summer, the lonely tenant of some secluded spring-hole in the upland swamps. Here, until late in September, his peculiar cry will be often heard, not only in the evening, but during dark and rainy days, and more than once have eager frog-hunters been led astray by it, and followed the "booming," thinking they heard bull-frogs, into the deepest recesses of the swamp.

I would not have it understood that they absolutely forsake the meadows during the summer, but practically they do.

For years I have been familiar with a corner of a neglected cranberry bog near which there grows a large cluster of oak and cedar trees. Here, year after year, I have found a solitary bittern, and no bird that I have yet seen passes, apparently, a more monotonous existence; yet could one be there at night and watch it the season through, doubtless many a little incident would be witnessed, showing that its life was really not a tiresome routine, day after day. This bittern in the upland bog has always been a mystery to me in one particular. He or she is always alone. I have never seen a pair there, and yet in the summer of 1877 I found a nest with four eggs. It was a loose bunching up of sticks and grass upon the ground. Two days after I found the nest, the eggs hatched, and, as usual, the young birds were the quintessence of helpless awkwardness. Even when two weeks old, there was little improvement. They were

> "Awkward, embarrassed, stiff; without the skill
> Of moving gracefully or standing still.
> Each leg, as if suspicious of its brother,
> Desirous seemed to run away from t'other."

The parent bird did not take kindly to my frequent visits, and when within a few paces, would ruffle up the feathers of its head and neck, partly raise its wings, and "look daggers" at me; but its courage availed it no further. As I came a step or two nearer, the bird always flew to a tree near by, uttering a petulant, rattling cry while on the wing. When three weeks old, and before the feathers of their wings were grown, the young birds, by some unknown means, had reached the lowest horizontal branch of an oak-tree that overhung the nest, and there they sat, near together, facing in the same direction, and solemn as owls. It was just two weeks later before they were able to fly. Like the young of the least bittern, when very young they uttered a shrill, fife-like *peep*, but their voices grew coarser as the weeks rolled by, and a harsh rattle was the last sound I heard them utter. I do not think that the peculiar cry of the adult bird is uttered by the young during the summer in which they are hatched.

Much has been written about the courage and fierceness of a wounded bittern. No exaggeration has, I think, crept into any of these accounts. My own experience, in one instance, leads me to conclude, that while they hold to discretion as the better part of valor, and do not seek a quarrel, they will, when necessitated so to do, show more courage than even the largest falcons.

While wandering along a very weedy portion of Poætquissings Creek, I chanced upon a bittern which I supposed, at first, to be wounded. I cautiously approached, and when within six feet of it, to my utter surprise, it made a dart at me, and with such vigorous use of both legs and wings that it was evident no limbs were broken. I stepped back quickly, and then dodging behind a tree, saw that my pursuer could or did progress but a few feet, and was held by a fragment of old fish-net, which had become entangled about the bittern's leg, and was also securely fastened to a branch of button-bush. It was now my turn to be brave, and I determined to capture or at least release the bird. How to accomplish this was another question. I tried coaxing, but the bittern had no faith in simple English, and replied to every word with a vicious stab of its beak, or a threat to use it, that was unmistakable. Finally, I cut a long stick with a deep crotch in one end, and after many efforts succeeded in getting the prongs of the forked stick about the bird's neck and holding its head to the ground. Then holding the stick with one hand, I cut the net from its leg with my left hand—an awkward job—and so set the bird free, so far as its legs were concerned. Immediately it found this out, and commenced using its claws with considerable effect. I was receiving more scratches than desirable, and let the bird up from the ground. For a moment it was undecided, and I thought meditated an attack. It had all the diabolism of expression ever seen in a wild-cat's face. I stood ready with my stick to strike it if it approached, but instead, it rose slowly upward and flew over the creek, and when over the middle of the stream, gave an unearthly cry, and fell dead.

I waited for many minutes, in hopes the bittern that I knew was skulking in the weeds on the shore would make his appearance; but in vain. In all probability, from some unseen outlook, he was just as patiently watching me, and wishing I would disappear. Well, I did as he wished, and slowly sculled the boat until opposite the clump of willows. While not so graceful as the weeping-willow, the kind here is a handsome one, and has the great merit of being attractive to most birds. During the early summer particularly, the newly arrived warblers congregate in its thick-set branches, and when, in November, it has dropped every leaf, its bared twigs are favorite resting-places for the enormous flocks of redwings which tarry until late in the marshy meadows.

My attention has recently been called to the fact that about the roots of these willows there are always many burrows, and the opinion expressed that the meadow-mice tenanted most of these and fed largely upon the delicate rootlets. I am inclined to believe that the burrows are there because the trees happen to be growing upon the banks of the creek, and the same would be the case were any other tree planted or growing in their stead. Still, I must admit that my examinations of other localities where there were no willows did not bear me out.

On landing, I found the usual burrows, but all were too large to be the work of meadow-mice. I endeavored to probe them and determine what creatures occupied them, but in this was altogether unsuccessful. No mammals appeared, and only from a pool of rain-water came crawling forth a half-grown, spotted turtle. I must confess to my disappointment. Yet what more suggestive creature could have appeared? Picking it up, I carried it a dozen paces back into the meadow and placed it in a shallow depression, thickly surrounded by a dense growth of grass. Once upon dry ground, the turtle looked about in every direction, craning its neck to the utmost, and then turning about, started in great haste directly towards the creek, distant about fifty feet. It could not have taken a straighter course had the stream been in full view. The weeds were high the entire way, and there was no beaten path. How, then, could it so unerringly take the shortest route to the creek? The waters were not rippling, and so could not be heard, and if the sense of sight availed nothing in the premises, was the creature guided by sense of smell? This seems probable, but is it not possible that the position of the creek was known to the turtle by the trees that grew upon the banks? Could a turtle not take its bearings by certain landmarks, and so be guided by sight, although the point sought was not within the range of its vision? Several years ago I made a large series of experiments with turtles and water-snakes, with reference to their possessing a special sense of direction, and I am quite ready to believe that these animals do take notice of the position of trees, and for such a purpose. Of a series of experiments with the common water-snake, I found that in ninety per cent. of the removals from the water to a point three hundred yards distant the snakes took the most direct course to the locality from which I had taken them. The meadows where I experimented were covered with short grass, and the nearest prominent objects were the trees upon the creek-bank. Under these the snakes were accustomed to remain most of the time when in the water, and in summer they basked in the sun near them. Could not this long familiarity have so impressed the general appearance of the trees upon the snake's brains that they could and did recognize them when carried to a distance of three hundred yards? In every case I was careful to blindfold the snakes, so that they could take no bearings during their inland journey. My experiments with turtles resulted similarly. These creatures may have been guided by the sense of smell, but I do not believe it.

It is somewhat different with fishes. If they do not possess a "sense of direction," it is impossible to account for their quick finding out of the precise localities of their nests. "Memory and recognition of localities seen one or more times" will not explain the matter when applied to such experiments as I have made; as, for instance, when I separated a mother catfish from her brood, and had a thick mat of water-milfoil between them; and again, a nesting sunfish was taken a long distance down a stream, and yet promptly returned to its nest, although it could thread its way only through a narrow and tortuous channel, flanked on each side with dense aquatic vegetation. Yet, when opposite the nest, which was near the shore, it came directly through the weeds to it. In this case there were no landmarks, and it is still to be explained how the fish could know which direction to take; for the creek was essentially the same in appearance for a much greater distance than it could see.

It is useless to dispute the claim of the palm to be the type of grace in the plant world; but were there no palms, the purple coxcomb grass, in August, and on these meadows, would bid fair to win the prize in a contest for that claim. I had already paused to admire a rank growth of cat-tail, about which was entangled a pretty climbing hempweed, with its pink and purple blossoms, and still remembered the beautiful oval clusters of purple "meadow-comb" grass, that as I came from home was sparkling with dew, and as it trembled in the passing breeze was the embodiment of grace. To eclipse the merits of these, the plant must indeed be beautiful, and this the purple coxcomb had the high honor of doing. I forgot, for the time, the outspread beauties of the earlier hours, while I sat and gazed at the tall, waving, purple plumes of this beautiful grass. One feature of the plant was here very noticeable: nearly one-half of it was pale-green, and so contrasted well with that which was deeply colored. Velvety sumach, with its crimson fruit, was a fitting background to the picture, and the spot needed nothing more. Nature had here finished her work for the time. I had, as I drew my boat close to the shore, a little tropic to myself—rich in color, rank in growth, wild in surroundings, and shared only with bees, butterflies, and birds.

A year ago, I met the owner of these meadows—a man of business—and when I spoke of the beauty of this purple panicum he snorted, and I heard a growl that it was "no use as fodder." To think that such men live, ay, and are in the majority! I would have been glad to kick him. If it ever occurs to one to feed the brain as well as the stomach, let such beautiful plants as this grass be lovingly looked upon. To this crabbed land-owner, it appeared to possess no beauty, because his cows preferred clover or timothy wherewith to fill their paunches. Whether this surly money-bags knows it or not, a pleasing view from one's dining-room windows is a safeguard against some of the dyspeptic ills that plague mankind. After your meal, let your eyes feast on beauty. My mid-day lunch, I am sure, was sweeter because of this beautiful purple grass waving its graceful plumes before me. Yes, it sweetened my crust and gave an additional sparkle to my cup of cold water.

At the lower end of Dead Willow Bend there is a pretty cove-inlet, through which the tides rush on their way to alternately submerge and uncover the low-lying meadows. A boat can pass up at high tide, and an exploring expedition on a very small scale is practicable. I have been in many such cove-inlets, and certainly they are all beautiful. Trees crowd their banks, and when in full leaf the sky is wholly shut out. It is water beneath, foliage on either side and above. I have never failed to find birds in such localities. However sultry the day, here it is cool, and however forsaken the open fields in the glare of an August noon, here there will be birds, and little if anything else is needed to make the surroundings all that we wish.

While lingering here I was surprised to find so many song-sparrows congregated about the creek, and particularly at this point. These birds belong to the garden, the gooseberry hedge, and not farther away than the road-side, where they welcomed us as we came from town. Now they would seem to prefer the most retired places. Can it be that the European sparrow has caused this change? Another reason for the extermination of the latter. It must be confessed, however, that these song-sparrows looked admirably well in their new quarters. They ran in and out among the roots of the trees, laid bare at low tide, and skipped so daintily over the mud as hardly to leave a track upon its shining, slimy surface. They chased spiders, I thought, as well as hunted for stranded seeds; and happy in the abundance that surrounded them, ever and anon mounted some projecting root, where their song would have free course, and the rippling melody float afar upon the bosom of the stream.

There is a point in our row-boat navigation which becomes at times monotonous — waiting for the tide to turn. To-day I waited until the deepest visible twig on the creek bottom was laid bare, thinking then surely the upward flow would commence; but no, the waters must recede yet a little more, and I marked another object just below the surface. This, in time, rippled the outward flow, and I looked for a telltale eddy which never appeared. A change took place at last, yet I could not determine at what precise fraction of a second. It happened between winks — without a sign. As I gazed intently at a water-soaked leaf, which just reached the surface, the water was flowing out, and before I could realize the change the tide had turned.

Although it is well known that the Indians were constantly fishing, and were expert fishermen, it is quite certain that there were far more large or fully grown specimens of our various fishes met with in their time than are now found in the creek or even in the river. It may, indeed, be doubted if we know what is the maximum size of some of our fishes. For a fish to escape nets, hook, and weirs for a dozen or twenty years must now be a very, very rare occurrence.

Among the ashes of the Indians' camp-fires it is well to look, when opportunity offers; for therein bones are frequently found which tell the story, without exaggeration, of what fishes these primitive folk were accustomed to capture.

Within a few rods of the Bend, on a knoll, there were, until recently, the unmistakable evidences of such camp-fires. By lucky chance I happened, not long ago, to be passing where a space was being ploughed and prepared for a basket-willow plantation. I noticed, long before I reached the spot, being on higher ground, that the upturned earth was very dark, and so went over to examine the spot. The soil was really black, the discoloration arising from the presence of great quantities of finely powdered charcoal. These camp-fire sites, two in number, were circular in outline, about fifteen feet in diameter, and so closely situated that when seen from a distance the outline of the two was that of an enormous figure eight.

I straightway commenced an exhaustive search for Indian relics, and was very successful. Bits of pottery were numerous, and the omnipresent arrow-heads were well represented. Two large circular plates of stone, quite thin, smooth, and well burned, were of much interest, as I had not gathered precisely similar forms in my earlier relic-hunting expeditions. The quantity of notched pebbles was remarkable, and their presence here was, I thought, evidence that, at least among the Indians of New Jersey, these stones were used as net-weights, rather than for other purposes, as has been suggested. Here was undoubtedly a temporary camp, near an excellent spot for fishing, and all the surroundings suggested fish and fishing. The fact that the locality was subject to overflow from freshets during the winter and early spring, at once put it out of the question that this was other than a temporary or periodically used site.

To return to the notched pebbles: because so simple an implement was used by the Ojibwa Indians of the

North-west as fuel-breakers, as has been stated by a correspondent of "Science," it does not follow that here in New Jersey our Indians broke their wood with such exceedingly awkward tools. A stone axe, with a well-sharpened edge, was too common an object among them not to have been put to such uses, instead of reserved exclusively for cracking skulls. Again, these notched pebbles have too frequently been found in alluvial deposits, so associated as to show that a large number of them were used together, as in weighting fish-nets. Here it would appear that a net had been lost or forgotten, and all traces of it had subsequently disappeared except the pebbles that were once attached to it.

But what more than all the stone implements that I gathered—a hundred or more—intensely interested me, were the remains of fishes and birds that were scattered all through the fire-discolored earth.

I gathered every bone and fragment of one that I could find, and after much labor finally determined the great majority to be the remains of the shad, rockfish, white-perch, catfish, and sunfish. I found also a few scales and a fragment of the jaw of the great bony gar and of the sturgeon.

Of the bird-bones, those identified were of geese and herons, except a single specimen which, although much broken, was ascertained to be the breastbone of a pelican. Of this bone, more hereafter.

It was after a study of these fish-bones that I became convinced that in Indian times our fishes attained a much larger size than now. Sunfish or bream were then frequently caught, which measured eight and nine inches in length. Such fish are not now seen on any of the strings of even our most successful anglers.

While it is true that the Delaware and its tributaries could not, even in Indian times, boast of such monstrous catfish as are found in the Mississippi, it is, on the other hand, equally true that our two or three species of catfish did, at this earlier time, attain a much larger size than now. Comparing the skull of one taken from the ashes of the old camp-fire with that of a fish weighing four pounds, I found that the former, estimating the weight by the proportionately greater breadth of the old skull, to have been nearly twice as great. The catfish that the Indian had caught weighed between seven and eight pounds, and none such have, I venture to state, been taken from the creek or river within the present century.

This is also true of the striped-bass or rockfish, so far as it is found in the river or its many tributary creeks. In other words, the Indians were accustomed to capture large numbers that weighed from ten to thirty pounds. Now, rockfish of even the lighter weight are not commonly found beyond the limits of the bay, and very seldom does a "ten-pounder" find its way into the creek.

With other species it became a matter of numbers or relative abundance, and not of weight. Even now sturgeon wander far up the creek, and specimens measuring six feet in length are not uncommon; but when the Indians were the sole possessors of the land, they depended upon trapping and spearing sturgeon in abundance, and its smoked flesh was an important article of food during the winter. Should the Indian return, his supply of sturgeon would go a very little way towards satisfying his winter needs.

Even more striking is the case of the bony gar. This fish is now so rare in the river, that but few people have any knowledge of it; yet, in pre-colonial times, it was exceedingly abundant, and judging from the fragments of jawbones, they were formerly found in Crosswicks Creek of the very largest size.

So few bird-bones were to be found, as compared with the remains of fishes, it would appear that the Indians, while they tarried here, were strictly ichthyophagi; the birds eaten being such as were met with while the men were engaged in fishing, and not regularly hunted. This seems the more probable, as all were aquatic, fish-eating birds—geese, ducks, and herons; with these was found the breastbone of a pelican; and a word here about this once abundant bird. Speaking of birds which have disappeared, Dr. Turnbull has written: "The rough-billed pelican was also frequent on the Hudson and the Delaware, but is now a very rare visitant to the last-mentioned river only." At how late a date it was frequent upon the Delaware I cannot satisfactorily determine, and probably the disappearance was largely synchronous with the English settlements upon the river two centuries ago. Early in the last century, however, flocks of pelicans came up the river as far as the head of tide-water, and their presence was recorded by a resident of the Falls of the Delaware. They were also seen by the farmer-residents of the Crosswicks valley, on the sand-bars and banks of the creek. I cannot learn of the presence of this bird during the past fifty years, and probably, in that time, not one has ventured on the river above Philadelphia.

Standing to-day upon this blackened earth that marks an ancient camp, it is not difficult to recall what time the fires burned brightly and all was active life about them. Was it day? The dense forest of nut-bearing trees cast a deep shadow over all, and not a ray of the torrid, midsummer sun ever reached the dank meadow turf. Was it night? Through the gloomy recesses of this same forest sounded the weird cry of the eagle-owl, the howl of the wolf, the bark of the fox, and blood-curdling scream of the wary cougar.

Then all this wide reach of open meadow was a forest, and the nuts that the Indians gathered were a no inconsiderable source of food. Walnut, butternut, shellbark hickory, chestnut, chinkapin, and hazel grew in great luxuriance.

The creek, and river too, were deeper then than now; their currents swifter, and the islands well defined, heavily timbered and stable. The trees that then grew upon the islands and the main shores stood as faithful guards, and resisted the encroachment of floating ice and the torrents of the yearly freshets. The shifting sand-bars were then far fewer and of inconsiderable areas, as compared with those that now choke up the channel and baffle the navigator's skill.

In May, 1749, long after the Indians had been displaced by the English settlers, Peter Kalm, the Swedish naturalist, described the bank of the river for a few miles above and below the mouth of Crosswicks Creek as follows: "About noon I left Philadelphia, and went on board a small yacht which sails continually up and down the river Delaware, between Trenton and Philadelphia. . . . Sturgeons leaped often a fathom into the air. We saw them continuing this exercise all day till we came to Trenton. The banks on the Pennsylvania side were low, and those on the New Jersey side, steep and sandy, but not very high. On both sides we perceived forests of tall trees with deciduous leaves. . . .

"The banks of the river were now chiefly high and steep (above Burlington) on the side of New Jersey, consisting of a pale, brick-colored soil. On the Pennsylvania side they were gently sloping, and consisted of a blackish, rich mould, mixed with particles of Glimmer (*Mica*). On the New Jersey side appeared some firs, but seldom on the other. . . .

"The river Delaware was very narrow here (at mouth of Crosswicks Creek), and the banks the same as we found them yesterday."

On his journey by stage from Trenton to New York he noticed, near the former place, "abundance of chestnut-trees in the woods. They often stood in excessive poor ground, which was neither too dry nor too wet," and, let me add, they grow in this manner still; but there is one difference in them: the nuts are good in proportion as the soil is suited to the tree. Too wet or too sandy a situation will render the nuts small and bitter.

Our author says: "Tulip-trees did not appear on the road, but the people said there were some in the woods." They might have said there were a great many; if not, then during the past century this tree has replaced others, which are now less abundant than formerly.

Again, he says: "The beaver-tree grows in the swamps. It was now (June 1st) in flower, and the fragrancy of its blossoms had so perfumed the air that one could enjoy it before one approached the swamps; and this fine smell likewise showed that a beaver-tree was near us, though we often happened not to see it." Probably this tree was much more abundant two centuries ago, and even when Kalm wrote, than now. In many local documents I have found that the term "beaver-tree swamp" was used as descriptive of such localities; which leads me to conclude that magnolias were prominent trees in such situations. They certainly are not so at present.

The bare and slender branches of the dead willow were now casting their longest shadows, and bade me seek a safe landing for my boat promptly, if I would not be benighted; for once on shore, there were four miles of meadows to be trudged over before I could lift the latch of my door-yard gate.

It quite often happens that when the naturalist is intently engaged with one object, another, wholly unexpected, forces itself upon his attention. A captive serpent may disgorge a frog, or a wounded heron vomit a fish; and so, this evening, while anxiously seeking for some sufficiently large and dense growth wherein to run my boat, I happened upon a black snake in a cluster of button-bushes, and much to my surprise, it "showed fight."

From what I have seen of these creatures, something very extraordinary must have occurred to induce them to attack, or even face, you when menaced. In this case, the snake disputed my approach as I proceeded to draw my boat into the bushes. It darted at me, full half its length, and suddenly withdrawing, again struck out. A moment's consideration of this unusual exhibition of courage on the part of a black snake revealed the fact that it was very fixed in its movements, not passing to any of the surrounding branches, as I moved from side to side to get a better view. This fixedness of position as well as of purpose so piqued my curiosity that I went within striking distance, and warding off the attack with one arm, pulled down the bushes with the other. This action on my part led to the discovery that I was not the first person the snake had recently encountered, and I am glad to add that I have never been so cruel, even towards snakes, as had the coward who had found this snake. It had its back injured, and had been impaled about the middle of its body upon a sharpened branch of the bushes. I quickly destroyed the snake. Perhaps the fellow who did this deed may meet with this record of his cruelty, and learn that I write him here a coward and a brute.

As I walked home this evening, I thought of the tenacity of life exhibited by many of the lower vertebrates. How long this tortured black snake had been impaled in the bushes I could not tell, but probably for twenty-four hours. How long it could have lived under such circumstances I should like much to know.

There is an old saying current in this neighborhood

that snakes, when fatally injured during the day, never die until after sundown; that so long as they can bask in the sun, however mangled they may be, they will remain alive. Of course this is an exaggeration, and yet I am not surprised that such an impression should have become common in the country. I have often seen hog-nosed snakes decapitated by the plough, and when the ploughman came again in his rounds to the spot, the headless snake would strike at him. At first it puzzled me to conceive how the reptile knew of the man's approach; but I found, by experimenting with one such headless snake, that the approach of the plough was recognized by the tremor in the earth caused by the tramp of the horses. Even in sandy soils this tremor is very considerable, and can be recognized very readily.

This is too painful a subject to enter into more fully, and let it suffice to say that a fracture of the spine, and sometimes a flattening of the skull, paralyzes, but does not kill, and consciousness returning, such injured snakes may linger for hours in agony. If people must kill snakes (harmless species ought never to be molested) let the work be done thoroughly.

Just as abruptly as my thoughts were turned towards snakes, so they forsook them when, touching my foot upon what I supposed to be a stone, I found it to be a large box-tortoise. As is my custom, I examined the plastron to see if any name or date had been cut thereon. In this case there was neither. I had better fortune, in this respect, during a hill-side ramble, in May, 1885, as I then came across one of these uncouth creatures, and to my surprise and delight, the following was found to be distinctly cut upon the plastron, " J. Abbott, 1821." A close examination conclusively showed there could be no mistake in the date, and it was evident that sixty-four years ago my grandfather had found and marked the tortoise in the manner described. I found the animal within a hundred yards of the house then occupied by my grandfather, and it is probable, therefore, that at or near this same spot the creature was found and marked more than half a century ago.

The tortoise was by no means a large specimen, measuring but four and one-half inches in length, by a little less than four in width. Evidences of great age, however, were not wanting. The edge of the upper shell had been broken, and the fractured part worn very smooth. The yellow markings of both the upper and lower shells were much less prominent than is usual. There was no evidence of any appreciable increase in size since the name and date mentioned were cut.

Previous to November, 1885, I had never found any very young box-tortoises. On the 19th of that month I met with a single specimen. It was found on the edge of a shallow pond, in very damp earth, and I judged from this fact that such a locality, if indeed not open water, was preferred by these creatures, when young, to the high and dry fields and woodland where the adults are usually found. How far I was right—if I am right— in my surmise, the subsequent eventful career of this young tortoise may serve to show. On the same day I placed it in a large aquarium, so arranged that it could remain on dry land, in or on damp earth, or beneath the water. The animal's actions clearly showed that water was necessary for its existence. To further test this, I placed it for twenty-four hours in a vessel containing dry earth, and it gave unquestionable evidences of suffering and inability to remain for any significant length of time in a comparatively dry atmosphere.

Replacing it in the aquarium, it immediately burrowed into the soft mud, as deeply as it could, and there remained without moving from these semi-aquatic quarters. By stretching its neck to the utmost, and rising upon its fore-feet, its nose reached just above the shallow film of open water, and I suppose that it occasionally refilled its lungs in this manner, as I found that by gently disturbing it, it invariably emitted a small bubble of air. In this position, and with only so much exercise as the stretching of its neck afforded it, the tortoise remained for thirty-four days.

I then placed it in a smaller vessel partly filled with sphagnum, and moved it to a warmer room. So long as there was sufficient water to enable the tortoise to keep submerged, it was contented, or at least quiet. As soon as, by evaporation, the water decreased to a certain point, the restlessness on the part of the tortoise indicated discomfort; which was promptly relieved by adding more water to the moss. One swallow does not make a summer, but the action of this box-tortoise leads me to believe that when so young that their under and upper shells do not meet, these Chelonians are more aquatic than terrestrial in their habits.

A word further as to their powers of withstanding the rigors of winter. That they hibernate is well known; but they do not get beyond the reach of frost when they burrow into the earth, nor need they, if all are as hardy as the little fellow I have kept so long.

January 13, 1886, the tortoise, while covered with water and sphagnum, was solidly frozen in. I carefully chipped him loose and allowed the adherent bits of ice to thaw very slowly. While this proceeded, the animal was apparently dead; but the disappearance of the last particle of ice was synchronous with the reappearance of vitality. This freezing was repeated, February 5th, and with like results.

Hereafter, I shall go to the swamps for young box-tortoises; nor shall I be surprised if in winter I find them incased in ice.

The strange absence of katydids caused the woods and meadows to be painfully silent as I hurried home; yet it was a silence that was distinctly audible, the air being filled with the trumpetings of a million atomies, and no one distinguishable voice.

At such a time how widely awake we are! The mere snapping of a twig beneath our feet thrills the body as with an electric shock. It is a feeling vastly different from fear, as some might call it. Something more tangible than the soul breaks out when we hear, "in the dwawm-like silence o' a glen, the sudden soun' o' a trumpet." Here in the home-woods, through which glinted the sparkle of the evening lamp, I disturbed my neighbor's peacock.

CHAPTER VI.
THE TWIN ISLANDS.

Passing by my neighbor's house, on my way to the creek, I was somewhat startled by seeing a chair come tumbling from the attic window. So odd an occurrence drew my steps in that direction. The inmates of this old mansion, I learned, were "cleaning house," as they called it, and to make room for some "old" things—I use their word—were pitching out of the lumber-room some that were still older.

Luckily I was there in time to stop the folly. The discarded chair, I grant, was not worth much, and could not, in safety, have supported more than a living skeleton; but it was of a curious pattern, and boasted of artistic carving. The bushes below had saved it from utter destruction, and the carved back and clawed feet will some day be utilized in a wonderful wooden mantle I have long had in contemplation.

I begged the privilege of a look in that old garret before further proceedings were undertaken by the cleaners, which was readily granted.

"He wants to ransack the garret and look at the trash up there," explained the daughter of the house to her mother.

"And he'll get stung by the wasps for his trouble;

but let him go, of course," added the perhaps not over-pleased mistress of the old farm-house.

So I went; and let me add here, if any who read this page should ever go on a similar errand, let him incase his precious cranium with a metal skull-cap. The old mansions erected in the past century were built to stand, and where you least expect to find them, there will be massive beams that are not to be left unconsidered. I entered, with some confidence, one of the dark closets under the eaves, and nearly decapitated myself. It seemed several moments before I recovered from the shock, and meanwhile wished the house, from turret to foundation-stone, in Jericho. Recovered at last, with all caution and no confidence I crawled in, for the roof was too low to enable any other position to be assumed, and when my eyes became adapted to the dim light, commenced the survey of the dusty, musty, waspish surroundings. The old lady was right. There were wasps there; and one came to the end of my nose and rested quietly thereon. I could use neither hand to dislodge it, and I wriggled my nose until my whole face ached. The wasp liked the seesaw motion and sat still. I tried to blow it off, but my mustache only soothed his wasp-ship, and he stroked each particular hair, I thought, and sat still. Slowly, then, I retraced my steps to the door of the closet, and once free, sent the wasp spinning through the air. It returned in hot haste — terribly hot to my bald pate—and I started to retreat; but no! I shall explore that garret, I vowed, and I did.

Again on all-fours in the closet, I moved towards an old trunk at the most distant point; but it was not so accessible as I thought. Across my path there lay an umbrella—and such a one! When it was carried, there were giants in those days, or should have been. A warming-pan, once silver-plated, but now brown with oxidation of the copper of which it was made, came next in view, and then a set of window-shades, something like Venetian blinds, but made of narrow strips securely held by hempen cord that still was strong. A roll of bed-curtain—this I captured—with small squares, portraying Old Testament scenes; and scattered everywhere, over and under these, were old boots, shoes, and knee-buckles; and best of all, warped, twisted, curled-leaved volumes—remnants of a little library gathered a century ago. As best I could I brought together my umbrella, bed-curtains, and what books I could, and backed into daylight. I had seven volumes before me, and sat down by the little window to inspect them. The first was a rheumatic specimen, with a back bent in all directions, and leaves as outstanding as the fur of a furious cat. After some search I found the title-page, and read, "The Journal of Thomas Chalkley, etc., etc.," and the books had the imprint of Benjamin Franklin. "This will do for a beginning;" and I laid it upon the bed-curtains; but it would not lie flat. The next was a little duodecimo, or smaller, and alas! I saw at a glance, was marked Vol. II. I turned to the title-page, for the title on the back was gone, and read, " History of Louisiana, etc., Le Sage Du Pratz." Was it possible the other volume was gone? A glance at the books beside me showed it was not there. If the gloomy corners of the garret closets must be again ransacked, so let it be—that missing volume must be brought to light. Again I crawled in, in spite of wasps, spiders, and millipeds, all of which took my presence grudgingly. I searched as thoroughly as practicable, and was about to return—for no book of that size could be found—when a glittering object, like a coin, attracted my attention. It was a pewter button on an old coat; and I saw then that a double row of them graced the front of the garment. I brought the coat into daylight, and for the moment forgot the missing volume of Du Pratz. It was such a garment as I have seen in pictures and nowhere else. Besides the two rows of buttons down the front, there were three on each of the great flaps covering the side-pockets, and three more on each of the wide-spreading pocketed tails. Forty metal buttons on a coat! I held it aloft by the shoulders and gazed admiringly; then laying it down, I proceeded to explore its capacious pockets. In one of them was the missing volume of Du Pratz! I pinched myself to see if it was I. Was it not a dream? No, there was the coveted book, and with a sigh of relief I sat down.

I made a third attempt to get a knowledge of what the closet contained, and particularly coveted an examination of an old trunk, but before I reached it, became tangled in a maze of spinning-wheels which I had hitherto escaped. My arms somehow were slipped in wheels of different machines, and to dislodge them was no easy matter. They resented by revolving to the full extent of the elasticity of my arms. It was a trial of both nerve and patience; but with one frantic effort I got through, and reached the great black box, hide-bound, and ornamented with rows of what had been shining, brass-headed tacks. I attempted to raise the lid, but the hinges were gone, and it slid back in an accommodating manner. The trunk was full of books! A slender thread of light kindly illumined the spot as I slowly deciphered the title-pages. Nine in every ten were Bibles or fragments of Bibles; but nearly at the bottom of the trunk was an uninjured copy of La Hontan's "Travels in America."

Had I been in the woods, I should have danced; had I been in a solitude, have shouted; but in a beseeming manner, I demurely walked down-stairs with my coat, umbrella, bed-curtains, and books. I offered payment, which was declined, and taking my neighbor's ridicule in good part, passed on with my antiquated burden.

How apt we are, when once a locality is associated with some unusual incident, to continue to half expect a repetition of it whenever we draw near. As I approached a pond-like expansion of a meadow brook, I found myself taking shorter and more cautious steps, as though it were probable that another Florida gallinule would be seen when I reached the bank of the weedy stream. I saw one here more than twenty years ago.

This bird is one of a considerable list that has almost wholly forsaken the Crosswicks meadows. The bird was new to me then, and with what unbounded delight I gazed upon it. I could have sat all day and watched it. Luckily, I was not seen, and crouching in the tall grass, where I could command a good view, I sat as nearly motionless as possible. The gallinule was wading in water about three inches deep, and at every step appeared to lift one foot quite above the surface and curl up the toes; then taking as great a stride as possible, plunged the foot, with the toes still curled, into the water. At every third or fourth step, the bird stopped and thrust its bill beneath the surface, and I suppose, judging from the subsequent motion, secured some morsel of food. While I watched, the bird appeared to be feeding only upon objects found on the bottom of the pool, and not at all from the rank vegetation that skirted the shores.

It had also another curious habit. At almost every other step the head would be thrown back until the occiput rested upon the shoulders, and at the same moment the wings were lifted slightly, as though the bird was about to fly.

At length, much to my annoyance, it was alarmed by a noisy troop of crows that swooped down near by, and flying directly over me, discovered my retreat. There was no reason to think it would ever return, so I shot it.

The purple gallinule, sometimes met with on the Crosswicks meadows, is quite as rare as the preceding; but their recurrence nearer the sea-coast has been frequently recorded, nor are they always found during the summer months.

I should be glad to know why this stream is so crooked. The alluvial flats through which it flows are very uniform in their composition; and unless lodged trees, borne hither and thither by freshets, have been the cause, there is nothing to show why the creek is not almost a straight line, instead of being as tortuous as a writhing serpent.

That it has changed its course for many a rod, even in historic times, there is evidence in maps attached to old deeds. That it was equally erratic in prehistoric times is also demonstrable, but not with so little labor. In several tracts of the lower lying meadows ancient channels can still be traced, and when ditches have been cut, I have gathered many a curious relic of the Indians, left upon what was the bank of the stream, centuries ago.

Where I have found relics of the Indians, I have long hoped to find the skeleton of a mastodon, or at least isolated bones of the creature. Very possibly I may never make such a discovery, yet there is no inherent improbability in the matter. Bones of the mastodon have been found on these meadows. My grandfather picked up a humerus, within a few rods of where I saw the gallinule, and the specimen was long in Peale's Philadelphia museum.

There has been an astonishing amount of twaddle written concerning the subject of the contemporaneity of man and the mastodon in this country. It would be just as rational to question man's sharing the primitive forests with the elk and cougar.

My friend Dr. Lockwood told us the story years ago in a few telling words. He wrote: "It is plain that the mastodon came into what is now New Jersey ere the ice-sheet began. It receded south before it. It followed the thawing northward, and so again possessed the land. It occupied this part of the country when its shore-line was miles farther out to sea than it is to-day. Here it was confronted by the human savage, in whom it found more than its match; for before this autochthonic Nimrod behemoth melted away."

Here we have not only the truth, but have it in a nutshell; something refreshing in these days of prolixity. I have but one criticism to offer concerning these admirable sentences. If by "autochthonic Nimrod" our author refers to that primitive man of the great ice age— palæolithic man—the ancestor of the Eskimo, who also antedated the Indian here, and supposes that the mastodon died out with these earlier folks, then I dissent. If the last mastodon in New Jersey died by the hand of man, it was the hand of a Delaware Indian that slew him; if he sank helplessly in some quicksand, while wandering over these meadows, then these later Indians knew it well, and told of the unhappy fate of the lonely beast, generation unto generation. Certainly not a score of centuries have passed since the shrill trumpeting of the mastodon awoke the echoes of our primeval woods.

Scarcely a rod from my neighbor's corduroy road, over which, in July, the hay-laden wagons creak ominously, is an ugly area of quicksand.

When Mink, a locally celebrated duck-shooter of the last century, got caught in it, he remarked, as soon as extricated, " The Lord left the materials of a good country about here and forgot 'em, so the devil did the mixin'." This covers the ground completely—I am glad the quicksands do not—for good in their way as are sand

and water, one does not want them mixed in such consistency.

The difference, so far as these meadows are concerned, between a "boiling" spring and a "quicksand," is one of dimension only; one being an intermitting, upward movement of a narrow column of water, bearing an insignificant amount of sand; the other a far greater bulk of water, so charged with sand that its movement is very deliberate: a spring is seldom more than a yard in diameter; a quicksand may extend over an area of several square rods. The fact that the temperature of the water in either case is always the same, 52° Fahr., shows that springs and quicksands do not materially differ except in size.

The danger attendant upon personal exploration of these quicksand areas, and a natural repugnance due to an adventure to be related hereafter, has deterred me from any extensive survey, and only one of them, two miles or more back from the creek, but in this valley, has been carefully examined. For years my neighbors have insisted that this particular quicksand is a veritable bottomless pit. To satisfy them I took a ten-pound lead, well greased, and brought up stiff clay from a depth of eighteen feet, and think I learned the difficulty about sounding the quicksand's depth, so far as my neighbors are concerned. Not one of them but admitted he had never used any other means of measurement than a fence-rail. As these are either twelve or sixteen feet in length, it is not at all strange my neighbors' never reached bottom. And this holds good not only with quicksands. How often it happens that they use but one probe in investigating the things of this life, and content themselves with the belief that there is no bottom, because they fail to reach it.

Marvellous stories were told of this quicksand or huge boiling spring by many old residents. One, current in my childhood, was to the effect that a dozen sheep were caught in its troubled waters and sucked out of sight, and nine of them turned up alive on Duck Island in the river about noon of the next day. Think of it! For more than a day tossed in the depths of a deep spring, carried half a mile through a subterranean passage, and landed upon an island alive! This was not told as a bit of fun to excite the wonder of children, but as a sober fact; and so firmly grounded was the belief that these quicksands were wellnigh fathomless, that every statement made concerning them, however absurd, was readily accepted as further evidence of their wonderful character. My own experience with quicksands is too full of horror to be related, at least I shudder when I recall a sunny summer afternoon of long ago. I stood upon a patch of quaking grass, pleased with its elastic yielding and too intent upon watching a pair of nesting finches to realize that I was slowly sinking. At last I noticed that my eyes were gradually approaching the horizon of the low-built nest, and looking about and beneath me, saw the treacherous waters creeping above the matted weeds upon which I stood. The latter were trembling more and more violently, and the fearful truth was plain. I was over a quicksand.

I had a double task to perform, and that right quickly—avoid fright and reach terra firma; but how? But one chance of escape appeared to offer, to distribute my weight, and at once I stooped and struck out, as though swimming. The theory was good, but not the application in this instance, for what I gained by the greater upholding power of additional vegetation under me was lost by my violence, and I broke through the raft of weeds upon which I depended. In the twinkling of an eye, in the fraction of a second, I lived a lifetime.

I have positive knowledge of nothing beyond this moment. I can only judge from the appearance of the tangled grass and weeds that my convulsive efforts to reach the meadow were finally successful. Once fairly beyond danger, my strength failed me and I fainted.

The clay that constitutes the "hard-pan" of these meadows, crops out here and there along the bluff that extends for miles parallel to the river. It is a tough dark-blue deposit, occasionally streaked with red, yellow, and pure white veins that are less tenacious. The blue clay is interesting in that it contains much fossil-wood, some amber, and an abundance of iron pyrites.

Let us consider these separately. The wood is not petrified, and still retains so much of its original condition that, when dry, it burns with a feeble flame and emits a pleasing aromatic odor. Dr. Cook, our efficient State geologist, describing another but similar clay-bed, remarks: "Trunks and branches of trees are everywhere to be found. . . . In opening some of the clay-pits, cart-loads of them might be saved. They have the structure of the wood, and the form, except that they are considerably flattened; sticks lying horizontal and two inches broad, may be only from a half inch to an inch thick. The wood is of a dark-brown color, and quite brittle.... When exposed to the air and dried, it cracks across or splits up into small fragments. Lumps of iron pyrites are found in the larger pieces, and it is very common to find the smaller sticks surrounded by knots and rings of the same substance. Some of the trees are quite large, two or three feet in diameter." There has been discovered, in one instance, "the trunk of a tree that was four feet in diameter," which as the clay was removed proved to be ninety-three feet in length, and ten inches in diameter at the top. Dr. Cook further states, that "the wood has not been examined microscopically; but from the leaves found, from the bark, and from the rings of annual growth, the evidence is conclusive that the age of broad-leaved plants was then begun." Dr. Cook makes no mention of the occurrence of amber in this clay, but refers to it as a "mineral . . . found irregularly distributed in all parts of the *marl* region;" and adds, "from its resemblance to resin it naturally attracts the attention of workmen, and becomes the subject of their experiments, and is burned up. Specimens have been seen from marl-pits in every county of the region, but there is no certainty of finding other specimens in the same localities. Pieces enough to have filled a barrel are said to have been taken from one marl-pit at Shark River about twelve years ago; but since that, in looking over many hundred tons of marl there, not a fragment was found."

It occurs in the clay near here, associated with the fossil-wood, and as little pebbles, in the bed of the creek.

Do not expect to find it, however. The search will prove like that of Dr. Cook at the Shark River marl-pits. It has been found, and will be again and again, but only by mere chance will you come across a specimen of it.

I do not know that the Quaker settlers ever believed that gold would be found near here, but the Swedes did. Here is a story from Campanius's quaint account of New Sweden, as Jersey was then called: "Lindstrom ... asserts that there is a great quantity of gold, and relates a fact in support of his assertion, which happened in the time of the Swedish governor, John Printz, and is as follows: 'Once an American Indian went to pay a visit to the said governor, and observing that his wife had a gold ring on her finger, asked her why she wore about her such paltry stuff; which, the governor hearing, he asked the Indian if he could procure him any of it, and said that, if he did, he would make him very fine presents; to which the Indian replied that he would, for he knew a mountain that was full of it. The governor then showed him cloth of various colors, with lead, gunpowder, mirrors, and several other things, and said to him, "I will give you all these if you will get me a piece of that stuff as a specimen. I will send two of my men with you to get it," but the Indian would not consent to that. "I will," said he, "go first and bring you a specimen, and then it will be time to send somebody with me." Some days after he returned, and brought a piece of ore as large as two fists, which the said governor caused to be assayed, and found it contained much gold, out of which he had rings and bracelets made. He then asked the Indian to take some men with him, which he promised to do, but had not time at that moment; he would, however, return in a few days and bring some more gold. But afterwards meeting with other Indians, he began to boast of what he had received from the governor, on which they asked him what he had given for it, which being informed of, they put him to death, in order that the place should remain unknown, fearing that its discovery might occasion to them some mischief; and so the gold mountain was never discovered,'" and never will be.

With this I leave the minerals in the bluff that guards, and the bed that sustains, the waters of the creek, and with a sigh of relief come back to the pretty creatures that dwell in the stream itself.

Wherever the clear, cool waters of a hill-side spring enter the creek, there many minnows of many kinds are sure to congregate. At one such spot I was attracted by the great gathering of blunt-headed minnows, the many barred cyprinodont that throngs every stream from Maine to Florida, or nearly so. Ordinarily I should have passed them by, but some individuals seemed different, even at a considerable distance, and I leaned over the boat to view them more closely. A large percentage were darker in color, with broader transverse bars, and prominent in that the dorsal fin was beautifully marked with a blue-black spot, encircled with clear, opaque white. After much effort, with an improvised net, I captured a number of them, and found, to my delight, that they were the "ornamented minnow" of Le

Sueur, described by him nearly seventy years ago. I thought I had seen all the fishes of the Delaware River and its tributaries, but here was one that had escaped me.

Such an incident as this is of far more importance than the fact of finding a fish I had not previously met with; it leads me to hope that other novelties are in store, and while I live I shall never take a ramble and return empty-handed; but perhaps better so than overburdened.

A captious critic has said, "He sees too much." It is true, sights and sounds crowd upon each other until I am bewildered. Could I have seen less, I should have learned more. I have never dared to recount the adventures of a single day. The sleepiest twenty-four hours of the year is more exciting than a battle-field, if one has the will to use his eyes and ears. I have seen too much. Alas! it is the one fact that saddens me, wherever I ramble.

Scarcely had I disposed of my burdens and pushed from shore than I was in sight of the goal of to-day's journey. The tide being with me, I was soon beyond the lone ash-leaved maple that stands upon a little "point no-point," and the pretty fringing of attractive shores, where wild-rice luxuriates in all its beauty. I feel the muddy bottom with the blade of my oars, I hear the soft *swish* of the prow as it ploughs the clustered yellow dock—I am at the Twin Islands.

Here are two small islands, together forming but a small fraction of an acre, yet each with features peculiarly its own. The one boasting of a single willow and a wilderness of weeds; the other, a tall ash, a dwarfed maple, and a garden that, excluding all else, grows in wildest luxuriance a golden bloom, the beautiful *Helenium autumnale*.

Whenever I come down the creek, I am tempted to draw up to the lone willow of the upper island, for to tarry there an hour, ay or for a day, is no hardship. For me, it is not to be

"Under the shade of melancholy boughs,"

but rather in the shadow of joyous branches, glittering with light and tremulous with the airy steps of many birds; nor, once here, do I

"Lose and neglect the creeping hours of time."

I may, perhaps, neglect to mechanically count the hours as they pass, but then, why should I? Tarrying here can never be accounted a loss of time. I always bear hence something to con over in the years to come —reap a fair harvest of food for thought.

Is there not much idle talk about losing time? Who is appointed among us to say this of his fellows?

He who, as the result of a meditative life, gives a single useful hint to his fellows, has accomplished more than any mere accumulator of a fortune. Surely it was better for us that Thoreau ceased to be a pencil-maker, and gave to the world "Walden" and "The Week."

To the poor toilers of the crowded town, who could not come hither without bringing thoughts of their ledgers and the state of trade, it might be a loss of time, but even such unfortunates should place some value on the pure air that has entered their lungs, and count that something of an offset to their "loss of time."

Herein lies one merit of Twin-island Bend; we are out of sight and hearing of man's industry. Nature, ever busy in her own wise way, has the region wholly to herself, and I encroach upon her domain merely as an eager spectator.

As I rested, still sitting in the weed-surrounded boat, I looked down the opening in the rank growth of aquatic plants made by the skiff, and saw upon the opposite shore a common rail-bird, or sora. The popular idea of this curious bird is that of a morsel of tender flesh, that conveniently awaits slaughter, late in September, after some weeks of fattening on the seeds of the wild-rice. But the sora is something else. It is a bird that puzzles every one who closely follows it. That many settle in the valley of the Delaware during the spring migration is unquestionable; they do not, however, remain and nest here, as I supposed, but passing on, leave us until the middle of August, sometimes earlier, and then remain until the frosts of October drive them away. My impression that they nested here arose not merely from the fact of finding them in May and August, but the nests of the little black rail were occasionally found, and attributed to the wrong species. I am glad to be able to record this fact, as it gives us an additional species.

Considering them collectively, we have then the following species: the king-rail, the Virginia, the sora, the little yellow, and the still smaller black rail. In the order of their abundance, of course, the sora leads, and to the ornithologist interest centres in it, early in its season, before persecuted by dogs and gunners. Probably one reason why so seldom seen, and so difficult to flush, is that it is more crepuscular than diurnal in its habits. The structure of its eyes may not suggest this, but I have often noticed its voluntary appearance upon the open mud-flats an hour or more after sundown, and seen them during moonlit nights continually rise above the reeds, and, flying a short distance, drop again from view. They fly, too, across the Delaware and across this creek far more frequently at night than during the day.

Like the smaller yellow and black rail-birds, the sora has a cry that is peculiar in its marked resemblance to the rattle of our green frog, *Rana clamitans*. The voice of the king-rail, on the other hand, is very different, and rather musical. It suggests the tapping of a hammer upon an anvil. A muffled, metallic ringing, perhaps intelligibly expressed by the following: Kĕ-link-kiṅk; kiṅk-kiṅk-kiṅk.

For several summers king-rails, perhaps but a single pair, have nested in a bit of marshy meadow near my home, and the summer long, all day, and often at night, its cry could be heard. A word more concerning the rail-birds of the Crosswicks valley, and of the nobler valley of the river beyond, for there are other and more extensive areas of marsh, where these birds congregate in far greater numbers than here. Dr. Turnbull writes of an European species: " The Corn-crake. A specimen shot at Salem is now in the collection of the Academy of Science (Philadelphia). Another was procured near

Bordentown, New Jersey, by Mr. John Krider. It is known as a summer visitant to Greenland." Now, as Mr. Krider shot a corn-crake on the shore of this creek, within a few miles of Twin-island Bend, why should not others? It is far more probable that a dozen migrated from Greenland, or came directly across the Atlantic, than one; and one old English gunner, familiar with the bird for years, assured me he had *heard* them on our meadows, but never had seen one. The truth is, a hundred of them might be killed by our professional gunners, and not one come to the notice of an ornithologist.

Passing from the upper to the lower and larger island, I landed near its two small trees, that from their branches, into which I climbed, I might survey to advantage the rank growth of sneeze-weed that covered the entire area to the water's edge.

There was absolutely nothing to be seen but a tremulous mass of brightest, unstained yellow. It was much like looking at the noonday sun through misty spectacles. Every blossom, like the buttercups, had "caught the sun in its chalice," and bees of every variety thronged the gilded forest.

The busy myriads of tuneful honey-hunters, indeed, added a charm to the novel scene, and their mingled voices, pitched upon every conceivable key, was much like the uncertain melody of an Æolian harp.

While watching and listening, I was surprised to find how remarkably free from molestation by birds were these bees. They hovered over this shimmering sea of golden bloom, always in plain sight, yet the birds, many of them true flycatchers at that, kept quite aloof. I saw several kingbirds in the branches of the trees on the creek bank, and heard the harsh screaming of the great crested flycatcher. Others of the tribe were heard, and one wood-peewee came from the woods and perched directly above me.

Perhaps, when purple martens were abundant, we had professional bee-eaters among us, but of this I am by no means certain. Dr. Brewer calls the kingbird a "bee martin," and has much to say of their being a pest where honey is a desideratum of the farmers.

No kingbird, while I was there, saw fit once to capture a bee, or even to fly among them. If they do so, how can we be sure it is a bee that is captured? Other insects swarm in the same localities, as I found to-day, and might not these be sought as food, in preference to the busy honey-gatherers? Wilson went so far as to say that the kingbirds fed only upon drones; but is it likely that a kingbird's vision is sufficiently acute to recognize drones from workers when they are flying?

I have found more than one bee-tree in my rambles, and always have looked out for bee-eating birds in their vicinity, but the kingbirds do not frequent the forests much; and the great crested flycatcher, although much more of a forest-dwelling species, never appeared to haunt the neighborhood of bee-trees. Kingbirds, no doubt, are willing to feed on bees, but that they prefer them to other forms of insect life is probably too rash a statement.

It was not far from here, in April, 1872, that a beautiful scissor-tail flycatcher was taken. It was a male, in full health and feather, weighing two and one-half ounces avoirdupois, and measuring thirteen and one-half inches from the tip of the beak to the extremity of the tail. The bird, when shot, was busily engaged in picking semi-dormant insects from the bark of trees—creeping about very much after the manner of a brown tree-creeper, and all the while opening and shutting the long scissor-like tail. The stomach proved to be full of small beetles, and remains of other kinds of insects.

This is the only specimen of this southern species known to have been taken so far north. Dr. Brewer quotes Dr. Turnbull as an authority for the capture of other specimens, but the latter does not mention the bird. The allied fork-tailed flycatcher has been twice found here, and to these Turnbull does refer.

It is of some interest to know that when this rare bird was taken the weather was chilly, and the season was unusually cold and backward. It would be easier to account for the presence of this bird had the season been far advanced, or had a southerly wind or storm prevailed at the time and for a few days previously, but the very opposite of this had been the case.

It would be interesting to watch during the year the movements of birds as rare as this, when they happen to wander so far from their proper habitat. Could a pair of such stragglers be left alone, is it not probable that they would breed here, and in so doing lead to the establishment of a race of summer migrants? Perhaps, if they once regained their southern home, they would stay, but I should like to have a few such stragglers spared, and learn the result of a summer's sojourn with us.

Speaking of bird migration, it is fitting to consider at

this time certain portions of Dr. Benjamin Smith Barton's "Fragments of Natural History," published at Philadelphia in 1799, and based upon observations made near that city. From it we gather evidence that a considerable change has been brought about in the habits of certain species, and many that he considered as summer or winter visitors are now strictly resident. It is, of course, possible that the doctor's observations were insufficiently extensive, and some birds were overlooked which were really to be found in the vicinity of Philadelphia at the time; but this supposition is scarcely tenable when we consider that Dr. Barton was an intimate friend of William Bartram, and depended largely upon the observations of that accurate observer for his facts. It will be seen, also, that in the ninety-six years since Barton wrote, there has been nothing suggestive of a greater regularity in the seasons. March and April were as fickle then as now, and the learned doctor would evidently have been sorely puzzled to give an accurate description of spring, of which he has so much to say.

Speaking of birds coming from the south, at the close of winter, Dr. Barton remarks: "It must not be imagined that the birds which I have enumerated arrive uniformly every year, at the times which are prefixed to their names.... I have long been persuaded that the uniformity of the arrival of the migratory birds, in any given country, is not so great as many naturalists have imagined. The attention which I have paid to this curious subject in Pennsylvania has convinced me that my suspicion was well founded. The migration of birds is not a 'determinate instinct,' but an act of volition or will. Hence the seasons and other circumstances will greatly regulate the arrival of birds in, and their flight or removal from, a particular country. Sometimes there is a difference of three weeks or a month between the arrival or appearance of the same species in two different years. This will appear from the following instances, which are selected from many others. . . . It will appear that the *Alauda alpestris* or shore lark; the *Alauda rubra* or red lark (titlark?); the *Fringilla tristis* or golden finch, and some others, were not observed in the vicinity of Philadelphia earlier than March 12, 1791; whereas the same birds were seen in the same neighborhood as early as February 28th, the following year, on their passage northward. . . ."

It would appear from this that these birds were merely birds of passage, which made no protracted stay in this neighborhood. As a matter of fact, the two larks arrive from the north in October, and tarry until April. They are characteristic features of our midwinter landscapes, and reside with us for nearly one-half of the year. Is it possible that, when Dr. Barton wrote, they passed us by in autumn, and after a protracted stay in more southern localities, only lingered in the vicinity of Philadelphia for a few days or weeks at most?

More strangely still, the "golden finch," our familiar thistle-bird, is now a resident species, and while wandering and erratic is in no sense migratory. Dr. Barton did not confound it with the pine-finch, for of the latter he has much to say, and was clearly well acquainted with both species. If not a blunder, which it is hard to believe, this bird has greatly changed its habits.

On referring to Dr. Barton's "Tables," we are at once struck with the inapplicability of the lists to the dates given. Thus, under that of March 12th, fourteen species are named as first seen at that time or about that time. Three of these have been commented upon; another, the white-throated sparrow, like the others, comes to us in early autumn and remains until every vestige of winter has disappeared.

Again, a more striking instance than all, is to mention the turkey-buzzard as appearing in this neighborhood as late as June 20th. Now it must be admitted that these birds are of a wandering disposition, and when the mercury falls close to zero, they are disposed to take shelter from the north winds; but of ordinary crisp winter mornings, provided there is plenty of sunshine, they have no fear, and it is quite within bounds to assert that there are fully one third as many of these birds floating in the upper air in January as in June. However the case may be, as to whether they are guided by scent or sight to their unsavory food, but let a sickly sheep wander afield in midwinter, and the attendant buzzards will not be far away.

Fully one-half of the birds Dr. Barton names are now strictly resident species. Are we to suppose that they were overlooked? Now, an autumn ramble or a winter walk, anywhere beyond the city's limits, will be rewarded by the presence of these very birds. The same is true of many species mentioned as "April arrivals." Some that are now migratory come much earlier, others are resident. One large diver, called by him an "eel crow," is said to appear about April 15th. This was true of the common "devil diver" or dabchick until recently, but of late years they are "irregularly" resident; but this may not be the "eel crow" of Dr. Barton, and all the other representatives of this family come to us in autumn and are winter residents; being more or less abundant, as the winter proves mild or severe; for while not scared by ice, they nevertheless delight in open water and an abundance of fish.

That the author we have quoted was acquainted with the winter birds of this neighborhood would appear from the following, and it would seem that the birds mentioned have really altered their habits to a certain extent. Dr. Barton writes: "How much the movements of birds from one country to another depend upon the state of the seasons, will appear from different parts of this little work, particularly from the Third Section. Here we find that during our mild winters several of those species of birds which, in general, are undoubtedly migratory, continue the winter through in the neighborhood of Philadelphia. Such, which I have denominated the Occasional or Accidental Resident Birds, are the *Ardea herodias*, or great heron; *Columba Carolinensis*, or turtle-dove; the *Fringilla melodia*, and several others: I doubt not many more than I have mentioned." Of these three species, the former only is "occasionally" resident; the others are strictly so. Dr. Barton continues, as follows: "The *Columba migratoria*, passenger pigeon, commonly returns from the northward late in the fall, and continues with us a few days or weeks, feeding in our fields upon the seed of the buckwheat, or in the woods upon acorns. But if the season

8*

be a very mild one, they continue with us for a much longer time. This was the case in the winter of 1792--93, when immense flocks of these birds continued about the city and did not migrate farther southward until the weather became more severe in the month of January."

At present, these pigeons find too little food to tarry long in this neighborhood, yet I believe I have never known a winter to pass without a few of them remaining about our woods, especially such as have many beeches growing therein. Dr. Turnbull, writing in and concerning the neighborhood of Philadelphia, remarks of this pigeon, that it is "plentiful, but is more frequent in spring and autumn, when it congregates in large flocks." This does not accord with my own observations, and I find on inquiry that fifty years ago flocks of pigeons annually wintered in the valley of Crosswicks Creek, about thirty miles from Philadelphia as the crow flies. It may be, therefore, that these birds were not as sensitive to cold as Dr. Barton supposed.

Another quotation from our author's "Fragments," and I have done. He writes: "It is highly probable that the periods of the migrations of birds will be found to be more or less uniform in proportion as the climates of the countries to which they migrate are more or less variable in their temperature. It is, perhaps, upon this principle that we are led to explain the difference of the times of arrival and departure of the birds of Pennsylvania, and other parts of North America. The climates of these countries are extremely variable; I suppose more so than most other countries that are known to us. If, as has been supposed by many writers, the hand of man, by clearing and by cultivating the surface of the earth, contributes essentially to the greater uniformity in the temperature of climates, it is reasonable to conjecture that the time will come when the periods of the migrations of our birds will be more constant and fixed. For in North America, especially the United States, the progress of population, and of clearing and cultivating the earth, is more rapid and immense than in any other portion of the world."

Whether it is reasonable to conjecture or not, certain it is, that our author did not correctly estimate the effects of that general deforesting of the country which has taken place since he wrote, nearly a century ago. The trees are gone; the countless acres of ploughed or weed-grown fields are here, and with them a climate as variable as ever. The birds come and go, as of yore, but with the same degree of uncertainty as to their arrival and departure. The birds have changed far more than the seasons, and so other causes have operated to bring this about, or it is, at least, an indirect effect of the climate. The destruction of the forests has affected plant life; this, of course, has its influence on insect life, and the birds must come and go, as their food supply determines. The change wrought is that migration has become less fixed and methodical than formerly—not more so, as Dr. Barton believed would be the case; and when any species learns to live upon food available at all seasons, it will probably cease to wander, unless forced to seek a suitable nesting place in some distant locality.

About 2 P.M. to-day the heat reached its maximum intensity; every bird became silent, the scuttlers and skaters ceased to fret the still waters, where they were nearly shut off from the incoming tide. Even the harvest-flies stridulated less frequently, and one naturally thought of those creatures in the tropics that escape intense heat by a prolonged sleep, somewhat akin to the hibernation of some of our mammals in winter. In equatorial regions there occurs a true æstivation among mammals. Does anything akin to it occur in New Jersey? Certainly, when we have days like this, it is probable that all animal life is affected by the heat, yet I find no reference to such influence of solar heat in any work descriptive of the habits of our fauna. What is æstivation? In Stormonth's dictionary the definition is as follows: "The sleep or dormancy of animals during the hot or dry season in warm climates; the analogue of hibernation in cold regions."

The condition of certain mammals, as reported to me during the summer of 1884, brought the subject prominently to mind, and I found that in past years I had made many memoranda concerning unconscious animals; but the full significance of which I did not, until recently, recognize; and, indeed, I may not now correctly interpret the facts.

The following is an instance of the supposed occurrence of æstivation, or something closely akin to it.

A family of white-footed mice was found in an exposed position in an open field; the nest being made of a few leaves and some thistle-down, under an old tin pan, the bottom of which had nearly rusted away.

When these mice were taken up—and they were handled with great care—they were found to be soft and warm, as when in full vigor, but gave no signs of life. The female mouse and her three young, which were more than full grown, constituted the family. As there was no apparent cause for the death of the mice, I determined to investigate the matter very carefully. One of the young was pricked on the ear with a needle, when it flinched slightly. The others were similarly tested, and all gave evidence of life to the same extent. Carrying these mice to a shady spot, and placing them in a comparatively cool position, they regained their ordinary activity in about seven hours, the process resembling closely the awaking from an ordinary sleep, but of course was much more gradually accomplished. They were then replaced in their nest in the field, which they promptly abandoned, but returned thereto in the course of the next day. Three days later these mice were found in precisely the same condition. Time, noon; thermometer 106° Fahr. These mice were taken directly to a cellar forty-two degrees cooler than the open field, and the sudden change proved too great a shock. The young died in one hour; the old mouse, in less than three hours. Had these mice, after their first removal, when replaced in the field, directly become stupid or actually dormant, it might naturally be inferred that the heat had seriously affected them; but, as we have seen, such was not the case. During the evening of the day following my replacing them in the field, the air became cooler by twenty-nine degrees, by 7 P.M., and was thirty-four degrees cooler four hours later, and the mice were active, and fed heartily upon breadcrumbs placed near their nest. Now why, it may be asked, did they not seek out a cooler retreat in the woods near by? I can only suggest that the supposed æstivating condition was not inconvenient nor unpleasant, and that it was preferable to the abandonment of their nest, which was suited to their needs for all time, except such extraordinary spells of hot weather. Either these mice were excessively stupid, or a dormant condition, caused by excessive heat, was nothing unusual with them.

There is in this instance a marked difference from a hibernating sleep, in that the period of dormancy was of but a few hours' duration; but was like the torpid slumber of a hibernating animal, in that the condition was one from which it was not possible to arouse them, as from ordinary slumber. The awakening had to come from a change of temperature; and just in proportion as the evenings were warm, the mice were tardy in returning to consciousness. To more effectually test this, I carefully removed these mice from the field, and placed them near a stove, so that the mid-day temperature could be maintained. The result was the continuance of the dormant condition for eighty-four hours.

When the effect of a protracted drought and heated terms upon our animals has been more fully worked out, I believe it will be found that many a mouse and other small mammal which is found lying dead, as supposed, is really not in a moribund but dormant condition, and if left undisturbed would revive. But what other evidence is there of this? The white-footed mice are not, of themselves, sufficient to prove that æstivation is an established habit. What other evidence among mammals have we?

In August, 1880, I found bats on four different occasions, all of which were apparently in full health, yet they did not, for some reason, which I supposed to be the excessive heat then prevailing, resume their crepuscular flights at the usual hour. These bats had "gone to roost" under leaves on trees and a grape-vine, and were, no doubt, fully intending to resume their activity after a nap of a day's length was over. Why did they not? The following days were excessively hot until the fourth, which was a few degrees cooler. It clouded over early in the afternoon; soon it became damp, and just before the commencement of a passing shower these bats were stirring a little as they hung—quivering their wings as though to see if all was in working order, and then away they flew, after, in each case, certainly ninety hours of rest. Does it adequately explain all the facts to say that these bats were overcome by the heat? They were resting in the shade during the day, and the nights, when they would be active, were cooler; but in these cases very little cooler. They were nights to be remembered for their sultriness; and may it not be that there was not sufficient difference in the mid-day and evening temperature to enable them to throw off the nervous prostration caused by the heat of the day? Explain it thus, and then we are left to consider what is this nervous prostration? In the case of the bats mentioned, they were all in a perfectly torpid state, and gave not the least sign of life when handled, and only flinched slightly when wounded by being pricked with a needle. Would not nervous prostration that produced insensibility, lasting several hours, almost certainly produce death? In the case of the bats, a torpid condition extending through ninety hours produced no ill effects. I am disposed to believe that the coming hot and dry weather was anticipated, and these bats retired for the purpose of escaping it, and entered into a condition widely different from ordinary sleep, which was to last until the so-called heated term was over, the lowering of the temperature being the one means through which they would be restored to consciousness. There occurs this deliberate action on the part of certain mammals which regularly hibernate —why should not the same be true of them when the extreme is one of heat instead of cold?

As bearing upon this question, let me quote a few lines from the *Encyclopædia Britannica* — ninth edition— article, Hibernation. It says: "The dormouse not only hibernates, in the strict sense of the term, but will sleep at intervals for several days together during mild weather. When a Myoxus—an allied animal inhabiting Africa — was brought to Europe, it hibernated as if this were its normal habit. Whether it æstivates in its native country is not known, but its hibernating in Europe shows a greater power of adapting itself to changed conditions of life than we should have been inclined to suspect."

I would briefly call attention to two points in the above: that in temperate climates prolonged sleep is not unknown among rodents, and also that some tropical rodents probably æstivate. In the case of the white-footed-mice, and, too, of the bats, I am very positive that their condition was not that of ordinary slumber; and the tropical temperature at the time, even through the night, certainly suggests æstivation as the most plausible explanation of the phenomena I have described.

As so often happens during hot August days, the afternoon draws to a close with a terrific thunder-shower. To-day I saw that one was coming. The threatening morning had been a combination of slight showers and intense heat—now for the climax. I knew what was to be, long enough before the shower reached me, to have escaped it all, but I had no desire to do so. I was prepared for all the rain that might fall, and willing to risk the inconvenient possibility of the night proving stormy. All needed preparation was soon made. I had but to draw my boat from the creek, and turning it up upon one side, let the other rest upon two short, crotched sticks. This done, and my gum blanket spread, I was provided with all necessary shelter. But I was none too prompt in making my arrangements, for by the time I was fairly under the boat and in a comfortable position, big drops came pattering down upon the meadows beyond, then upon the creek, and finally upon the bottom of the upturned boat. It was music to my ears. At times the rain seemed to descend in thin sheets of water, one closely following the other; and the sudden splash of these upon the surface of the creek produced a series of very distinct, sharp reports, like slapping the flat side of an oar-blade upon still water. This at times was varied by the effect of sudden puffs of wind which converted the rain into mist-like particles that penetrated everywhere, even under my boat. Once the wind gathered the descending waters and produced of them a miniature water-spout. This shot erratically up the creek, leaving a white line of bubbles that marked its zigzag track. But once in my life did I ever see it rain more violently.

Interesting as was this shower, viewed under such circumstances, I was more struck by the effects that the thunder had upon the fishes than by anything else that I saw. The lightning played about me at uncomfortably short distances, and a large tulip-tree, not many rods away, was somewhat shattered. But of the fishes: at every clap hundreds came suddenly to the surface, and the small minnows leaped several inches above it. This was not an occasional but a uniform effect of the thunder. I have been on and near this and other creeks before during showers, but never saw this effect produced upon fish to anything like the same extent.

After the shower passed, by the dim light of a cloudy sunset I hunted for fishes that I thought might have been killed by the concussions that shook them up so thoroughly, but found none; and so, while I could yet see, sought for a cluster of bushes, wherein to leave my boat for the night.

I have referred to a harder shower than this of to-day. It occurred on August 24, 1877; and although its force was largely spent upon meadows three or four miles away, it may properly be included among the eventful occurrences of this creek's valley.

I quote from my notes concerning it, published in the State Geologist's report for 1881: "Previously to 1.30 P.M. the day offered no peculiar meteorological features. The temperature was 78° Fahr. at noon, wind south-east. About 1.30 P.M. the wind shifted to the south-west, and a heavy bank of blue-black clouds formed in the north-west. The appearance at this time was that of an ordinary summer shower. I did not notice any lightning or hear any distant thunder. While standing on the brow of the hill, near where my house stands, and facing the south-west, I noticed that a bank of cloud somewhat similar to that in the north-west was also rapidly forming, and the two appeared to be approaching each other, although, of course, not from opposite directions. In a few moments there was a sudden change in the several conditions then existing. The stiff north-west breeze suddenly ceased. A remarkable stillness pervaded the atmosphere, and a feeling of oppression was very noticeable. Just at this time the two masses of clouds came in contact, apparently (and really, I think), directly over the extensive stretch of meadows lying north of Bordentown, New Jersey, along the Delaware River. At the moment of contact of these cloud-masses there was a loud, humming sound clearly audible, but not caused by a wind, as the leaves on all the trees were motionless. The two cloud-masses formed one, but each retained its peculiar coloring, and in less than a minute, I should think, a huge water-spout formed —or at least the clouds became a single conical mass, with the apex downward. As suddenly as it formed it broke, and in ten minutes at most thereafter the meadows were flooded. The storm now took the form of a general rain, and extended over a considerable area.

"Such a rain, however, I have never witnessed either before or since. I found by experiment that it was impossible to breathe while facing it unless by protecting my nose and mouth with my hand. At a distance of one hundred feet objects were wholly obscured from view. This fearful rainfall continued for about forty minutes and then began to abate, but it was not until 5 P.M. that the rain ceased and the sky became comparatively clear. This storm was remarkable for one feature other than that of the quantity of water that fell; this was the absence of lightning.

"No ordinary means would have proved available for measuring the rainfall in this case. I have no doubt that it was considerably in excess of what I ascertained at the time to be, we will say, the minimum; and here, certainly, in the immediate vicinity of the water-spout, was a rainfall of nine inches in the three hours of that day, from 2 until 5 P.M.

"Perhaps it may not be without interest to add that the storm caused a considerable destruction of life. Calves and sheep were drowned, and many birds and small mammals were destroyed. I found numbers of drowned crows and some smaller birds immediately afterwards, and several mice and squirrels. Insect life, also, was greatly affected by the storm, their ordinary means of shelter during showers proving quite inadequate to protect them against the violence of this remarkable rainfall."

My eventful day had drawn to a close, but my labors did not end with the gloaming. It was no light task, with my treasures mined from a neighbor's dark attic, and an arm-load of meadow bloom, to wend my way homeward through tangled grass still dripping with the recent rain. An occasional stumble was not submitted to with the best of grace. But the climax was to come. I had thought that my exposure to a storm would have excited sympathy, and my heaped-up treasures arouse the interest of all who saw them. Alas! straightway on entering the house I was reminded that I had not washed my hands.

Washed my hands! For what then had I been gathering the glory of the marshes, if not that their essence might cling to me? Washed my hands! No, and to free them from such honorable soiling never will. I would that my heart was as stained as my hands; that the virtues of waste-land pierced me through and through. All that is lovable in this world has not yet been garnered.

CHAPTER VII.
MILL CREEK.

THE wanderer in waste-lands comes continually upon localities, shady nooks in the woods, quiet corners of neglected fields, and weed-hidden recesses of forest streams, that are suggestive of contemplation. Eagerness for active exploration gives way to a desire for passive enjoyment. Such a spot is Mill Creek. One must, indeed, have urgent business who can hurry over its brief course.

My purpose was to pass the day in quiet, or at most to watch the fishes that swarm the shallower portions of the stream.

While I have always urged the desirability of being forearmed with a plan, when bent upon a day's outing, I do not claim it can always be carried out. Some stranger may, at the same time, come up to spy out the land, and you have then nothing to do but to spy him out. Count it good-fortune when so it happens.

Years ago I met with pleasant surprises when here; still, I could not, from this fact, expect them to continue. To-day, at least, I hoped that the suggestive quiet of these shades would not be disturbed, and had not proceeded a dozen rods beyond the bar that nearly closes the reedy entrance to the creek, when down from above the tree-tops dropped a dainty sand-piper.

Quietly as possible I sought the drooping branches

of an overhanging oak, hoping to observe the bird to advantage. In this I failed. It saw that my movements referred to itself, and wheeling upward rose far above the trees and disappeared.

It tarried a second before speeding riverward, and suggested, in so doing, that a view from some such height would prove a pleasant variation in my outings. Forthwith I left my boat to climb a tree.

To most people, I suppose, tree-tops fifty feet above their heads are quite as inaccessible as the antipodes. But this inaccessibility is not real in every case.

The truth is, I envied the slight breeze overhead, and determined it should fan my brow. It did, and now I am ready to proclaim, happy is he who has sufficient "scansorial ability" to climb inviting trees and take his comfort in their upper branches.

Before fashion turns the tide that way, let me chronicle what I conceive to be the charms of such a journey; for it is equal to a day's tramp to reach the summit of a towering tree—one which has disposed of its branches in such a manner that a man needs to be ten feet long to reach from one limb to the next above him. The climber must exercise a deal of ingenuity at times, and perhaps run something of a risk; but once at the top, what happiness awaits him!

There is an inborn disposition in all to look down upon our fellows, as well as to look up to a few individuals. Climb a tree and look down upon the world without giving any one offence. From my tall tree's upper branches I looked down upon toiling harvesters, and then looking upward saw a cloud of mosquitoes looking down on me. Was my boasting to come to naught, thought I; but before I heard the faintest trumpeting a breeze had carried them to the distant hills. It was but an intimation that pride was liable to a fall at all times, so I became humble—a curious sensation—and essayed to study life from my novel point of view. The first bird that I saw was a swallow. I marked it as it passed a gaunt-armed chestnut, tardy with its bloom. Tarrying not, it circled the leafy crown of clustered beeches, scanned the deep caverns of a gnarly oak, traversed a maze of birches, elms, and maples, threaded its way through tangled growths beneath, and twittering to its fellows as it passed, hurried to greet a passing feathery cloud, and from the upper regions viewed afar the misty mountains, miles and miles away.

Perhaps a threatening storm-cloud drove it thence, but swift as an arrow back again it came, and I felt my cheek fanned by the creature's wing. Off then to the river shore it sped, and tricked each leaping wave that sought to catch it, peered into every nook and cranny of the stream, cast a fleet shadow upon every rock, bathed in the spray, basked in the sunshine, and then outspeeding vision sought the cool shadows of a wild ravine. Then, upward and outward in a flood of light, it circled a sink-hole in an upland field, counted the queer corners of a zigzag fence, and played bopeep with a little whirlwind, as it bore a dust pillar to my neighbor's woods. Checking its course, it turned abruptly and sought the Mill Creek shadows whence it started.

Was it gone an hour? By my watch not five minutes. I saw almost at the same moment the steam from the locomotive as the "limited express" went hurrying westward, and that marvellous train seemed not half so wonderful as the swallow's wing.

So far as these birds are concerned, one need not wonder at their migrations. In less than a day and a half they can transport themselves to the tropics, or as near them as they see fit to go, when winter's rigor drives them from their summer haunts. And the other birds? You rouse their curiosity when you sit in a tree and can study them at leisure. The first to come after the swallow's fleeting visit was a cuckoo. It perched upon a twig but a few feet away, and failed at first to recognize me. Then what I was slowly dawned upon it, and it spluttered a guttural exclamation that you, kind reader, and I would probably translate quite differently. After long intercourse with birds of many kinds and a few representative mammals, I am inclined to look upon profanity as a product of evolution. But the cuckoo was not mad. It merely took a back seat and contemplated me. What the cuckoo thought, do not ask, but if a bird has once been seen sitting and watching a man as that one did, it will not be denied that it does think.

I glanced about to see if there was any attraction for the bird, and saw a group of caterpillars almost within my reach. I wished that I was a little farther off, that the cuckoo might eat them, and then wondered if he would not in time muster up the necessary courage. This he finally did. Finding that I was perfectly quiet, he ventured a little nearer, and at last reached the outer side of the group of caterpillars. Like lightning he seized perhaps a dozen, and then his courage failed him.

9

I might prove dangerous, he thought, and afar over the meadows he flew.

I heard him croaking, when a quarter of a mile away, I am sure, and straightway his hoarse cry was answered from my tree. "Another cuckoo here?" I asked myself, and looked everywhere above, below, and about me. I strained every muscle to see the outermost branches of the tree that I was in, and scanned each neighboring tree as carefully. There was no bird visible, and yet a guttural "cuck, cuck, cuck," was continually rung in my ears. Finally, looking directly below me, I saw a shallow hole, where a weak side-branch had rotted off, and in it, squatted in the rain-water lodged therein, sat a tree-toad. The creature was far in advance of me in tree topics. Here he was with his bath-tub and certain of a moderate food supply, even if he sat still. A snugger nest I never found, and am only puzzled that its occupant should croak instead of sing. Why any bird or batrachian should ever express itself in such doleful tones is a hard nut, I take it, for evolutionists to crack. It does not seem, in any case, to subserve any good purpose. It is not a call to its mate, and tree-toads can hardly be said to ever be mated; it brings no food and frightens no enemies. Like dyspeptics among mankind, in the case of the tree-toads they sit still and croak pretty much their whole lives; or in that of cuckoos, wander the country over and never cease croaking. The truth is, the cuckoo has a far easier time than most birds, and its voice suggests that it is a natural fault-finder.

> Ofttimes the fool the universe would rule.
> The world moves on, and disregards the fool.

While contemplating the pretty tree-toad in its cosey quarters, I was startled by a multiplicity of sounds: a passing flock of redwings, a family of pigeon-woodpeckers, the hum of excited bees uncomfortably near, and more strange than musical, more suggestive than entertaining, the hoarse, rattling cacophony of a yellow-breasted chat. It fluttered up from a tangled thicket of briers below me, and when in mid-air gave utterance to such varied cries as would baffle a mocking-bird.

How rudely, sometimes, our dreams of bliss are dispelled! The time came for me to descend, and I discovered that my limbs had rebelled against their long confinement in a cramped position. I was very wide awake, but they had gone to sleep, nor would they be awakened. Clinging with my arms to the stout branches, I kicked at the outer air, and then for a moment, though it seemed an hour, could not withdraw my legs to a more substantial footing. Here was a veritable thorn clinging to my pet rose, and one not easily got rid of. I as nearly lost my life as I care to, and will not ignore my legs in the future when I go a-climbing. So a word of advice. However comfortable you may be, whether in a tree-top or the laziest of rests aground, secure your comfort, if not safety, by occasionally shifting your limbs.

Scarcely had I reached my boat, when the dainty sandpiper returned. It is larger than the common speckled-breasted "teeter," as it is usually called, of more slender build and darker plumage.

The bird before me, which for quite insufficient reason is often called the "solitary," and by some the "wood-tattler"—a much better name—comes early or late in April, according to the weather. It does not make much of a stay, but hurries northward, and reappears in August and September. Every summer, however, a few remain and breed.

When the wood-tattlers arrive in May, they are mostly found in the wet meadows, often in flocks of from twelve to twenty, and are usually so silent that, if not seen, their prerence would not be suspected. Many a time, when crouching in the long grass on the margin of a meadow brook, watching the frogs or fish, as the case might be, I have seen these sand-pipers alight within a few feet of me, and wander about in full view, yet never uttering a sound. After a long flight, to see them set their wings and pitch towards the ground, and when very near it, to check their course and settle, is to witness the acme of graceful motion. Another exquisite movement is that of raising their wings as their feet touch the ground, and then folding them gracefully. I know of no ordinary habit of our many birds that is so uniformly attractive.

But if quiet during the day, it is not so always. Towards the close of the day, and sometimes until long after sunset, instead of hunting for food in a staid, methodical manner, they indulge in aerial antics that exceed the wooing woodcock in fantastic high and lofty tumbling. A half-dozen or more will dart at one another when at a great elevation, yet never come into actual contact, and then, with loud and pleasing whistling, dart down and perch upon the very top of some tall tree, and there bow and bend with all the fussiness of a dancing-master.

These antics occur towards the end of their spring-tide sojourn here, and probably then mating occurs among young birds, and former vows are renewed by the older birds, if it is true of these, as of some others, that they are mated for life.

Wood-tattlers are contradictory creatures. They appear to be very timid, yet in fact are not very readily frightened. As the bird before me was standing quietly at the edge of the water, not then engaged in feeding, I sharply slapped my hands together. At the report, up went the delicate, slender wings until they touched above the bird's back, and then were deliberately folded. Again I made the same noise, with the same effect; and then, repeating the sounds at shorter and shorter intervals, kept the poor bird's wings trembling in a very ludicrous manner. As soon as I ceased clapping my hands, the bird resumed its position of contemplative rest, except when stirred to action by the sight of some delicate morsel of food creeping in the mud or water before it.

In time, as the outgoing tide enlarged the mud-flat, and brought newer feeding-ground to view, the sand-piper became more active and ran from side to side, as though fearing some of the available food-supply might be overlooked or escape. While so doing, a shadow passed over the creek; it was that of a buzzard, half a mile away, and yet the sand-piper would run no risk, and squatted so closely to the mud that I could not see it. In this concealed position it remained fully one minute, and then resumed its food-hunting calmly as before.

At no time did the bird leave the little island and wade out into the water. This was quite interesting to me, as it often does wade until the water laps its breast, and then, if it happens to keep its body bobbing forward as it walks, you would suppose that it was taking a bath.

At length, being very tired of my cramped position, I concluded to flush the bird by making my appearance from beneath the drooping boughs of the oak. As I did so, the sand-piper gave a shrill whistle, and flew up the creek to another mud-flat. Here, however, it was not satisfied, and returning flew to within a dozen paces of my boat, and then commenced an upward circling flight, until nearly out of sight.

This wood-tattler, the first I have seen since May, recalled the finding of a pair in the chinkapin swamp more than twenty years ago. It was a perfect June morning, and all that that implies was to be enjoyed in the sprout lands and the chinkapin swamp beyond.

That June morning of long ago was a naturalist's red-letter day. Here, for the first time, I found the pretty prairie warblers in abundance; not as tardy migrants on their way north, but here for the summer. They were busy insect-hunting among the dwarfish oak-sprouts, and some busier with their nests and young, which I found after an easy search. Occasionally a brilliant redstart would dart through the bushes, and add to the animation of the scene. All these birds sang constantly.

An individual prairie warbler cannot be classed among our accomplished songsters, but the united voices of a dozen or more as I heard them, mingled with the distant ringing tones of wagtails and the nearer and clearer whistle of the oriole, made delightful music.

Even better than my experience with the warblers was the fact that while I was stooping over a little spring that bubbled and sparkled among emerald mosses, down like an arrow came a wood-tattler and settled scarcely six feet away. I turned my face towards it, and the bird, while evidently much puzzled, could not make up its mind as to what sort of a creature I was, and remained at its post staring back at me. To preserve such a cramped position for any length of time was, of course, impracticable, and suddenly regaining the perpendicular, my identity was revealed so abruptly that for a moment the bird was helpless from fear; but as suddenly as it had been overcome with surprise, it recovered its mental equilibrium and darted away. Notwithstanding such a strange adventure on its part, the tattler quickly returned to the very spot where it had recently been sorely frightened. Its actions were all peculiar. It did not bob its head and shoulders, as they constantly do when on the meadows, but held its head well up, trailed its wings and spread its short fan-like tail, and in this strange fix ran in short circles about the long grass, just beyond the moss-hidden spring. I thought of a nest and commenced a careful search, much to the annoyance of the nervous little tattler, that now kept twenty paces distant, and was often hidden from me by the tall weeds.

It seemed, at last, as though I must have scanned closely every square foot of the ground within a reasonable distance of the spring, and finding nothing, I withdrew. As soon as I was away, the tattler, which had evidently been watching my movements, returned to the spot near the spring and acted just as strangely as before. This more strongly than ever aroused my curiosity, and I resumed the search. After several minutes I at length touched with my foot an enormous bullfrog, which gave a mighty leap and a loud grunt expressive of displeasure. It had been squatting closely in what was evidently a tattler's nest, a structure identical with those of the common spotted sand-piper I had often found. This threw some light on the mystery. The frog had been up to mischief, and the distressed wood-tattler was the sufferer. I captured the criminal, which was suspiciously aldermanic, and dissection proved that it had swallowed four young tattlers, just emerged from the shell.

Running my boat under a cluster of hornbeams, draped with Virginia creeper and daintily trimmed with feathery thalictrum, I was quite concealed even from any inquisitive creatures that might pass, and yet could assume a comfortable position, as was far from being the case when watching the wood-tattler.

Here, with birds, trees, flowers, and rippling waters, I proposed to take the world very easily and pursue the most delightful occupation that is possible for man—to follow the whim of the moment.

Feeling equally ready to meet and discuss a mammoth or a mouse, a heron or a humming-bird, I was certain not to be disappointed whatever appeared, and in the course of half an hour it proved to be a mouse. From the opposite bank of the creek it crept slowly over the muddy shore left bare by the receding tide, and then bravely plunging into the water, swam laboriously across the stream and directly towards the boat. Seeing it coming, I very quietly slipped an oar in its course, and, as I hoped would be the case, upon reaching the oar the mouse ceased swimming, and crawled up the blade until it was quite out of the water, when it gave a vigorous shake and commenced licking its fur, much as a cat would do after an involuntary bath.

It has not appeared to me that the meadow-mouse is an amphibious mammal, yet I know when occasion requires it can swim for a considerable distance, and in more ways than one proves itself by no means hopeless when sudden freshets submerge its subterranean retreats. I have so often been assured by my neighbors that at such times they catch to the first bit of floating wood which they find, and float thereon until the wind or tide carries them within reach of dry land, that I cannot but accept the statement; and yet, guided solely by my own observation, I believe they trust far more to their natatorial powers in such crises, and I do know that such a freshet as that of June, 1860, results in the death by drowning of hundreds of these mice.

Mr. Ord, who described this species of *Arvicola*, says: "This species is fond of the seeds of the wild-oats (*Zizania aquatica*), and is found in the autumn in those fresh-water marshes which are frequented by the common rail (*Gallinula carolina, Lath*). When the tide is high the animal may be observed sitting upon the fallen reeds, patiently waiting for the recession of the water. From its position when at rest it has much the appearance of a lump of mud, and is commonly mistaken for
9*

such by those who are unacquainted with its habits. It swims and dives well." This would indicate that somewhere the meadow-mouse is quite as amphibious as terrestrial in its habits; but into the marsh, only a few rods distant, with its acres of wild-rice, or "oats" as Mr. Ord calls it, the mice nowadays seldom if ever come. The pretty picture of their sitting at high tide upon tangled blades of the reeds, I have never seen; and why should they, if they desired to go elsewhere? Mr. Ord says, "it swims and dives well." That it can swim we know. Until recently I had never seen it dive, but did not question its ability so to do because I had not seen it.

As with all mammals, their proper habits, as indicated by their anatomical structure, are not closely adhered to, for not only do we find land animals at home in the water when necessity requires it, but this meadow-mouse, so generally supposed to be a vegetarian, is by preference as carnivorous as a cat. During the early weeks of the current summer I found them to be systematic egg-hunters, and that they had destroyed both the eggs and young of song-sparrows, brown thrushes, and one nest of a chewink. If I have ever, in earlier writings, spoken a good word for this little mammal, let me recall it. A creature that will destroy a song-bird's nest is a pest, and whether furred, feathered, four-legged, two-legged, or a small boy, ought to be exterminated.

It is probable that nests placed but a little way above the ground are not molested, and equally probable that the persistent persecution suffered by the song-sparrows and brown thrushes has induced them generally to abandon the practice of placing nests upon the ground, and to locate them in bushes or trees. It is a rather curious fact that of nineteen song-sparrows' nests found in the lowlands, where meadow-mice abounded, fifteen were in bushes, and ranging from two to five feet from the ground, while in the upland fields, where there are very few of these mice, of twenty-three nests found, eleven were on the ground, but all so placed at the base of some rank growth that their detection would not be easy. Of the brown thrush, or thrasher, it is now to be said that it has pretty generally abandoned nesting upon the ground. It is one of several species that is partial to a locality once chosen, and will return to it year after year if not disturbed; and now the densest thicket of smilax, or a vine-hidden branch of a gnarly oak, is far more apt to be chosen than any spot upon the ground. That mice, snakes, and all egg-loving creatures have brought about this change, is quite likely to be true. Indeed, it is hard to understand why any of our small inland birds should ever select such a locality as the bare ground, yet one little sparrow, the vesper-bird, never builds anywhere else, and escapes the many dangers that beset it, for no bird is more abundant, both young and old.

To return to my Mill Creek meadow-mouse—marsh-campagnol, as Godman calls it. After it had straightened its fur and had so far recovered from fatigue as to feel equal to continuing its journey, it started up the oar towards the boat, and apparently not until it had reached the gunwale did it notice me. Its sudden stopping, that nearly caused it to fall over backward, was very funny, but not more so than its quick recovery from astonishment, and prompt resolve to consider the remarkable situation. It sat upright on its haunches, like a marmot, and looked in every direction, but seeing no other dry route to shore than over the boat, and not desiring a second swim, it cautiously approached until within a few inches of me, when it gave a shrill squeak and broke into a run. In a moment it was out of sight.

An empty nest of a wood-thrush, directly above my head, recalled another wild mouse that is exceedingly abundant on the wooded bluff that faces the terrace. I refer to the white-footed or deer-mouse. The nest above me recalled them, because in October very many of the larger birds'-nests, especially if in thickets, will be found to have been converted into cosey winter retreats by these beautiful little mammals.

Notwithstanding my having given much attention to the subject, autumn after autumn, for several years, I have never been able to clear up several points in the histories of these bush-nests of the white-footed mice. In the first place, how far are these old birds'-nests remodelled; and again, are not a certain number of these mouse retreats constructed *de novo*, the builders using the abandoned nest of the bird for the exterior of the new structure?

In the months of October and November of the past year I examined a series of forty-two bush-nests, as I prefer to call them. Every one was materially different from an ordinary bird's-nest, none being open above, nor having the lining that birds use. They were all occupied, and I believe the full number of individuals occupying them was ascertained. In most cases I captured every individual—and released them.

Of the series, thirty-one nests were placed in a dense tangle of smilax or green-brier. None was near the surface of the thicket, but usually about one-third the distance from its uppermost surface; for instance, if the thicket was six feet high, the nest would be at an elevation of four feet, or very near it. This was a very uniform feature of the nests examined, and if the mice merely occupy old nests of birds where they find them, indicates a uniformity in the matter of nest-building of which I was not aware.

Again, the smilax was so very dense, or closely interwoven, that it seemed to me impossible that a bird as large as a robin or cat-bird could have penetrated it. Perhaps the continuous growth of the vine, after the birds abandoned the nest, made it inaccessible to them by early autumn. I did determine one interesting fact about the impenetrability of these growths of green-brier—that the small hawks found sparrows and the mice quite inaccessible when they took refuge therein. In one case, a sharp-shinned hawk, a little more rash than usual, struck at a snow-bird as it dived into the smilax, and instead of capturing it, was himself hopelessly entangled. At least, before he could extricate himself, I was able to secure his hawkship.

Four of the forty-two nests were among blackberry canes, and this growth also was exceedingly dense and difficult to penetrate. The remaining seven nests were in a mixed tangle of Virginia creeper and grape. These seven nests were all at a greater elevation than any found in smilax or other thorn-bearing growths, one being thirteen feet from the ground.

All these nests were distinctly globular in shape. The original structures were not merely covered at the top, but distinctly arched over, so as to give a greater capacity to the nests than when occupied by their original builders.

Careful examination convinced me that twenty-nine were the preceding summer's nests of cat-birds, wood-thrushes, and robins; those of the latter not being so popular, apparently, on account of their partial or complete mud-lining. I think this, because I found several of these nests that were not utilized, even when so strong an incentive was brought to play as the removal of the nearest available nests of other birds, which they had chosen, and from which they were forced to retreat.

The foundation and lower halves of the sides of these twenty-nine nests were unaltered; and many appeared as if a smaller nest had been bodily removed, inverted, and so used as a roof to the lower structure. Eight others were quite unlike birds'-nests in their construction. The interlacing of the twigs was not like the ordinary work of birds, and the diameter of each one of this series was nearly one-third smaller than that of an ordinary cat-bird's nest. Three of them I picked to pieces, and the lining was small feathers and the silk of the milk-weed, materials not used by any one of the thrushes I have named; and, indeed, the silk of the milk-weed would not be available until nesting was over, unless a little of the preceding year's could be gathered, which is not probable.

Nevertheless, I am not prepared to say that these mice do build bush-nests without at least the base of a bird's-nest as a starting-point. Yet why they should not does not readily appear. They build beautifully constructed nests in hollow logs and under bits of boards and old tin pans, carrying the materials therefor from quite distant points; so why not carry them up a few feet into tangled growths, offering almost as sure a footing as the ground itself? One difficulty that besets the investigator is that these creatures do next to nothing by daylight. Hours of patient waiting, during dark days and throughout the gloaming, have availed me nothing. As a day-time feature of our woods, I know of no sleepier creatures than a family of white-footed mice.

Judging from the number of nests mentioned—another such series might give different results—these bush retreats are usually modified birds'-nests, but in some instances the modification appears to be extended to practically the construction of a new nest.

A feature of much interest that is worthy of detailed mention concerns the occupants of these nests rather than the structures themselves. Thirty-six nests contained each a female mouse with a litter of young, either old enough to run alone or clinging to the teats of their dam. In not one case did I see a male mouse; while in the other six nests each contained a single adult male mouse, and no other occupant. This appears to me the more peculiar experience, as in several nests placed upon the ground both parents were found in the same nest in every instance. Still, it is not safe to draw any conclusions without hundreds of nests are carefully examined.

It was a pretty sight to see the mice when forced to quit their airy quarters in a smilax thicket. Be the vine ever so slender, they took no uncertain steps, but tripped lightly down from point to point, always descending and never arriving at a confusing corner, and so at a loss as to what direction next to take. One female mouse with two young ones clinging to her teats turned just twenty corners before she reached the ground. Once there, she suddenly disappeared. This is always the case, but just where they go when they reach terra firma remains to be shown. The prevalent impression is that every mouse has a subterranean retreat directly beneath the bush-nest, and passes from one to the other as fancy dictates. Their actions, indeed, seem to bear out the truth of this, but I have never been able to discover these supposed underground retreats. In some cases it was clearly impossible that such should exist. That they take refuge, at times, in the intricate tunnels of the meadow-mice, I know, and that any burrow would be entered, when these mice are driven from the bushes, is quite certain; that they construct one expressly for such a contingency is quite another question.

Why, it will probably be asked, do so many of these mice quit their cosey quarters in or on the ground, and which have served them every purpose, and take all this trouble to build a new home in the bushes for the winter? It has been suggested that the old nest was worn out, and better fitted for entomological research than for hesperomoid habitation. I had myself thought of this, but have never detected such abundant evidences of this disastrous condition as would warrant the removal; and certainly the fur of these creatures would carry, in all cases, a sufficient number of acari to bring about, in a short time, a repetition of the plague.

The supposed excessive dampness during autumn and winter of many situations where the summer nests of the mice abound has also been urged as a probable reason for the marked exodus that, as we have seen, occurs on the approach of cooler and wetter weather; but the exposure to sudden summer showers would, in this respect, be more objectionable than the steadier rains and gradual melting of snow during winter, when, as a matter of fact, they are less apt to suffer from water encroaching upon their nests than at other times, the frozen condition of the rough surface tending to carry off the water and prevent its soaking into the ground. I have never found a nest that could not have been better guarded from the damps of winter than from those terrific cloud-bursts that recall the vivid description in Genesis of the Noachian deluge. During such rainfalls, for which August is noted, very many white-footed mice are drowned.

I have not been able to determine how late in the spring they remain in these nests in the bushes; but some time before the arrival of the cat-birds and thrushes they have all sought again their earth retreats or cosey nests in prostrate hollow logs, where they quietly pass their summers.

The slanting rays of the slowly setting sun penetrated the shallow waters on either side of the boat; and so gentle was the current that I had the wished-for opportunity to observe the many small fishes that were constantly passing and repassing there, and which also were congregated upon the smooth sandy bottom of the stream. The smaller minnows were generally too restless to be studied satisfactorily, and indeed they do not offer much attraction to the student; but fortunately there was a goodly company of little darters or etheostomoids, and these were pitching about over the rippled sands in so sprightly a manner that I gave most of the remaining hours of daylight to them. They were all of one species—the common tessellated darter—chestnut-brown, and covered with inky-black lines, dots, and little squares; and when resting upon the mottled sandy mud were very difficult to detect. These fish are not pretty, but what they lack in attractive coloring is compensated for by the methods, all their own, of their lives. As the water was but a foot in depth, and steadily decreasing, I found many individuals were lying on the sand directly beneath me, as I leaned over the gunwales. I found very few by looking for them, but many by waiting until they gave a start and then watching where they settled. Often several would be almost in contact, but there was no concert of action as when small shiners or cyprinoids are associated. Occasionally two, and sometimes three or four, would see the same object move, and within the fraction of a second all would pounce upon it. This seemed to lead to no ill-tempered demonstrations on the part of those which were unsuccessful in capturing the coveted morsel.

As is well known, darters are poor swimmers. With a great effort they can move ahead for a foot or two, and then, unable to remain afloat, they come to rest upon the bottom of the stream. If the bottom be of sand or sandy mud, the imprint of their ventral and pectoral fins can be seen; and always when they make a plunge for some minute crustacean or insect, the print of their pig-like snout can always be seen.

I began a series of simple experiments by dropping coarse grains of sand into the water directly in front of them. These they seemed to recognize as such, and did not heed them beyond approaching a little nearer to the spot where the sand-grains lodged, or turning so as to directly face the spot if the grains fell a little to one side or the other. Continuing to watch the darters closely, I found that this was a customary movement with reference to all animate objects upon which they fed. The first motion a water-mite or cypris might make caused the darter to assume a make-ready attitude; the next assured the fish that the object moving was alive, and immediately it was pounced upon.

Having a quantity of mustard-seed shot with me, I conceived the plan of controlling the movements of these fishes by dropping single grains of it in front of one or two near together, and while they were waiting for the grains to move a second time, bring up others that were behind. Experience showed that theory and practice were very different, in this as in many another matter, but finally I got seven in a row, and by placing a row of shot-grains on a stick and letting them fall overboard together, I kept these seven together and without confusion; they faced to the right or left or advanced, in obedience to my order expressed by the dropping of the shot. While thus engaged a school of small minnows came trooping along and disturbed the scene. They darted after the shot that I dropped among them and scattered the darters, so that I could not regather them. After tarrying a few moments the minnows passed under the boat, and when out of sight I threw a few grains of shot into the water with some violence. Immediately they returned as one body, and searched for the supposed food which they heard but could not have seen.

I have often been puzzled by similar concerted action on the part of roach, and how it is accomplished is not readily explained. It has been said to be due to experience and memory; but how? Can experience have anything to do with it? It begins with their earliest infancy, and unquestionably some means must exist of conveying the fact that a companion fish, behind his fellows and therefore unseen, has changed his course. What this method of conveying intelligence is remains to be determined. Experience, at least, can be ruled out of court. May it be that the hindmost of a school of fishes, suddenly reversing its position, gives an impression to the water that is promptly felt by those immediately in advance? Probably if but two or three fishes were swimming single file, and the hindmost one turned about, the others might not notice it at once; but when there is a large school of these gregarious fishes, then they swim many abreast, and an object falling behind the school would be seen by several, who turning together would give a peculiar motion to the water that would be felt by the preceding individuals. If to remember that this impression means that the fishes behind have changed their course, then I can agree with my critic; but then what of those very young fishes who have had no experience?

A repetition of the experiment with five shot showed me quite conclusively that these little fish cannot be fooled indefinitely by such means. After a reasonable amount of patient waiting for the falling shot to prove its vitality, the darters become satisfied that it is inanimate, and pay no further attention to it. Here we have a genuine exhibition of the operations of "experience," and a proof that if fish may be temporarily fooled they are not necessarily foolish.

My second experiment ended rather curiously. Remembering having noticed in a meadow-pool vast numbers of water-fleas, I left my boat and proceeded to gather a quantity. Returning, I inverted the glass jar with its indefinite thousands of fleas, and when it was nearly at the bottom of the creek, removed the cover and pulled up the jar. Immediately all the darters were wild with excitement, and whirled about in the most remarkable manner, and then, before I could ascertain any reason for so doing, suddenly vanished. I was thoroughly astonished, until I saw a pair of voracious turtles rooting up the mud where the busy darters had been. These carnivorous creatures had seen the commotion, and either desired to be guests at the darters' feast or to dine off the fish. Either case would doubtless have pleased the turtles. Where the fish hid themselves so quickly and effectually I could not ascertain.

Thomas Campanius, in his quaint little history of New Sweden, credits the Delaware with two fishes I have not yet been able to capture, to see, or hear of as captured or seen by others. Campanius says: "Opposite to *Poaetquessingh*—which, I take it, is not far from here — there is a kind of fish with great long teeth, which the Indians call *Manitto*, which means spirit or devil; it plunges very deep into the water, and spouts it up like a whale; the like is not to be seen elsewhere in the river." It is scarcely likely that such a remarkable creature will ever be found in Crosswicks Creek, and so, wondering what our author meant, let us turn to his second description. He says: "There is here an abundance of a certain kind of fish, which the Swedes call *tarm-fisk* (gut-fish). It has no head, and is like a small rope, one quarter of a yard in length, and four fingers thick, and somewhat bowed in the middle. At each of the four corners there runs out a small gut, or bowel, three yards long, and thick as coarse twine : with two of these guts they suck in their food, and with the two others eject it from them. They can put out these guts at pleasure, and draw them in again, so that they are entirely concealed, by which means they can move their body about as they like, which is truly wonderful to look upon. They are enclosed in a house, or shell of brown horn."

Here our author refers, I take it, to the egg-cases of skates, and as a description, *it* "is wonderful to look upon." Campanius doubtless saw these somewhere in the lower bay, and received at second-hand all that he finds to say about them.

Such palpably absurd descriptions of animals found in the Delaware are of some interest to the naturalist, in that they open up the question whether, even so recently as two centuries, marine forms may not, far more frequently than now, have wandered up the river very near or quite to the termination of the tidal portion of the stream?

I have been told by very old men that the common harbor porpoise was seen nearly every year as far from the bay as Bristol and Burlington; the seal is still no stranger, and a skate was taken near Bordentown in 1860, and exhibited in the Trenton markets. These now strictly marine forms can live in fresh water, as we have seen—why may not the navigation of the river by steam-vessels, and the general disturbance of its waters by so many means, have driven them oceanward, as the general settlement of the river's shores caused all the larger mammals to retire?

Mill Creek is the only running water, I believe, where the pretty water-shield is to be found, except in the mill-ponds scattered at intervals along the valley of Mechen-tschiholens-sipu; but as the prettiest of mill-ponds is necessarily somewhat artificial, I do not consider them, visit them, or feel interested particularly in what I hear of them.

Of this pretty water-plant, the *Brasenia*, I gathered a number of floating, delicate leaves, and endeavored to secure the entire stem also, but this was too difficult a task for an August afternoon. The under side of the leaf and the stem are purplish brown, and were covered with a translucent jelly, embedded in which were millions of what I took to be insects' eggs. They certainly had that appearance. I was far more interested to find that usually beneath each leaf of the water-shield there was hiding a little pike. The largest was not two inches in length. When disturbed they swam a few inches, and seemed wholly "at sea" if there was not another leaf near by to afford them shelter. They were remarkably tame or stupid, and I caught several with my hand-net. One was far more obese than the others, so I sacrificed him in the cause of science. In his stomach was a minute cyprinoid, about one-half an inch in length, which had been swallowed but a very short time. I should have been glad to find a still smaller fish in the stomach of the cyprinoid, but — I didn't. Not many years ago I did, however, find something more marvellous than this would have been. I caught an unusually large mud-minnow, which had swallowed a pike; and in the pike's stomach was a small mud-minnow, and in its stomach were *the remains of a pike.* Four fish as one! This will do; and were it not for the prejudice against fish stories, I would beat this earlier record of my own by narrating a more recent occurrence.

While speaking of the pike, let me add the following from a recent publication. It quite accords with my own impressions about their intelligence, as compared with other fishes—even the black bass.

"There can be little doubt that the pike is decidedly an exception to the rule that fish have little or no intelligence. Even the size of his brain is worthy of respect. Its proportionate size as compared to the rest of the body is as 1 to 1300; in the shark, whose intelligence has so often been vaunted, it is only as 1 to 2500; while in the tunny it is but as 1 to 3700. The only thing that dulls the pike's intelligence is his greed; but even this may perhaps only be caused by an overweening confidence in his own gastric juices. Like many other voracious animals, to swallow seems to be his only joy; palate he has little or none."

Pushing the boat a little nearer to the channel, I came to a long narrow strip of dark green growth that completely covered the bottom of the creek where it grew, but did not reach to the surface. It was the eel-grass. It was slimy to the touch, but not coated with jelly, like the water-shield. Some of the leaves were gritty from the thick studding of minute shells.

The water was sufficiently clear to enable me to see the grass plainly, so I peered for some time into the dense growth, which moved gracefully with a life-like, wavy motion, as the current bore its free ends up the stream. Like all dense, aquatic vegetation, it harbors many fishes, and it is surprising how great a variety will often issue from their hiding-places when once they have become accustomed to the presence of the boat above them. For a while to-day I saw nothing but waving grass; then an eel peered forth and quickly withdrew to the waving wilderness; then a number of sticklebacks rushed out, and as quickly returned; then in turn came a water-snake, a turtle, a perfect swarm of water-bugs of large size, and finally, as a fitting close of the day's exhibit, a number of beautiful silvery bill-fish.

Of the entire range of fish-life of the river or its tributaries there is no one species more attractive than this. Its manner is as peculiarly its own as its anatomical features are unique, and he who doubts that fishes play, just as children do, should watch a number of these fishes. In the first place, they never go about singly. Always there are a dozen or more, and often as many as a hundred are seen. When they come into the creek and get among the eel-grass the fun commences. They glide in and out of the waving ribbons of the slender water-weed with all the gracefulness of the undulations of the plant. Very frequently they chase each other or play a game of hide-and-seek, and however fast and furious the fun, their gracefulness of movement is never lost. They seldom are at rest. Perhaps, as is said of carp, they never sleep. Whether swimming onward, as though only anxious to reach a distant point, or playfully wandering about some attractive spot, the body always has that sigmoid curve which is so attractive, and tends even to lessen the ugliness of the most repulsive forms of animal life. All know how very different is a gracefully coiled serpent from one that is stretched out in a nearly straight line.

The billfishes have one habit, quite frequently indulged in, which I am not aware is common to any other species occurring in our waters—that of turning over upon their backs while rapidly swimming, and in this position continuing their course for some distance. Had I not often witnessed this, during the past three years, I should have considered it an error in observation on the part of the reporter. To-day, the many billfish that I saw were not so disposed to gymnastics as is often the case, and all remained very properly with their backs to the sky; but I have seen half a dozen at once, in a school of perhaps twenty, swim in circles in this reversed position, and less commonly in a nearly direct line. It is, I believe, merely a peculiarity of their own, when engaged in a game of romps.

The sun has long since sunk beneath the horizon. Even the topmost twigs of the tall liquidambars are no longer gilded by the stray beams that struggled through the sunset clouds. The gloaming has set in. The darkened waters hide their treasures; and it is fitting, after so full a day, to be afield, and homeward bound, rather than afloat.

This may be true, but the truth is, I am always eager to go to and never ready to leave, for the day, my little boat, that for years has carried me safely so many miles up and down the charming bends and winsome reaches of Mechen-tschiholens-sipu.

It was time to return home, yet I could not make up my mind to start. Was there not yet something that I could watch even by the gloaming's uncertain and steadily waning light? The full moon was rising, and there was every prospect of a perfect night. At least for a little longer I would remain. Had I not need of food and sleep, to have sat quietly in my boat until the day dawned would have been no hardship. Behind me, for I was now on the main creek once more, rose the steep bluff that forms the south bank of the stream, and the shadows cast by the magnificent trees that covered it had wooed the birds of the neighborhood to rest therein, until now their dream-songs floated creekward, and blended with the ceaseless hum and rattle of the tireless crickets. Before me the never-resting current of the stream glittered in the moonlight, and the vast marshy meadow beyond was a wilderness of weeds teeming with noisy life. From the tall trees upon the bluff there came a troop of noisy herons, that after circling high overhead and sailing far over the meadows, returned to the shallows of the creek, and ranged themselves in convenient shadows in wait for fish. Would it not be worth the labor to watch them through the night?

From the rippling waters there leaped many a fish; even what I took to be a sturgeon plashed and rolled over the sand-bar, to the terror of all smaller fry, as their bodies glancing in the moonlight proved. Every projecting stick supported its full complement of turtles. Muskrats crossed and recrossed the creek, leaving long lines of silvery bubbles in their wakes. The whippoorwills were holding high carnival on every prostrate tree in the woods, and over all there fell a shower of uncertain light as the myriads of fire-flies were wafted hither and yon by every passing breeze. Would it not be worth the while to watch all these even until dawn?

Now, I have always contended that animals of all kinds were unreliable weather prophets, and not a creature of the many that were abroad to-night but expected to remain. Why not? There was no indication of any change in the weather, and be it man or insect, all was favorable for an outing, with no other shelter than the starry sky. Would that I possessed a pocket aneroid, rather than an indifferent timepiece. Without a moment's warning a raw east wind swept across the water and sent a chill to my very bones. The crickets ceased to stridulate, the whippoorwills to sing; the moping herons rose, with impatient cries, and sought the shelter of the woods. In a minute, at most, there was the fearful, unnerving change from sound to silence. I hurried to a safe shelter for my boat. The dipping of my oars was a hollow, mocking sound. I was as one deserted, absolutely alone, and it was with a sweet sense of relief that I reached the highway and neared the habitations of man.

Quickly following in the track of that chilling wind came up from the east a great bank of leaden clouds, and before I reached the threshold of my home, the steady pattering of rain-drops on the oaks foretold, in no uncertain terms, the coming of a storm.

CHAPTER VIII.
THE LANDING.

TAKING a most erratic course, a flock of cow-birds, with silent, undulatory flight, preceded me this morning on my way to the creek. They brushed the dew from the taller bushes as they progressed, and caused the clustered growths to look inky-black in contrast with the dew-gemmed grasses beneath and dripping branches of the trees overhead. The effect was very striking. Until the sun had dried every twig, the route of this flock of birds could be distinctly traced.

Why they rested for a moment, in nearly every clump of bushes in their path, remains a mystery. They certainly were not in search of food, nor did they tarry long enough to rest themselves. They stopped, and then hurried on, as though led by the whim of a witless leader.

I clip the following from a paper, as it refers to these Crosswicks meadows and the nearest village: "For upwards of an hour yesterday morning (November 5) a continuous flock of cow-blackbirds flew over this town. They came from a northerly direction, and were moving southward. An old gunner says that cow-blackbirds have not been very numerous hereabouts of late years."

The day referred to was clear and warm, and I was within a mile or two of this wonderful flock of birds, and yet saw nothing of them. It is additional and unneeded evidence that the horizon of one individual's observation is very limited. On the other hand, the report of the gunner that the cow-blackbirds have been scarce of late is quite an error. I can speak with confidence concerning the past twenty years, and in no one of these have I failed to find them in abundance; but, unlike him, I never saw such a flock as he reported.

The redwings, too, are flocking now. Their cheerful chatter is heard everywhere over the meadows, and at intervals great flocks pass swiftly by. Nor have they yet forgotten their spring-tide songs. Above the roar of beating wings and the shrill chirping of their companions can be heard the sweet singing of many that no thought of frosty autumn seems to sadden.

As early as the middle of July the redwings begin to congregate on the willow hedges, and a dozen or more birds flying together, their wings keeping

"time, time, time,
In a sort of Runic rhyme,"

give us the earliest intimation of the approach of autumn. It is six weeks off, to be sure, even according to the almanac, and nine weeks really; but when the wavy, concerted flight of a few blackbirds fans the outlying leaves of the tree-tops, know then that the active days of summer—days of nesting and bird-youth—are over, and with the gathering of the clans a new era is ushered in; and these wide meadows, rich in tangled weeds, and all spotted and scarred with thicket, hedge, and pool, are their gathering grounds.

A word as to their numbers: we have all heard of those wonderful flights of passenger pigeons, that, like the clouds of a summer shower, obscure the sun for hours. Nothing like them is now to be seen in this valley; but a year ago, while near the starting-point of this day's journey, I witnessed the passage of a vast throng of redwings, which, if it did not wholly shut out the sun, at least cast an enormous and well-defined shadow.

Their numbers can only be estimated; but allowing one bird to every square foot of surface as they flew, there was certainly an acre of them. I think it is safe to say that there were fifty thousand birds in the flock.

Before I had passed a hundred yards down stream I rounded an abrupt bend in the creek, and all that remains of a once busy spot came into view.

The unceasing tides for more than two centuries have ebbed and flowed since a thrifty young Englishman traced the half-hidden Indian path that led to the uplands, then a gloomy forest, and discovered amid a wilderness of undergrowth a noble spring issuing from the low bluff a few rods distant.

Here, he thought, of all points between the river and the back country is the one whereat to build a wharf; and before half a decade it was ready to receive the passing shallops, and his own were being builded.

At low tide to-day I saw several of the old wharf logs still in place. But could this pioneer merchant of the Crosswicks valley return, he would scarcely recognize the site of the "landing," as it was then called.

Not one of several landmarks, of which tradition makes mention, now remains.

I drew my boat ashore upon the clean sand brought from subterranean recesses by the spring, and first paused at a slight depression on a grassy knoll, which is the site of the old warehouse. Wild roses cover the spot now.

Before following up the spring brook to its source, let me recall one bit of early colonial history connected with the wharf and its belongings. It was during the winter of 1741–42 that the shallop *Anne* lay at the wharf, not temporarily storm-stayed, but ice-bound. The winter had "set in" before she could sail for Philadelphia, and, as it proved, not a rod of open water was visible until the middle of the ensuing March. So she was made fast and guarded from the ice, should there come a sudden break-up.

It was the business of one Jemmy Cumberford to look after the boat, and this he did faithfully and well, except upon such occasions as rendered him unable to look after himself. One such was late in January of that notably severe winter, when about midnight he roused the merchant's family by his shrill cries for help. It happened thus: all through the night before and all that day it had been snowing. Not drifting snow-flakes scattering through the air, but steadily descending from a leaden sky hidden behind the feathery rain. Not a vestige of any familiar object was to be seen that did not bear its load of snow. Jemmy Cumberford that afternoon, wandered to the boat instead of going home, and when he closed the door of the little cabin behind

10*

him the snow was still falling. But the storm was at an end, and soon the moon was struggling through the broken clouds, and shone out in all its splendor. All nature was profoundly quiet, and Jemmy asleep.

Now it so happened that a troop of a dozen snowy owls had been journeying for days, winging their way southward above the storm, and ready to rest, when the breaking clouds gave them sight of mother earth again. They reached the Crosswicks valley when the storm ceased; and mistaking the ice-bound, snow-clad shallop for some great tree set adrift by the tempest, they chuckled to themselves that it offered so good a resting-place, and in the rigging, upon the deck, and directly by the cabin-door, these grave-visaged owls sat, peacefully scanning the congenial surroundings, as arctic then as ever they found their native haunts within the polar circle.

Being silent birds, their scarcely audible chuckling could not have aroused Jemmy from his slumbers, and their promenading about the snow-covered deck could not have reached his muffled ears; but quite certain it is that he was suddenly roused, and, half-awake, slowly emerged from the cabin. The opening door pushed aside one of the owls; but no owl was it to Jemmy. He saw two fiery eyes and a mass of snow rise up and settle in the rigging overhead. Completely dazed, Jemmy dared not retreat or advance, until his presence excited the suspicion of the others, and everywhere, as he thought, the snow with fiery eyes was conspiring to crush him. With one mighty leap he reached the wharf and floundered, with all the energy of despair, to the house, a hundred rods distant, and uphill at that. With what strength remained he pounded the door and called, in husky tones, for help.

In a moment the family were aroused, and as excited as he, and it was long before they could get a word in reply to their many questions. Regaining a little of his usual composure, he whispered, "The snow's alive, and chased me off the boat."

The record of this occurrence, a mere fragment now, concludes thus: "Father found that James had been scared by a number of great white owls, not quite of the bigness of turkey-cocks. Father saw them the day following in the woods near by, and they were very tame. No one of us had seen birds like to them, but an Indian told us their name in his own tongue."

My impression, twenty years ago, was that these snowy owls came into New Jersey every winter, but I now am equally confident that such is not the case. That, being arctic birds, they should remain until summer, is remarkable, yet several such cases have come to my knowledge. My first meeting with these owls was in December, 1857. It was a perfect winter day, with a steel-blue sky, and every object covered with snow. Even in the sun not a flake melted; yet the perfectly still air did not feel cold. The chinkapin swamp, with its bush-like growths, was full of sparrows, and to hear them sing I wandered thither. The snow-birds twittered merrily; the white-throats whistled, and the dear old foxy finches warbled now and then. I was repaid for my tramp, but in time longed for novelty. "Is there nothing else?" I asked myself, and, boy-like, began to grow impatient. At last, plunging into the denser growth of another swamp near by, I was brought face to face with a novelty, and very abruptly too. In a small cedar-tree sat a magnificent snowy owl.

In witless, blank astonishment I stared at the owl, and it, without winking, stared at me.

An owl's solemn visage is meant for the world; what is behind it is meant for itself, and this great snow-white bird was thinking quite as rapidly and far more rationally than I was. It was not at all alarmed. I was; for the appearance of the bird was suggestive of direful results should it assume the offensive. But my courage gradually returned, and I very cautiously approached a little nearer. How the owl watched my every step! A few yards nearer, and I was so close that the feathers of the bird were distinguishable, and I began to examine more critically every feature, when it stepped backward, and brought the trunk of the tree, close to which it had been sitting, between me and itself, and then took flight, going still deeper into the dismal swamp.

I had no little difficulty in following; for the undergrowths were thickly matted, and afforded no footing for mammals larger than mice, but in time reached quite to the tree where the owl had alighted. It was a dense cedar, heavily weighted with snow, and showing but little of its green foliage; and yet, with so gentle a motion had the owl sought its perch, that not a flake seemed to have been disturbed, and by mere chance was I able to learn the bird's precise whereabouts.

Being now much nearer the owl than before, it pursued quite different tactics; and instead of flying, although I was so near, it first pressed all its feathers closely to its body and reached out its head, so that it became long and slender, and the few dark spots of its plumage aided in making it represent a portion of the snow-covered tree. It was done so quickly that I was fortunate in being able to watch the process. Had my attention been diverted for a second, the owl would simply have disappeared.

After waiting for perhaps a minute, I took hold of the outer ends of the nearest bushes and shook them vigorously. At once the owl spread his wings and disappeared in a growth of blueberry-bushes, too dense, indeed, for me to follow.

I was struck, as I watched the bird's retreating form, with a marvellous feature of its flight. Howsoever dense the growth, the bird penetrated it without touching a twig, or brushing a flake of snow from any bough. The impression I then received—now nearly thirty years ago—was that the flight through a forest of the snowy owl was one of the most striking exhibitions of wing power to be witnessed, and this impression remains.

It is unquestionable that a small proportion of these owls do not return north, when in March or April there is a decided change in the temperature, such as affects the movements of winter migrants generally. There is no reason to believe, however, that such birds ever breed here, although they have been taken in the cedar swamps of southern New Jersey as late as the middle of June.

When kept in confinement they become quite gentle, except towards strangers, and give much evidence of being more intelligent than our smaller native owls.

So far as my own observation extends, they do not appear to suffer, even during the extreme heat of our midsummer. The late Dr. Richard Harlan, of Philadelphia, a noted naturalist of his day and generation, kept one in his cellar for seven years. It became quite tame, but was averse to being approached by strangers. The doctor might have kept it even longer, had he not so frequently made use of it to frighten the children in the neighborhood. This finally caused it to suddenly disappear, much to the satisfaction of the young people and chagrin of the surly, grim-visaged doctor. I have this from my mother, who was once badly frightened by the owl, and who, shortly afterwards, headed the conspiracy that succeeded in making way with the bird.

The last considerable flight of snowy owls into New Jersey was in the winter of 1876–77. Notices of specimens shot were frequent in the local papers, and quite a number were offered for sale in the markets.

It has been frequently stated that the flesh of these owls is fine and delicate; but such has not proved true of specimens killed in this neighborhood. All were very tough, and of a disagreeable musky flavor.

The one prominent feature of the landing is the spring. From a little ravine that extends back into the bluff there issues a considerable stream of purest water, cold, colorless, and sparkling. Towards the creek it hurries rippling over snow-white pebbles, tarrying a second by some projecting root, and then with greater speed passes it by, "to join the brimming river."

One naturally pauses at a bubbling spring, even if not

thirsty. No one is so insensible to nature's beauties as to find nothing attractive in it. It is a point where life gathers in greatest profusion, and so the naturalist, be his specialty what it may, is sure to find something to bid him pause.

In the little basin where the eager waters rush upward to the light, and in the little brook beyond, not twenty rods in length, I have gathered many plants, beautiful shells, silvery fish, swift salamanders, and once chased a cunning shrew that at last out-witted me.

One feature of this spring, unlikely to escape the notice of a naturalist, is the quantity of pure white sand that is carried to the creek by the water. Dip but a tumblerful of the water, and in a moment many fine grains will settle in the bottom of the glass. That this, in the course of a day, is a considerable amount, is most readily shown by examining the sand-bar in the creek. Were it not that every tide bears quantities of this sand, so fine is it, both up and down the stream, the ever-growing bar would choke the channel of the creek and dam up the very waters that have carried it from unknown subterranean depths. As it is, the ever-present bar is constantly built up and unbuilded, as the tides roll by.

Think, for one moment, of the age of this spring. Its crystal waters have been flowing without a check since the close of the glacial epoch, which some too enthusiastic modernists date back but ten thousand years. Think then of the enormous bulk of sand which has been washed from beneath our upland fields and carried meadow-ward. What a cavern is beneath our feet if this sand once occupied space by itself; what a certain lowering of upland levels if it is washed from extensive areas! The growth and disintegration of a continent is epitomized in the work unceasingly performed by this bubbling spring.

In the immediate vicinity and even along the little brook, where there is more of sunshine, is little if any August bloom. The plants are green, luxuriant, and of many kinds, but all flower at the commencement of the season instead of at its close. It is in May, when the spring is hedged in with bloom—dog-wood, azalea, and other shrubs. Each succeeding month the brilliancy of bloom is more and more replaced by a wilderness of leaves only. Here is one of the few spots where lamb-lettuce, with deep blue flowers, suggesting the forget-me-not, grows in great profusion, and nearer the creek there is, each returning spring, a never-to-be-forgotten display of blooming golden-club. This is, except the yellow lotus, our least abundant water-plant, and so never fails to attract attention when in bloom. The plant itself, later in the summer, is pretty, but liable to be overlooked amid the wealth of growths that crowd the valley. Not so in May, when the plant is in bloom. The long, tapering spathes, densely covered with minute blossoms of the richest yellow, are the most conspicuous objects on the water's edge.

I examined many clusters of this plant when in bloom, during the past spring, and failed to find any evidence that insects habitually visited it. This surprised me the more, because I found the plant generally tenanted by a small black spider, which placed its web at the base of the finger-like stalks of bloom.

Kalm makes interesting reference to this plant. He writes: "Taw-Kee is another plant, so called by the Indians, who eat it.... The plant grows in marshes, near moist and low grounds, and is very plentiful in North America. The cattle, hogs, and stags are very fond of the leaves in spring, for they are some of the earliest. The leaves are broad, like those of the *Convaleria*, or Lily of the Valley, green on the upper side, and covered with very minute hair, so that they looked like a fine velvet. The Indians pluck the seeds, and keep them for eating. They cannot be eaten fresh or raw, but must be dried. The Indians were forced to boil them repeatedly in water before they were fit for use, and then they ate them like pease. When the Swedes gave them butter or milk, they boiled ... the seeds in it. Sometimes they employ these seeds instead of bread, and they taste like pease. Some of the Swedes likewise ate them; and the old men among them told me they liked this food better than any of the other plants which the Indians formerly made use of. This Taw-Kee was the *Orontium aquaticum*."

Just as two centuries ago this splendid spring was looked upon by my paternal ancestor as a spot very desirable to possess, so the Indians, in earlier days, were attracted to it, and lived, no one can say for how long, within hearing of its rippling waters. The ashes of their fires are mingled with every clod that is now upturned by the spade. I lately gathered from among the pebbles in the brook a tiny arrow-point, and tracing the probable course of the little weapon, which must necessarily have been washed from the hill-side, I found that the crumbling bluff had, by the recent uprooting of a tree directly above the spring, exposed the site of an arrow-maker's workshop.

Such evidences of the aborigines are not novelties in this vicinity. I have found dozens such, and thousands of beautiful arrow-points, spears, scrapers, and all the variety of chipped flints, now rest in museum cases, gathered from these places and the intervening fields.

The one I found so recently told the same story as have the others. Here were bowlders of jasper and flinty rocks, such as are common to the gravel-beds that form the eastern bank of the river, five miles away as the crow flies; also cores or remnants of the selected pebbles and bowlders, which were too small or too irregular in shape to be further available. With these were large flakes, some of which may have been used as knives, or intended for such use; for just such specimens are frequently found, with undoubtedly finished tools, on wigwam sites. I found too, as is always the case, blocked out and subsequently discarded specimens, and others that had been nearly or quite finished and then irreparably injured by some unlucky finishing touch. Of course, fine chips and splinters were abundant; but I failed to find any hammer-stones or other flint-clipping tools. Had the arrow-maker, when he left, carried these away with him? It is certainly a plausible explanation of their absence.

What I have mentioned of another and much larger workshop-site I can repeat of this: here, shaded by dense woods, on a slightly elevated knoll, in the midst of a meadow-like expanse of low-lying ground, through which trickled a sparkling spring brook, had tarried, for years, an arrow-maker, shaping with marvellous skill those varied patterns of spear-points and delicate tools which are still gathered from the adjoining fields. Unlike localities of many acres in extent, where the traces of former occupation are scattered throughout the whole area, and indicate that manufacturing had once been in progress simply by the abundance of chips, we have in this workshop-site the evidences of the toil of a single skilled workman, who, in the quiet of his forest retreat, spent the greater portion of a long and useful life.

What gave zest to a pleasant hour spent here, a year ago, in archæological research was the finding of a small smooth horn-stone pebble, upon one side of which was a rude but unmistakable carving of a human face. What may we call such objects? If worn upon the person, and treasured beyond all other possessions, it became in fact an idol, and so perhaps we are warranted in considering it. Larger and more pretentious carvings have been found not far away, and these are held to be such if the smaller but otherwise similar ones are not. John Brainerd, while a missionary among the Indians of New Jersey, recorded of one of these people that "she had an aunt . . . who kept an idol image, which indeed partly belonged to her, and that she had a mind to go and fetch her aunt and the image, that it might be burnt; but when she went to the place she found nobody at home, and the image also was taken away." While this, indeed, is slender evidence of the occurrence of idol worship among the Delaware Indians, it is of interest in showing that images were not unknown, and that they possessed other significance and value than as mere ornaments. Any carving in wood or stone, merely used for personal decoration, as the one I found in the workshop-site may have been, would not have become sinful in the mind of an Indian woman through the preaching of the missionary; and a desire to destroy the object she reported as in her possession must necessarily have arisen from the fact that it was regarded with superstitious reverence, and invested with supernatural powers in their belief.

A word more concerning Indian idols, and I have done. Dr. Brinton remarks: "They—the Lenâpè or Delaware Indians—rarely attempted to set forth the divinity in image. The rude representation of a human head, cut in wood, small enough to be carried on their person, or life size on a post, was their only idol. This was called *wsinkhoalican*. They also drew and perhaps carved emblems of their totemic guardian. Mr. Beatty describes the head chief's home as a long building of wood. 'Over the door a turtle is drawn, which is the ensign of this particular tribe. On each door-post was cut the face of a grave old man.'

"Occasionally, rude representations of the human head, chipped out of stone, are exhumed in those parts of Pennsylvania and New Jersey once inhabited by the Lenâpè. These are doubtless the *wsinkhoalican* above mentioned." So much for the Indians of the Crosswicks valley.

It is easier to keep out of trouble than to get out of

it. The truth of this, as regards both birds and men, was illustrated by a recent adventure near the spring, which had its comical as well as serious features. I saw a purple grakle's nest that had every appearance of being suspended in the tree-top like an oriole's—a position wholly out of the rule. It was too high up to let me solve the mystery by viewing it from below, and to satisfy a laudable curiosity I resolved to climb the tree.

Having done so, I was well repaid for the labor. The nest had been displaced by the wind, but had strangely lodged between two nearly parallel branches, which, however, held it only by its rim and threatened to let it fall at any moment. The poor birds, which were plainly in great distress, had vainly tried to secure it anew, and had built up its edges until they overlapped the supporting limbs, but had not the skill to interweave the new stuff with the old, and thus make one structure of it all. Their intentions were good; the means adopted to secure the desired result deplorably bad. They were merely adding weight above, when they required support below. Many of our birds would have been engineers equal to the emergency; but the grakles were not. I made the nest as secure as I could by drawing it to where the space between the branches was narrower, and so gave it sufficient support. The birds looked on approvingly, and I was well repaid by what I imagined to be their grateful thanks.

It now remained for me to descend and leave the birds in peace. I started to do so, when through some strange miscalculation I failed to secure a footing, and fell. I have heard it remarked that there is an art in falling. What one does when spinning through the air for a second or less is not easily recalled; but the descent seemed a great deal longer than a minute. I can only be sure that I started face downward, and came to a short stop, with the sun shining in my face. I was still six feet from the ground, lying at full length across the densest growth of smilax on the farm. Now smilax has thorns—a fact that had never troubled me before; and these resented my abrupt intrusion by penetrating into and through my clothes, and beyond. This may seem trivial as you read it, but do not test the matter. Accept my assurances that a thorn to every square inch of one's back and limbs is not trivial; and when smilax confronts you, go round, and not through it.

Perhaps those who have so much to say about reclining on beds of roses, have never realized the accompaniment of thorns. Here was I upon a bed of thorns, with no very rosy prospect of getting from it. There was a cat-bird hard by who looked at me for a moment, laughed, flirted his contemptuous tail, and departed. The gesture was irritating. Man vaunts himself the climax of animal creation; yet this saucy cat-bird could, without an effort, skip over the smilax, where I was helpless.

A happy thought struck me. I would crawl out of my clothes! Alas, that seemed only the beginning of a reduction which would have no end before I had escaped from that piercing and clinging smilax, short of having reduced myself to a bare, hard skeleton, and I feared I never could put myself together again. What *was* I to do? Planning on a bed of thorns, even if they do not prick us, is not an exhilarating pastime. The surroundings are not conducive to quick-wittedness, and the sunshine from above and mosquitoes from everywhere distract attention. The most feasible and natural thing of all occurred to me at the last of a long series—to call for help.

I combined the penetrative elements of shriek, yell, howl, and squeal, hoping some receptive ear might recognize the meaning. It startled the birds, and they quickly came to see what manner of creature had happened into their midst. First, of course, came the tantalizing cat-bird. He investigated closely—too closely—and then contemplated me, perched within arm's-length of my fist. His ultimate conclusion was a spiteful *ba-a*. Every robin and thrush of the whole hill-side came, and the volume of their united voices, in discussion, brought the jays and a pair of crows.

The crows were more clamorous and bolder than the smaller birds; and knowing their fancy for a luncheon of the eyes of sick sheep and helpless lambs, I began to have some fear for the safety of mine. I called again in no uncertain tones. It had the initial effect of driving away the avian congress, and then, to my inexpressible relief, I heard a voice answering. Again I shouted, and a quick reply assured me that help was at hand. A moment more, and my rescuer was ready—but his ingenuity was not equal to his desire to aid me. He could no more get into the smilax than I could get out of it. Scratching his head, he remarked, "I don't suppose it will do to burn the briers and let you drop on the ashes, will it?"

I gave a faint groan in reply, and suggested his devising some other means.

"I have it!" he exclaimed, and turning to the tree I had climbed, he drew himself to the lowest of the long, out-stretching branches, and bearing it down within my reach, gave me a chance to pull myself upward from the smilax; the only thing, indeed, that I could do. As I secured my hold he withdrew, and I finally, by the resistance of the bended limb, was free of the briers, and left to painfully work my way to the trunk of the tree. This took all my strength, and I needed much help to enable me to reach home. It was no slight mishap I had suffered, and the scars on my back made an excellent map of the Micronesian archipelago.

Prominent in the modest landscape, as we view the "landing" from the boat, is a shapely beech, that midway between the spring and the creek overhangs a sparkling brook. It possesses no very marked features, and certainly is not so large as one might think a tree two hundred years old should be; but it is a tree with a history, and has had the honor of sheltering many a naturalist, and bearing upon its bark their names or initials, cut by the naturalists themselves. These traces of distinguished visitors have all disappeared; but the tree is still singled out for like attentions from others, for contemplative ramblers and happy lovers have carved either their names or initials in suggestive proximity.

While endeavoring to decipher some of the older of these names, cut half a century ago, I was somewhat startled by a great roaring overhead, and the world of to-day was promptly recalled. The sound proceeded from a swarm of bees that literally rolled over the tops of the trees. It crossed the creek, and sped over the meadow, and when almost beyond sight the peculiar roar could be distinctly heard.

This incident recalled a remarkable flight of mosquitoes which I once witnessed from this point. It occurred too at the same time of year. Since sunrise there had been no noticeable peculiarity of the weather; the temperature, perhaps, being a little below the average of a midsummer day. The sky was clear, and while I was rowing slowly down the creek, suddenly, almost between winks, I saw a long, narrow line of dark-gray cloud rising rapidly and extending over half the western horizon. In a few moments I heard a faint humming sound, which grew louder and louder, and I thought of a tornado. I was too frightened to plan for my safety, and indeed there was no time in which to act. Heading for the shore, I reached an overhanging elm, and clinging to a projecting root, I awaited the oncoming of the supposed tornado. It came, but not as wind. The tempest proved a cloud of mosquitoes. It rose higher and higher as it approached, and when directly overhead quite cleared the tree-tops. Nevertheless, it was no pleasant, although novel, experience to be beneath such a cloud.

Had a sudden change in the wind checked their course and caused them to settle, I do not suppose I could have escaped being fatally stung by them. A rough estimate made on the spot led to the conclusion that this cloud of mosquitoes was half a mile wide, and one hundred yards from front to rear. The depth of the mass

I could not ascertain, but it effectually excluded the sunlight. The sound, as they passed, is best described by likening it to a long train of cars passing over a bridge.

My duties as a naturalist called me to determine if the meadows were unusually free from these pests, after the exodus of so many millions, but I could not see that this was the case. By careless exposure of my hands and face on the following evening, I found that there were enough left to render a night in the marsh exceedingly painful, if not absolutely dangerous through their attacks. I had also the task before me of determining the fate of the migrants, but this was never accomplished. The wind apparently carried them to the river and dispersed them over the flourishing county of Bucks, much to the annoyance of many a Pennsylvania farmer.

While standing by the beech-tree to-day I killed several "striped-stockings," as they are locally called, a species of *Culex* that out-buzz and out-sting the ordinary variety. They are twice as large, and the distinct black and white markings on their legs serve to distinguish the species. It is rarely the case that mosquitoes are too troublesome to enable one to carry out any plans, however much the hands and face are exposed; but occasionally, when in the low marshes at low tide, there will be a dozen or twenty "striped-stockings" which will make a simultaneous attack, and then prudence suggests beating an immediate retreat.

It has lately been ascertained that mosquitoes destroy young trout: "When the latter came to the surface of the water, so that the tops of their heads were level with the surface of the water . . . a mosquito would alight and immediately transfix the trout by inserting his proboscis or bill into the brain of the fish, which seemed incapable of escaping. The mosquito would hold his victim steady until he had extracted all the life juices, and when this was accomplished, and he flew away, the dead trout would turn over on his back and float down the stream."

It was early in September when I read the above, and I straightway took my stand on the bank of Faxon's Brook, then teeming with young cyprinoids, to see if such attacks were made upon these fish by our mosquitoes. The conditions were all favorable, but not a minnow was molested. I did find, however, in a sink-hole in an upland field, that these "striped-stockings" occasionally settled upon the tadpoles there, and puncturing the tail, caused it to bleed and often to swell and become congested. The water in the sink-hole was very shallow, and the tadpoles—of *Rana clamitans*, probably—were often put to it to keep wholly submerged. It is not at all improbable, I think, that under certain circumstances numbers of very small fish are destroyed in the manner described; for I find frequent reference in my note-books to the occurrence of quantities of dead young fish, the cause of the mortality among which I was unable to ascertain. Now it is no uncommon sight to see the surface of the water thickly dotted with the projecting snouts and even heads of small fishes, and such an occasion would afford excellent opportunity for the mosquitoes to attack them.

A peculiarly angry buzzing in the grass near by soon

called my attention from winged to wingless insects, and I saw, moving hurriedly along, that beautiful but dangerous creature popularly known as the velvet ant. It had better be called a sulphur-breathing imp of sheol. It is not an ant really, but the wingless female of a Hymenopter allied to them — the family *Mutillidæ* — and without further reference to her position in the textbooks, it may be added that she is the incarnation of ill-temper. One often hears the phrase, "as mad as a hornet;" but these are really peaceful, compared to the velvet ant, and angry only on occasion. Hornets can be provoked to anger, but do not systematically get out of bed, day in and week out, in a fit of fiery passion. This is just what the scarlet velvet ant does. If astir before the sun is well up, they are angered by the low temperature; at hot, high noon they venture abroad, berating even the grass blades, and killing or torturing with their poisoned sting every creature that crosses their path. Brave, indeed, must be their winged mates, to be willing to approach, and ever alert to take flight the instant any additional frowns darken these viragoes' foreheads. If it is true that anger is hot, then it is strange the frost can penetrate to their winter's subterranean abode. Packard says it quickly conceals itself when disturbed. Not always. I have found that it was by no means cowardly, even when pursued by man. On the contrary, often has it shown itself ready to fight, as though well aware that it possesses a terribly effective weapon. Whether undisturbed or when pursued, it at all times utters a loud and ireful buzzing that strangely enough has been recorded as a "faint squeaking sound."

I have often heard it at a distance of twenty feet, above the hum and stir of myriads of other insects. It is a sound much like the z-ing of a harvest-fly (cicada), but even more steady, uniform, and unceasing. Not even is the creature quiet when at home. Although the burrow is often half a metre in depth, still, by placing the ear to the entrance of the retreat, we can hear the ominous, angry buzzing, a casting of curses at every living creature that it can by any possibility afflict. Let him who would witness the climax of ill-temper watch for a while a velvet stinging ant, the formidable scarlet *Mutilla occidentalis*.

Had I not seen the Mutilla enter her subterranean abode, I should never have suspected that here, in the clean, closely shorn sod was the entrance to a considerable excavation. Not a trace of her tunnelling was now visible except the clean circular opening in the ground. Had there ever been? If so, what had become of the earth removed by this insect? The same may be asked of many another animal earth retreat.

It is presumed that whenever a mammal burrows into the ground, the earth removed is brought to the surface and scattered about the entrance, and there it remains until slowly removed by the rain, or blown away by some high wind, or, if not thus scattered abroad, that the grass springs up through it, and so effectually conceals all trace of it. Is all this presumption true? As a matter of fact, does every burrowing animal bring to the surface all the earth it displaces in making its burrow?

My attention having been called to this subject early

in the past summer, I have since then taken every precaution to let no new burrows near home escape detection and very careful examination; and as a result, I have concluded that there is in the minds of most people a misconception concerning these underground retreats, whether made by mammals or insects.

When a burrowing mammal is cut off from its retreat, and finding escape by running impracticable, instead of turning about and facing a pursuing foe, it will, as a desperate resort, start to burrowing. In the case of skunks, chipmunks, and star-nosed moles, it needs but an incredibly short time for the animal to conceal itself; but of course, in all such cases, the displaced earth is thrown upon the surface, and is a certain indication of the creature's whereabouts. Nevertheless, escape by such uncertain means is often effected, in consequence of the animal's being able to round a bowlder or large root, and so place it between the pursuer and pursued. In every such case the amount of dirt displaced is not all brought to the surface. Does the animal then worm its way through the soil, pressing it to either side of the tunnel as it progresses? There is certainly much evidence that this is true; but, of course, the practicability of such tunnelling by pressure depends upon the character of the earth and its relative density.

This has been pronounced impossible; and the assertion made that earth of so loose a texture that a mammal could worm through it, as loose sand, would immediately cave behind the animal as it progressed.

The striped ground-squirrel or chipmunk affords, in its burrow, a good opportunity to examine into this matter. I have carefully noted the conditions of thirteen such burrows, which ranged from seven to thirty feet in length. Every one was tortuous except the longest, which can better be described as wavy. In no instance could I find any evidence that dirt had been brought to the surface more than sufficient to fill about one-twentieth to one-fiftieth of the area of the tunnel, and probably in every case this was an over-estimate. Of this series of thirteen burrows none was more than a month old, and there had been no rains in that time sufficiently copious to have washed away all trace of newly exposed dirt. The main entrance to five was a perpendicular descent varying from two to five feet in depth, and I claim that this animal has no power to bring to the surface, when forced to back out of its burrow, any significant quantity of loose earth; and even if the diameter of the burrow was sufficient to enable it to turn about, it could not then remove any important amount of loose soil except it spent hours at the work; and this I am positive it does not do. The excavation of a tunnel is not the labor of a month, and so long a time would be necessary if every particle of detached earth was brought to the entrance of the burrow.

Some of the tunnels examined by me extended in from the face of the bluff about three feet, and then turned at a right angle and ran parallel to it for a considerable distance. Some made two or three abrupt turns, and had one or more roomy excavations besides, wherein food is stored. Now if the displaced earth was removed by these animals in small quantities, as by filling their cheek pouches with it—which they probably do not do—it would require a much longer time to complete a burrow, say fifteen feet in length and with a magazine for winter food of an area of one cubic foot, than is really consumed in the construction of such a subterranean home.

I have dispossessed chipmunks of their burrows and found that they made for themselves others in the course of a night—the length of such varying with the character of the soil in which they burrowed. I am free to admit that it seems quite impossible for an animal to penetrate the earth by pressing it from side to side as it progresses; and yet there seems to be no other method open to them after an ingress of a foot or more has been effected. The diameter of the burrow is simply sufficient for the animal to proceed forward. It cannot turn about and reach the entrance face forward. In burrowing, therefore, the earth detached by the fore-paws is forced under the belly, and it is to be supposed that this loose material can be continually collected by the animal in a pellet and pushed forward towards the entrance of the tunnel by the animal's hind-feet, as it slowly backs out, and often turning two or three corners. This absurdity has been seriously claimed as what must necessarily take place. I will not pretend to explain the methods of a chipmunk when burrowing, but that it is essentially different from the above supposed method I am confident.

As bearing upon this, let me refer to what I have witnessed in the case of a land-tortoise when preparing to go into winter-quarters. It was one that I had had in my yard for several years. Twice I saw it preparing for hibernation, and the process in each case was precisely the same. The animal chose a spot at some distance from any tree, as though desirous of escaping contact with roots as it descended into the earth. Without protruding its head, the tortoise first dug a shallow pit but a mere trace larger in circumference than its shell. The fore-feet only were used to displace the earth, but with its hind-feet, at times, it would effectually scatter this loose earth in every direction. When the depth of the pit was such that the animal could no longer dig without standing on its head, it rested upon all-fours in the shallow pit, and commenced immediately the task of lowering itself still deeper into the earth. By exercising great care, I was enabled to see the beginning of the work, and the same method was doubtless continued unto the end. By a vigorous scratching with all four feet the earth beneath the creature's plastron was first brought to the sides of the little pit, and then slowly was pushed upward until it formed a rim of sand about the margin of the carapace. There was a slight sidewise dipping motion of the creature's body all the while, but I judged that by the feet alone it not only loosened the earth beneath but worked it upward. However this may be, the quantity of this displaced earth was gradually increased until the tortoise disappeared. Just a day later I dug down to the animal and found that it had gone to a depth of fifteen inches, and the earth displaced and scattered was not one-twentieth of what it had actually removed from beneath and worked above it in the manner I have described.

Here was a case where an animal buried itself without difficulty, and passed through a layer of very compact earth. Scores of tortoises do the same every year, and possibly reach greater depths.

If, then, such excavations without removal to the surface of the displaced earth is practicable for a tortoise, may it not be equally so for a chipmunk, that works in far less compact earth and in a horizontal direction? The task is different in the case of the mammal, to be sure, but this difference is less significant than may at first be thought. I refer to preserving the burrow open as it proceeds. I find that in the sandy hill-side, where all the burrows are which I have examined, if you push a stout tube into the earth and remove so much as the tube will contain, then the side of the excavation made will soon crumble; but if a stick of the same size is pushed into the earth, the displaced portion, by being made more compact, is firmly fixed, and the little tunnel is comparatively permanent. Does not the peculiar digging motion of a burrowing mammal have the effect necessarily of compacting the sides of the tunnel as it progresses? The particles detached by the projecting fore-feet must unavoidably fall under the neck and belly of the animal, and the motion of the rapidly moving limbs must pat this material, which again is pressed down by the weight of the animal's abdomen. In such soils as I have examined, all of very loose texture, there did not seem to be any difficulty in rapidly tunnelling, but skill was required in so compacting the sides of the excavation that they would remain intact.

But what positive evidence have we that a mammal can penetrate even sandy soils and form a tunnel as it goes? I have finally met with what appears to be such evidence. Twice I have found where moles had made loose tunnels by heaving up the surface of the ground, and coming in contact with a projecting bowlder, had passed beneath it and reappeared at the surface at a point precisely opposite where the descent had been made. In these cases not a particle of earth had been brought to the surface; indeed, could have been so brought.

More recently I have been fortunate enough to surprise chipmunks in short tunnels, and securely closed the openings, and in every case I found that these tunnels were largely increased in depth, or a curve was made and the animal came to the face of the bluff not far from the opening which I had closed.

Because a dog, when in pursuit of an animal hidden in some burrow, may scatter the dirt in every direction as he digs, it does not follow that the pursued mammal "made any dirt" at all in excavating his subterranean retreat. Whatever may be true of marmots in other localities, of foxes and prairie-dogs, it is quite evident that where the earth is of so loose a texture as on our sloping terrace fronts, the chipmunk, the mole, the shrew, various snakes and certain insects, find it practicable to construct underground retreats by other means than the complete removal to the surface of the displaced earth; and further, such is the character of the soil, that actual removal would be fatal to the preservation of the walls of such retreats. Finally, if the earth is not removed, what can become of it, if not compacted by the animal's body as it makes its way forward?

Reluctantly leaving the beech-tree, about which cluster so many pleasant memories, and of which I have heard so many pleasant things told me in former years by graybeards no longer with us, I wandered to a sunny nook where orange-yellow touch-me-not filled the entire space, to the exclusion of every other plant. A walk through the little thicket was quite amusing. On every side the petty musketry of their exploding seed-pods filled the air. The little seeds fairly stung when they struck me in the face. I remained for several minutes in the midst of these plants, to determine how far the countless bees and butterflies provoked the seed-vessels to burst. They would seem to be too gentle in their movements generally. One burly humblebee did indeed appear to receive a broadside on his "ribs," as he turned over in mid-air, buzzed a loud guffaw at the fun, and sped off to more hospitable quarters.

As the day drew to a close, I again sought my boat upon the sandy beach, and met, while journeying thither, an employé of the United States Geological Survey. He had been mapping Crosswicks Creek, and kindly gave me some interesting information. The cornerstone at the blacksmith's shop is ninety-nine feet eleven and one-half inches above high-water mark at Sandy Hook. My neighbor's big brick house stands ninety-seven feet six inches above the same level, but where my house stands there is only seventy-seven feet elevation of which to boast. (I had always been told before that it was eighty feet.)

Perhaps I ought to feel unhappy because the blacksmith's shop is more than twenty feet nearer heaven, but I do not. If I am "farther off from heaven than when I was a boy," I still have no lack of company in the wee beasties, pretty birds, and brilliant butterflies that forty years have never failed to make this lower region all that I wished.

Again afloat, I pushed, since it was a little past high tide, into the wild-rice that clusters on a marshy island near, and there, hid from the outside world, watched the slowly descending sun. It was a fit place wherein to realize what is solitude. The marsh-wrens for a while seemed to stand in awe of me, and I heard no sound save the distant cawing of a crow. Somewhat weary, I lay flat upon my back and kept company with the clouds. But the feathered world soon spied me out. The wrens grew bold, and anon a "moping heron," that for long had been standing "motionless and stiff," came slowly towards me, and with one wild barbaric yawp, published my whereabouts to every creature. As once before, I soon became an object of interest, and while returning the curious gaze of many birds, forgot that the tide never takes a rest; and so, when the increasing darkness bade me hurry home, I found myself stranded on a fathomless expanse of quivering mud. The mud would not bear my weight, or else I could have waded to the running water and dragged the boat after me; so I settled down, with no good grace, to wait for hours before I could go home.

Had I desired to spend an evening on the marsh, no doubt but I should have found an abundance of entertainment; as it was, my plans being quite frustrated, I saw no beauty or interest in any object. Such is the perversity of human nature. Never before had I heard such a concert of owls; never before had the marsh-wrens twittered so cheerily, nor the wild-rice teemed with such a wealth of nocturnal insect life. Nature was celebrating the advent of the harvest-moon; and yet, because I had planned otherwise, I was in no mood to enjoy a rare opportunity for studying the meadows by moonlight.

A little later, circumstances forced me to be less fretful and more studious. While slowly urging my skiff over the soft mud by very short and most uneasy stages, I reached the carcass of a dog that was being gradually devoured by myriads of small eels.

This grewsome sight recalled the unfortunate

> "Sir Thomas's body,
> It looked so odd—he
> Was half eaten up by the eels!
> His waistcoat and hose, and the rest of his clothes,
> Were all gnawed through and through;
> And out of each shoe
> An eel they drew,
> And from each of his pockets they pulled out two!"

I would refer these lines to those who of late have insisted upon the fact that eels are very dainty, and refuse all food that they do not capture and kill.

At last I reached the running water and was again afloat, but not until long after the day had closed—a day that I could wish different but in one respect; it had been too full of pleasant sights and sounds.

CHAPTER IX.
THE DRAWBRIDGE.

I HAVE yet to see the rambler who finds the jumping of fences exhilarating. When one crosses his path there may be no audible comment, but thoughts multiply. Particularly is this the case when the barrier to his progress is constructed of spiked wire.

The fence that gives least offence is the quaint old zigzag series of chestnut rails, staked up with twisted cedar saplings and chunked by moss-covered bowlders just peeping above the ground. This once common feature of all our fields merits a word in its defence.

What feature of a long cultivated country can boast of so many attractions to a rambling naturalist as one of these worm-fences? Indeed, the very existence of not a few animals, in many localities, depends upon these roomy structures, that secure to them a strip of land eight to ten feet wide. Insignificant as bare earth, it is true; but far from it when densely overgrown with impenetrable tangles of thorn-bearing vegetation.

Here congregate in confidence weasels, skunks, mink, chipmunks, and mice. Bluebirds and wrens find convenient nesting-places in the hollow rails, sparrows in the low bushes filling all the angles. The lithe green lizard is happy among the upper rails, where he can still bask with safety in the glowing August sunshine.

And whenever any of these chance to wander far a-field, they well know it is to a city of refuge to which they speed when hurrying to the little forest that hedges an old worm-fence.

The pretty tree-toad, quaint batrachian philosopher, is not loath to squat about the lichen patches of the older rails, and finds a safe home in the hollows of such as are slowly decaying and hold the chance-caught rain-drops in their mossy nooks.

Of fish as dwellers about fences I can say but little; yet one worm-fence in a distant meadow will ever remain memorable, from the fact that a herring dropped by a fish-hawk safely lodged thereon, and was carried home in triumph by me, years before I reached my teens. Would that subsequent days a-fishing had proved half so happy!

Of insect and arachnian life there is literally no end. Flies, beetles, and wingless crawling life; spiders, both great and small, of sombre tints and the most brilliant hues.

And the botany! There is no need to catalogue the plants actually gathered from the angles of the fence. Recall the smilax, blackberry, ivy, wild-grape, and Virginia creeper, for the little thickets that delight the thrush and make glad the heart of the to-whee bunting; recall the cedars that tower above these sinuous growths, and, too, the palm-like foliage of the sapling sumacs. Where else so completely at home is that embodiment of midsummer vivacity, the indigo-bird? The chinkapin bushes wherein jays gather—what more suggestive picture does a farming country offer?

A fact or two statistical concerning these fences. When Kalm, the Swedish naturalist, travelled through New Jersey, he studied these structures, as well as the animals they harbor, and his account is of considerable interest: "The enclosures made use of in . . . New Jersey," he says, "are those which, on account of their serpentine form resembling worms, are called worm-fences. . . . Experience has shown that an enclosure made of chestnut or white-oak seldom holds out above ten or twelve years before the poles and posts are thoroughly rotten," and then wonders "what sort of an appearance the country will have forty or fifty years hence"—he wrote in 1749—if some new fencing methods are not devised.

As a matter of fact, Kalm was misinformed as to the durability of our woods when thus used, or a great change has taken place. I know of a fence erected in 1826 that is at present in fairly good condition, and contains a large percentage of the original cedar rails; and the newer chestnut rails, with which the fence was last repaired, are nearly thirty years old. So, too, Kalm was in error about posts placed in the ground. White-oak now will last for twenty years, and cedar as long; locust posts are still in use, and are yet firm, which have been in the ground for half a century. The catalpa, too, is quite equal to locust, perhaps better. Much depends, I take it, upon the condition of the wood when placed in position. It should be thoroughly dry. Perhaps Kalm's informers were not acquainted with this fact; and I cannot but think that the earth had some corrosive element in it two centuries ago which it does not now possess, or in far less degree.

Our author's fears that general deforesting of the country would prove disastrous were better founded; yet we have not wholly come to grief. Let one climb to the top of a tall tree and look over the most open country—he will often have to look sharply to see the fields, farm-houses, and even villages, so hidden are they by the abundance of trees. Scattered along the roadside and by the cross fences, they are ignored by the pedestrian, unless he seeks their shade; but when seen from an elevation, these comparatively few trees about our farms aggregate many thousands, and we realize that while there are next to no forests left, we yet are preserved from the dreariness of a desert.

And now, having generalized to the degree of tediousness, what of some old worm-fence particularized?

Partly because the ground is rather unproductive, and more because there is a superabundance of it, one such fence within the range of my wanderings has been left undisturbed for more than half a century. To cross it, except at the bars, which are themselves not always free from weeds, is absolutely impossible. The impenetrable tangle of vines in this case extends fully half a rod on either side, and up through it tower trees that are models—tall, shapely, and so widely scattered that never a twig has suffered for want of room.

I clambered over the splintery, half-decayed bars of this old fence on my way to the creek to-day, purposely taking a new and circuitous route, because of an early start. I crossed over carefully, and let me add parenthetically, that I am tempted to assert that misfortune awaits me whenever I quit the firm earth. It is, of course, necessary for a naturalist to climb trees, to leap fences, to cross quicksands; and one devoid of skill can readily come to grief. How confidently, but a few days ago, I sprang to the top rail of a fence near by, and spinning quarter way around, not simply did I face in the direction I desired to go, but screwed myself fast to an unseen projection of that same top rail—then dangled hopelessly among the weeds. The result was as likely to be serious as ludicrous, but fortune favored me so far as to grant a release, with a large percentage of an important garment left as toll with that inexorable fence. Besides the loss of time, it was exasperating to stand amid briers with half-clad limbs, and see how easily all the trouble might have been avoided. It was worse to return in so dilapidated a condition and run the gantlet of anxious inquirers as I sought the clothes-press.

The history of a chestnut rail can be read almost without an effort. How vividly there comes to me the picture of one old woodman, as he shouldered his keen axe and started for the woods! How plainly I see him in the snow-clad forest, resting a moment from his work, and telling of some wild hunt or strange mishap that befell him when a boy! Then, too, looms up the patient ox-team, with the load of rails upon the sled; and better than all, the pile of gnarly sticks not even the woodman's axe could conquer, and which, in due time, blazed in that cavernous fireplace before which I passed so many glorious winter nights—nights, if a storm raged, which were sure to recall the thrilling stories of those early days when forests enclosed the scattered fields, not fields that surrounded mere remnants of the forest.

I do not know whether any of the original rails are still remaining, probably not; but a fence of this rude pattern has been here for two centuries, and portions of it have every appearance of long antedating the very oldest inhabitant. Many a rail can be found that is no longer an obstacle to man or beast. Indeed, some of them depend for their very existence upon the aid of the dense growths that uphold them. One giant sassafras has actually incorporated a portion of a sturdy cedar rail, which, if removed, would leave a hole directly through the trunk of the tree.

To the few remaining old worm-fences, then, the thanks of the rambler are due for many favors; for where else than in the densely overgrown headlands that divide our fields could many a creature find so safe a retreat in a neighborhood like this? It takes the place of extensive forests, of trackless swamps, of immovable rocks. Let the rambler be patient, then, when such a worm-fence crosses his path. Let him stop and study it, panel by panel, unless abroad upon some special errand.

Here he is surest, perhaps, of meeting with weasels, if they are abroad by day; nor let him be too bold if there be a number of them. They well know that in union there is strength, and it is no unusual occurrence for them to show fight at such a time; and no creature can bite more savagely, or aim for vital spots more surely.

The weasel's distant cousin, the skunk, is also a lover

of these old fences, and knows their nooks and corners as well as his northern brethren know the safe crannies of an old stone wall.

The raccoon, too, has occasion to think well of fences. From his hollow tree he will carefully crawl to the top rail of the fence below, and run a long distance, a dozen panels, perhaps, before touching the ground, and so the prowling dogs are hopelessly baffled.

Bats have learned the comfort, if they do not know the security, of a weed-encompassed fence, and hang by day from the lower side of a broad rail in blissful expectation of the coming night.

Lastly, the pert chipmunks. The first lesson in geography taught them, I take it, is the zigzag coast-line of the nearest fence. And once learned, what more graceful sight than to see them dart from panel to panel, dodging the knot-holes, leaping the projections, hugging the under side of a rail for an instant, and then peeping slyly at you from some coigne of vantage that it seeks when danger threatens. It does not appear that chipmunks are at a disadvantage upon any uneven surface, but their grace culminates scurrying at utmost speed adown the warped sections of an old worm-fence.

The ornithology of these fences is half the bird history of the county. It cannot be dwelt upon now, but a few marked features of it may be briefly mentioned. Here, about the rank growths of poke, thistle, and Jamestown weed, congregate those beautiful yellow and black finches,

> Whose wavy flight and cheery whistle
> Adorn the wastes o'ergrown with thistle:

> No field so foul with noisome weeds
> But there the dainty goldfinch feeds,
> And greets with song the fervent rays
> That flood high noon of August days.

Here, swinging upon the tips of bending weeds, or curving the uppermost twig of some tall tree, the no less beautiful indigo finch sings with an ardor no other bird excels. The hotter the day the sweeter the song; and if the gloaming brings no coolness, even through the night this little finch will repeat the songs that gave life to the fields at noon.

And later, when the winter migrants come, nowhere else am I so sure to find that prince of sparrows, the royal foxy finch, and surely nowhere do the flocking white-throats congregate as here, and sing with such full-voiced energy, morning, noon, and night. When winter nears its end they are all impatience, it would seem, to reach their northern home; for when the glimmer of the April moon fills the dense hedge-row with uncertain light, these birds still sing, and even start from their perches, as though their homeward journey had commenced.

That they are dreaming there can be no doubt, and not the weird chat alone is given to curious antics long after the world is supposed to be at rest.

Bluebirds, of course, love the old hollow rails, and perched upon the out-reaching stakes, sing their best songs.

Wrens have long since learned that an old fence is their best hunting-ground.

Woodpeckers, both great and small, even to the little

downy fellow, flit from stake to stake watching the plodding ploughman at his toil, and scolding mildly when he comes too near.

It was at these weed-hidden bars that I once witnessed a riot in wrendom. A pair of vigorous Carolinas and four irate house-wrens had met to settle a dispute. They had no judge to which to appeal, nor was there an attentive jury, but every bush was crowded with spectators.

As my old friend Uz Gaunt once remarked, "When any smooth-headed bird raises its crest, look out for fun." I saw something like this, and was at once on the alert for interesting developments. Not one of the six wrens but had every feather of its head pointing upward, and with it all each spluttered, stuttered, screamed, and hissed until nearly exhausted. Every syllable of the wrenish language was uttered with emphasis. Every few seconds one or more would withdraw, as though to recover breath, and then reappear, excited and disputatious as ever. But it was a war of words only, and became monotonous. In hopes of determining the cause of the difficulty, I thrust myself among them and scattered the spectators, but not the wrens. They resented my interference; and while not quite willing to attack me, became allies for the time, and vented their spleen in no uncertain manner. I withdrew to a short distance, when the wrens reassembled at the fence, and the quarrel soon waxed louder than ever, and thus engaged I left them.

Two days later I found the Carolina wrens in peaceful possession of the spot, and in an adjoining panel they had a roomy nest. May not the wrangle have been a lawsuit concerning this desirable bit of real estate?

There are very few people who know a wren when they see it. Do not take me up, captious critic, and insist that this is too sweeping a statement. Have you tested the matter? In all probability not. I have. It is not enough to know only the pair that nest in cosey quarters you have provided for them. There are wrens and wrens, as there are people and people, and your door-yard couples are sadly uninteresting when compared with their wilder brethren that have roughed it for the season in a hollow fence-rail—suffer in comparison, just as the gilded youths of large cities so often dwindle to absolute insignificance when seen by the side of their wide-awake country cousins.

But the tenants of the wild woods know the wrens full well, and usually give them a wide berth. They realize that they are petty tyrants, suffering no intrusion and excusing no blunder; particularly so when something has gone wrong with them; then it is "a word and a blow, and the blow first." Even hornets stand back when there is a riot in wrendom.

Nowhere do the few remaining black-snakes find so sure a retreat as beneath the bottom rail of the fence, where it is beyond the reach of every foe; and where, too, it has the entrance to a snug underground retreat. From such weedy coverts these shy serpents occasionally venture far a-field, and it is as instructive as amusing to see with what promptness they dart directly towards the fence, even if you happen to be between the snake and its home. However high the weeds, the direction is never mistaken, and they seek shelter with that celerity of movement no other creeping creature can obtain.

A friend of my early boyhood, and now but a chance acquaintance, is the pretty, vivacious, amusing lizard that years ago made this same fence its home. I should be glad to know why it has forsaken us. There certainly has been no change in the fence, and next to nothing in the surroundings, since it was as common a feature of our fauna as tree-sparrows in winter. But it has left us. For years I have not seen one, and have nothing to say concerning them save what I recall of a distant but not shadowy past. Year after year, about the middle of June, I was teased with visions of a dewberry-pie, and straightway sought certain briery fields, where for the labor of gathering was to be had an abundance of the coal-black fruit. The task performed, how inviting were the shady nooks of the old worm-fence! With no laggard steps I hurried thither, and catching the scented breezes fluttering through the rails, revelled in the luxury of a well-earned rest. My friends crowded about me. The chipmunks stared, whistled a welcome, and were gone; the dainty field-sparrow trilled from the tapering cedar's top; the tree-toads croaked; the burly carpenter-bee hummed heartily; and darting past me as swift shadows were the shy lizards, whose presence made me forgetful of all discomfort, as I wistfully gazed after them far down the sunny reaches of the fence.

All my ingenuity was exercised in efforts to capture
12

them, and summer after summer passed without success attending them. Not one but was too swift for me. Time after time I struck at them with long switches, always aiming well ahead, yet never succeeding in accomplishing more than the amputation of their tails. They seemed always bent upon going forward, and dodged me successfully when I attempted to check their progress. "Forward!" was their motto; forward they went, and disappeared.

I could never find their nests, nor see their young; never could discover their winter retreats, nor learn how far they are affected by the weather. They came and went along the sunny highway of the ancient fence; travelled it from April till October, and were gone. Strangers as they were, I always hailed them as my friends, and look for them now, listening for their fleeting footsteps where the hot sunshine falls, and seeing them only when, with closed eyes, I recall the happy wanderings of many a year ago.

Even when the grasping farmer raids upon the pretty tangle of wild growths that another furrow may be added to his field, the naked fence becomes no eyesore to the wanderer. Wild life will love it still, though shorn of half its glory. But set in its little wilderness, it is a country worthy of exploration, and fruitful, be it in summer or in winter, of strange adventure, curious knowledge, and facts that are treasures to him who delves for Nature's mysteries.

The voyage of to-day was but the rounding of a little

bend. Scarcely had the boat rippled the flood-tide of the glittering waters when I checked its course, and from my point of view in mid-stream gazed upon an ancient bridge that here spans the creek. It is an uncouth structure that the close-fisted freeholders of that day saw fit to build sixty years ago; and the farmers finding no name so easy as that learned in their childhood, called it the "drawbridge," as though it was but a second edition of the open structure that preceded it, and which had a "draw" in it for the accommodation of those masted vessels that, as we have seen, passed far up the creek. I wish heartily that the Quaker settlers who dwelt here had handed down some pretty romance or details of some bloody tragedy concerning this earlier bridge. It certainly was old enough when, in 1827, it was removed, to have a thrilling history, and in a spot romantic enough to have made poets of some of the sturdy youths who for years were accustomed to pass to and fro over its oaken planks.

I might, indeed, fearless of contradiction, have purpled the stream with the blood of innocents, and peopled the woods hard by with headless ghosts; but alas! just here, colonial days were days of colorless prose, nothing more exciting than the arrival of a travelling preacher—John Woolman or Thomas Chalkley—ever causing the Crosswicks Friends to so much as raise their eyebrows.

But why, it may be asked, is there a bridge here at all? Let us go back to even earlier than colonial times. On Lindstrom's map, 1654, the surveyor caused to be printed, besides the various Indian names, certain interesting facts; and at the mouth of this creek, "Mechansio sipu," as he calls it, he states that "here commences Manahattan's Wägar, or Road to Manhattan." If a highway existed, as there pointed out, it must have been but rarely travelled by Europeans so early as 1654; for it was not until nearly forty years later that any land was occupied between the Delaware and the Raritan. It is now, and has been for over two hundred years, a public road, and before the building of railroads was the stage route, or one of them, from the Delaware eastward to the towns between Bordentown and New York. And long years before all this—who shall say how many?—it was the well-worn trail of the Indians, who crossed the river from Pennsylvania near the mouth of the creek, and passed along the terrace that forms the bold east shore of the stream, and crossed it where now it is spanned by this shapeless structure. The European in many ways followed closely in the footsteps of his dusky predecessors; and at this spot, where the Indians' steppingstones were lying in the sand, the early settlers drove down pilings and rested thereupon the ancient drawbridge. Some of these are still to be seen at low tide.

But if there be no startling colonial history, the bridge, the creek, and the valley have a bit of revolutionary record that might have been famous had it been, like the fight at Concord bridge, of some significance.

The original drawbridge spanned the stream in June, 1778, when the British soldiers "attempted to cross Crosswicks Creek over a drawbridge . . . three regiments (of militia) remaining near, after a general withdrawal of the Continental troops. A party of the enemy appearing, with great zeal began to repair the bridge, the planks of which had been pulled up and the draw raised. For this purpose they ripped off the planks from an adjoining hay-house. Upon their approach the militia rushed down with the greatest impetuosity, and a small party from one of the regiments, happening to be considerably advanced, caused them to retire with the loss of four killed and several wounded." It would appear from this that none of them came across, yet years after, in regrading the public road, a few bits of metal were found that seemed to indicate that an officer had been buried on the north side of the creek. Well, it matters not, and patriotic Americans can only regret that a great many more than four had not fallen in that June skirmish.

The Quakers about here were, almost to a man, very lukewarm in the cause of independence, and very grudgingly gave aid to the soldiers who defended the bridge. They claimed to be non-combatants, and so were passive spectators of the stirring scenes enacted at Trenton, Princeton, and Monmouth. Their caution prevented their suffering persecution, but it was far different with the more outspoken Tories. One Isaac Pearson, a Church of England man, was less fortunate than his neighbors. He was too outspoken, and, wearing no Quaker garb, was singled out as a dangerous man. While at Hightstown, not far away, he was apprised that soldiers were in pursuit. He rushed for his horse, and just as he entered the stable was shot.

He it was who built, some years before, a once famous hostelry that stood within sight of the old bridge. When the new road was laid out, about 1795, the tavern was moved to its present site. Pearson's Inn it had been; but now a new name was desired, as well as a sign to swing from the old buttonwood that still is standing. The writer's grandfather agreed to furnish the sign, but found, when he commenced the task, that he had only a single pot of white paint. He sketched a horse at full gallop, used the paint he had to color it, and so gave the name of "White Horse" to the tavern, which it still retains.

Near this place until July, 1869, stood the largest white-oak in the county, and probably in the State. It was something to stand under the wide-spreading boughs of a tree that was well grown before Columbus pleaded with Isabella for permission to cross the seas. This oak had dropped its acorns over a sod pressed by no human foot, save that of the Indian, before the continent of America was heard of by our European ancestry; and as one of the few trees of Indian times that remained to us, it very appropriately contained a flint arrow in its heart, and had buried among its deepest roots a grooved stone axe.

This mighty oak, which measured twenty-seven feet in circumference three feet from the ground, was so injured by a violent gale of wind that its removal became necessary. It stood upon a knoll, and from this the immense stump was subsequently removed. The excavation was seven feet in depth and nearly twelve in diameter. Four feet below the bottom of the pit, or eleven feet from the surface of the ground, I found a very rude stone axe entangled in a mass of fibrous roots. The appearances were all such as to indicate that the axe had been lost and buried before the acorn sprouted which became this greatest of our oaks. As the age of trees is usually estimated, and in this case correctly, it is quite certain that the tree was a thousand years old, and that prior to this the Indian axe had been lost. Some little clew, therefore, have we to the length of time during which New Jersey was occupied by the Indians.

A feature of the creek shore, not only at the bridge but for some little distance above and below, was the abundance of plum-trees. Campanius, in describing the various fruits and nuts found on the Jersey shore of the river, mentions "great quantities of walnuts, chestnuts, peaches, *damsons*, cypresses, mulberry, fish-trees, and many other rare trees . . . not found anywhere else but on this river;" and again, writing of the opposite shore of the Delaware, says, near "Plum Point there grow great numbers of beech, *plum*, mulberry, and chestnut trees."

Plommons Udden, or Plum Point, was a common name with the Swedes, they giving every bold river shore such designation if it grew a cluster of these trees. Where the bridge now stands was not long since a Plum Point, and from a careful examination of the surroundings I am disposed to think that plum orchards were commonly planted by the Indians. It is certain that they had other orchards, and therefore it is reasonable to suppose that the clusters of plum-trees were likewise the work of this people.

With so much palatable wild fruit, it is strange that such miserable food as the wild-bean and golden-club should have been ever used. All of our fruits, except the persimmon, can be dried, and kept indefinitely; and notwithstanding no mention is made of the practice, I am inclined to believe that dried plums and other fruits were used, as well as the fruit eaten in a fresh state. Certainly if it is true that plum orchards were designedly planted by the Indians, this latter inference must be true.

While yet discussing the botanical features of this neighborhood, what, it may be asked, is the fish-tree? Somewhere not far away, according to Campanius, there grew, in his time, "the fish-tree, which resembles boxwood, and smells like raw fish. It cannot be split, but if a fire be lighted around it with some other kind of wood, it melts away." I have tested on my andirons all our native trees, and there is not one that can be said to melt away. The persimmon when newly split has a more fish-like smell than any other, but then it can be split. It is indifferent firewood, I am sure; so perhaps this is the tree referred to.

But the present bridge: what of it? Like many another rude structure far away from the bustle of a town, it is the home of a host of creatures, furred and feathered, for mice hide in its roof and musk-rats in the abutment walls; while under the eaves cliff swallows have dwelt for years, and upon the rough framework that sustains the floor peewees have nested since the bridge was built. I have counted seven such nests, all occupied at the same time, and never a quarrelsome word between these near neighbors. In one of the abutments for years a pair of Carolina wrens have nested, and, strange to say, without quarrelling with the swallows, the peewees, or the marsh-wrens that throng the wild-rice not twenty yards away. So much for the ornithology of this quaint bridge.

The entomology would require a volume to exhaust; yet I cannot forbear brief mention of the wonderful borings of the sturdy carpenter-bees.

Belonging also to the zoology of the bridge is the list of fishes to be taken from a deep hole between the stone pier and the north bank of the creek. Here the remains of the ancient drawbridge make fishing somewhat difficult, and the eager anglers hurry by to the wide reaches of deep waters farther down the stream. In this deep hole beneath the bridge have been caught the largest specimens of rockfish, catfish, and perch ever taken in the creek. So at least I have been told by one born near by, and who for years was familiar with the stream and those who fished in it. Of course it will not do to indulge in fish stories, and yet, in the interest of ichthyology, I am tempted to give some figures of weight and measurement — am tempted, but will not yield. Let this intimation, however, stand for an assurance that the largest catfish, sunfish, and other kinds have not yet been recorded. If museums were considered more and kitchens less, our knowledge of fishes would be considerably advanced. Many and many a valuable specimen has gone to the frying-pan that should have filled a jar on the museum shelf.

This, in brief, shows how much natural history may linger about an old country bridge. Let us now return to the birds that frequent it and study the cliff swallows nesting under the eaves.

12*

As summer swallows darting through the air, or lightly skimming the rippling surface of the sparkling waters, this pretty species presents no peculiarity not common to the tribe. It is its nesting habits alone that make the bird so very interesting. Dr. Brewer states that "the nests of this swallow, when built on the side of a cliff or in any exposed position, are constructed in the shape of a retort ... since they have sought the shelter of man and built under the eaves of barns and houses, the old style of their nests has been greatly changed, and the retort-like shape has nearly disappeared."

Early or late in April, for very much depends upon rain-storms, sure to occur during this uncertain month, the cliff swallows return. Not a few at a time, and day by day the colony increasing in numbers, but promptly, unitedly. Yesterday the bridge was silent as a tomb; to-day it fairly trembles with the excited chattering of their united voices.

A word concerning early swallows. It has caused much hasty comment to speak of swallows appearing in New Jersey as early as March. Is a March swallow such a *rara avis?* Turnbull says of the sand-martin: "Not uncommon on the high bank of a river or the seashore, *arriving early in March*, and leaving about the middle of October."

And of the white-bellied swallow the same excellent authority remarks: "Rather plentiful. Comes late *in March*, and leaves early in September."

Unlike the warblers or finches, there is no possibility of mistaking swallows for other birds; nor need they be slaughtered to be identified. Any country schoolboy can tell one when he sees it; and when I say that I have seen them in March, year after year, I mean this and nothing more.

Perhaps the common saying, "one swallow does not make a summer," referred originally to those pioneer birds that come in advance of the main flight, and are often driven away, and sometimes killed, by severe storms that follow their arrival. But this subject need not be pursued further. March swallows were known to Turnbull, and I have seen them. I regret man has yet no means of informing them that to visit New Jersey in March, and to tarry until November, is to transgress the laws of official ornithology.

To return to the pretty cliff swallows: their nests, now no longer retort-shape, but each a semi-globular cup of clay, are always on the south side of the barn or bridge; or, if this is not available, a south-eastern exposure will be accepted, provided the surroundings afford some shelter from wind and rain. While our swallows are somewhat sensitive to cold, none so promptly yield to a "cold snap" as do these cliff-dwellers, or "rocky mountain" swallows, as they are usually called in this neighborhood. It is for this reason, I think, they so often forsake, suddenly and permanently, a locality like a bridge or any outbuilding. If a violent storm arises and they are not sufficiently sheltered, they will promptly leave, even when they have young in their nests. I have known this to happen twice, besides the instance to be mentioned with reference to the drawbridge. In the latter case, a violent storm with wind, on July 3, 1869, so disturbed the colony of swallows, which had been here every summer since 1850, that on the morning of the fourth not a bird was to be seen, nor have others since then made their appearance. In this case there were young in about one-half of the row of forty-seven nests.

This colony, which occupied the eaves of the drawbridge for eighteen years, did not increase in size. I was informed by one who had watched them yearly, that the first summer as many nests were built as were forsaken in 1869. I know from personal observation that for seven summers the number of nests remained the same. This may arise from the fact that any structure like a bridge or barn would afford but a limited amount of space available for nest-building; yet in the case of the former, to my eyes, there was room for several times as many as the birds erected.

There was no courtship among these birds after their arrival from the south; no waste of time in idle compliment; nothing analogous to human small talk. The long row of nests was before them, and every one needed some repairs. About this they held no consultation, but straightway commenced the work. There was not an idle bird among them; and strange to say, there appeared to be no special ownership of the nests, at least when they were being repaired. Every bird did whatsoever he found to do, be it on this, that, or the other nest. A week later there was a more methodical manner observable, and each Jill may have had her Jack, but the appearances were otherwise. I thought at times that the male birds were considerably in excess, and that here was a case of polyandry, but I may be mistaken.

My attention was called by an old observer to the fact that, in clear weather, these swallows never alighted upon the roof of the bridge; but when there was a gentle rain, without wind, they would line the peak of the roof facing the storm, and chatter incessantly. They seemed to enjoy this method of bathing more than by dipping into the water always beneath them. Later, I found that this did not hold good of a colony of these swallows nesting against a barn. These birds appeared never to alight upon the roof, and when it rained clung to the outsides of the nests, or flew about as usual, unless the storm was violent.

Speaking of swallows recalls the fact that the purple martins, princes of their race, have within the past quarter of a century become less and less abundant in this neighborhood. This has not arisen in consequence of the removal of the boxes erected for their accommodation. They were abandoned gradually, here and there a colony, until not a twentieth part of those here twenty-five years ago remain. Very many of the old boxes are still standing, and usually are tenanted by the pestiferous foreign sparrow.

Many causes have been assigned for the withdrawal of the martins, mostly quite untenable ones, and even that one which is most plausible not holding good. It has been supposed that the annual cold storm in May proved fatal to many; and again, by lessening for the time being the amount of active insect life, the survivors became utterly discouraged. But cold storms in May were as frequent in the last century as in this. Dr. Benjamin Smith Barton, whom I have so frequently quoted, writing of this bird in 1798, remarks, "I have observed that several weeks after the first appearance of the swallows in the spring, the coming on of a cold day has occasioned in them great distress. The following fact will strikingly illustrate what I am saying. The beginning of the month of April, 1773, was unusually warm. In the vicinity of Philadelphia the clover in some of the fields was five or six inches high. The martins (*Hirundo purpurea*) were seen about the city: at this time there came on suddenly a very severe spell of cold weather. It destroyed many of these birds, several of which were seen to drop down, benumbed or dead, among the clover."

This clearly shows that no peculiarity of our climate has caused these birds to remain away from their old-time haunts. The reason is not known, and probably unascertainable. It is to be classed with the changes of habits of many other species, as the Carolina parrot, mocking-bird, summer redbird, and sand-hill crane. Once they were prominent features of our avi-fauna; now they are so no longer.

My grandfather told me, many years ago, of the sudden appearance here of a colony of martins. In April, 1794, a pair of sparrow-hawks nested in a hollow in the trunk of a tall tulip-tree, and remained with their young in and about the spot until the following autumn. Early in April, 1795, a large number of martins made their appearance, and finding no more suitable locality took possession of the tulip-tree. Immediately after, a pair of sparrow-hawks came upon the scene, and at once disputed the right of the swallows to it. Had there been but a pair of each, the contest would have been of short duration, so unequally matched are hawks and martins; but this was a case of twenty or more to two; and the battle, which was bloody, ended in victory for the smaller birds, the sparrow-hawks being driven off.

The hollow tree was occupied all that summer by the swallows, and many young birds were reared, but they did not return to it the following spring. In 1797 a box was placed upon a pole for their accommodation at the cross-roads, a short distance off, and not a summer passed that it was not occupied, until 1849, when the martins failed to appear, and none have been seen since in the immediate neighborhood.

It would be strange, indeed, to find even a country bridge an aviary, and yet we have seen already that this one has an instructive ornithological history. The wrens and peewees have already been mentioned, but one bird-feature of the structure remains to be noted. For years a pair of barn-swallows have found a convenient nook beneath the roof, and have never yet been disturbed by prowling urchins bent upon destruction. These barn swallows, the most beautiful and graceful of the family, were never disturbed by the eave-dwellers, although always associated during the day. I had abundant opportunity to compare their flight with that of the others, and found it to be more rapid and artistic. They could curve, dive, mount upward, reverse their flight, and fantastically tumble in mid-air, with greater precision and command of wing than the eave-dwellers, and certainly were less often at rest. Dr. Barton states that the Mohegan Indians call the martin "pons-pau-cloo-moose: the bird that never rests." The name is much more applicable to the barn swallow. While resting one sunny afternoon in the shadow of the bridge, my attention was called to these birds, and I noticed that they dipped into the water very frequently, and always at one spot, where the wild-rice grew closely to the edge of the channel. Believing that they were in search of food, I concealed myself in the rice and watched the birds as well as circumstances would allow. Their movements were too quick to enable one to be positive, but I think they partly dived rather than merely dipped, and caught each time a very small fish; for at this place there were literally thousands of minute minnows crowding a limited space, and so near the surface of the water as to faintly ripple it.

The impenetrable tangle of blackberry briers, dwarfed trees, wild-rose, and smilax that covers much of the bank on the creek's north shore below the bridge is a favorite locality for winter sparrows, and so too of shrikes. Were the latter more abundantly represented a century ago than now? In an interesting letter from the Moravian missionary Heckewelder to Dr. Barton, dated December 18, 1795, I find the following: " I went to a farm . . . to visit a young orchard . . . where on viewing the trees I found, to my great astonishment, almost on every one of them one, and on some two and three grasshoppers, stuck down on the sharp thorny branches, which were not pruned when the trees were planted. I . . . was informed that these grasshoppers were stuck up by a small bird of prey which the Germans called *Neuntoedter* . . . that this bird had a practice of catching and sticking up nine grasshoppers a day, and that, as he well knew they did not devour the grasshopper nor any other insects, he thought they must do it for pleasure."

This quotation is suggestive in more ways than one. Certainly no such abundant evidences of the shrikes are now to be met with, and Mr. Heckewelder's experience in the orchard implies that they were very abundant about Bethlehem (in eastern Pennsylvania) when he wrote, for no one bird would have visited every tree in a comparatively small enclosure. Again, our northern shrike is not here now, nor is it about Bethlehem, mountainous region as it is, when large grasshoppers are abundant. The latter have generally disappeared prior to the arrival of the shrikes, nine-killers, or butcher-birds, as they are variously called.

On the other hand, the mention of grasshoppers as the prey of, if not food of, the shrikes, suggests the southern species, which may have been as constant a summer visitor as the other is during winter, and even more abundant. If so, a change took place about the time that Heckewelder wrote—ninety years ago—in its habits, and it ceased to come north, as we have seen other migrants have ceased to do since then. Very recently, however, they have returned, and in the interests of the anti-English sparrow clubs, let us hope their numbers will steadily increase.

This August afternoon was peculiarly quiet. The hum of many insects was to be heard only by careful listening, so subdued was every sound. Scarcely a bird chirped, and few were to be seen. It may seem a rather startling assertion, but an August day in the bird-world is more apt to be silent than a day in January. With the wind blowing at the rate of thirty miles an hour, the air thick with falling flakes of snow, and the temperature 20° Fahr. or less, one is, perhaps naturally, disposed to stay in-doors, and to take it for granted that the entire bird-world is of a like way of thinking; but herein mankind sadly errs; for even during such days, both in the woods and fields, there are birds and birds. As a proof of this, one need only mention crows and snow-birds; but I am not speaking ironically, but soberly, discreetly, cautiously, when I say that our woods, at least in midwinter, often contain as many species, usually even more individuals, than in midsummer, and almost equal the early spring when the northward trooping warblers throng every nook and corner, even to the very outskirts of the town. The merit of the pudding is the presence of the plums, and winter is by no means a fruitless batter if there be birds among the boughs.

Early in the winter there is pretty sure to come rain after rain, and often snow upon snow; and if succeeding these we have a wide-reaching rain-storm, the snows are melted, the river swollen, and a freshet results. The gently sloping banks of the creek here at the bridge offer no barrier to the encroaching waters, and the narrow stream becomes for a time a noble river in every feature except depth.

A freshet, whether it happens in summer or winter, is a thoroughly enjoyable and instructive occurrence; but is peculiarly attractive in winter if followed by freezing weather. I can recall several such during the past decade, when firm ice offered a safe foothold over every rod of the treacherous marshes. Tangled nooks in the boggy meadows, familiar only to the heron and wary mallard, are now open to all comers, and we can boldly explore where before we have not ventured to approach. But it is not of these in all their varied aspects that I have now to speak. Beyond the flooded meadows, now a field of ice, along the steep north bank are sheltered crannies, where there is sure to be found abundant warmth, light, color, and music. Even if there be no birds within sight or hearing it is all the same, scattered everywhere are half acres of emerald set in miles of crystal.

The background of glistening snow, flecked only by faint shadows, gives cheerful prominence to the leafless branches of winter-berry, crowded to the tips of their tiniest twigs with brilliant scarlet fruit. The dark, tapering spires of the cedar are as green and gloomy as in June. The varied lichens still clothe many a tree-trunk with a motley gray-green garb. The intricate maze of the smilax is as fresh as when its spring-time growth first twined and twisted upon itself until both beginning and end were irrecoverably lost. The white-oaks still flutter and rattle their dusty golden leaves in every passing breeze. Beneath the sheltering branches of taller growths trim sassafras sprouts still keep their dark-green, lengthy, leathery leaves, as rich in color and in freshness as ferns at the flood-tide of summer sunshine. Surely there is no lack of color.

The ice, fashioned fantastically by the deft fingers of Frost, yields to the searching rays of the noontide sun, and is now dripping from the moss, the dead grass, and overhanging banks of frozen earth, and every drop tinkles with bell-like music as it strikes the pebbles beneath, and its shattered glories are lost in the rippling brook. This, with the rustling of crisp leaves and sighing of the wind, will it not suffice for music?

Add to these the birds, and we have the jubilee. I have been present at scores of them in a single winter. Omitting all reference to hawks and owls, although these are very far from being devoid of interest, let me recall, while I sit in the shadow of the bridge, those birds that I have seen here and hereabouts every winter since I systematically rambled in search of them.

There are robins, of course. Not a poor straggler now and then in search of its fellows, but hale, hearty birds, full of song even, and never disheartened because the frozen sod no longer yields them an abundance of earthworms. The berries of the cedar, and what they left in the autumn of the gumberries, afford them sufficient food, and so no cause to complain have they.

Restless, rambling, rollicking bluebirds. Be it clear or cloudy, they come and go with as much uncertainty as the weather. To-day a hundred perch upon the stakes of worm-fences, warbling their May-day songs, and chasing imaginary insects in the clear cold air—to-morrow not one is to be seen. Nor have they merely hidden in some secluded corner. They have taken a fairly long journey, and will return, not in accordance with the weather, waiting for a mild day, but always following the whim of the moment, instead of, like so many birds, the dictation of Jack Frost.

Then there are the two kinglets, wren-like in all their ways; wee bits of impatience, wrapped in light-brown feathers. They climb and twitter among the tall trees, and at times dip down to the very ground to snap their little beaks in the cat's-ears; then, clutching a twig, will sometimes warble a bar or two of some half-forgotten summer song before mounting to the tall tree's very top and launching into dreary space, regardless alike of wind or rain, of sleet or snow.

Two titmice—cheerful birds the world would sadly miss; the lordly tomtit, with his jaunty crest; the merry chickadee—the former making the woods ring with his earnest invitation to ramble therein: *here—here—here!* the latter ever winsome as it chirps, in more subdued tones, *chick-a-dee-dee—dee-dee; winter no terror has for me—for me.*

Titmice will never allow you to be lonely if you walk in the woods. They are honestly pleased with your presence, and mean every chirp and twitter as a hearty welcome. They will follow you at times, and when they flit from bush to bush it is not to avoid you, but lead you on—guide you to the pleasant places, to the tallest trees, the warmest, cosiest corners. Evolution did itself honor in producing such a bird.

And we have two nuthatches—marked features of a winter day. They are near cousins, creatures of like tastes, and, happily, never at loggerheads. One has a ruddy waistband—if a bird has a waist—the other is clad beneath in white; by this you may know them. All day long, and even far into the moonlight night, these birds clatter over the crisp, frost-nipped bark of the forest-trees, uttering, with scarcely a trace of variation in their tones, *quank-quank—tat-a-tat*. In every phase of winter it is all the same with them; the mercury may creep to zero, they will only creep a little faster; and going the rounds of the door-yard trees they never stop to ask if it is tiresome, but greet you, as they did the first man who wintered in America, with a strongly nasal *quank-quank—tat-a-tat*, all of which no ornithologist has as yet been able to interpret.

We have also the very pretty brown tree-creeper—curious grub-hunter of two continents. He chatters alike to European and American; and although familiar with so much of the world, is positively happy away off here in the benighted region of central New Jersey. Like the kinglets, the creeper will pause in his wild career and sing exquisitely; not at the close of winter, or in deceptive, spring-like days, merely, but in January, with its ice and snow, north winds and arctic cold. These but stir him to action, and I have often heard his cheering song during such bitter days that even the titmice clung to the sunny sides of the oaks.

Of the Carolina wren I must speak with caution. He is such a favorite I fear I may exaggerate his merits. This splendid bird is not so ready, as a creeper, to face a cutting north wind, yet is never a coward. Only give him a ghost of a chance and he will sing such songs in January as those with which his summer cousin, the house-wren, charms the world in June. Like others I have mentioned, his spirits often rise with the growing violence of an approaching storm, and far above the wind whistling through the leafless branches of the wood could be heard the Carolina wren's clear call of defiance, mocking the rage of an angry winter day.

And how different the smaller winter wren!—shy, wood-haunting, thicket-loving, silent, and so, to very many, even though they are often abroad, unseen, unsuspected, quite unknown. His close acquaintance is well worth making, and I can promise that his many pleasant ways will cause the rambler to forget the usual drawbacks of a winter walk. The winter wren only chirps at this season, it is true; but it is such a hearty, ringing chirp that it may well pass for a song; acceptable, because it appears to be uttered for your pleasure as much as for the bird's. I have said it was a shy bird: it is shy of approaching us and our ordinary surroundings; but go to its home in the retired nooks and corners of the wood, and it will not fear you; indeed, in an hour's time it may become quite familiar.

Another winter bird, and one of both great beauty and accomplishments, is the horned lark. You are not treated to a glimpse of one merely, nor a meagre dozen, but of a hundred. They are never in the woods, even during violent storms, but out in the open fields. Possibly you may have to tramp knee-deep to find them, but if you do, the walk will never be regretted. I have so often mentioned these larks that I can only name them now.

But a word concerning the pipit. In him we have a lark, a splendid songster, and altogether a bird of many attractions, even were it mute; yet far and near, both in town and country, my neighbors do not know it. Pipits come in October, scattering about the least frequented fields, always on the ground, or flitting, like wind-tossed feathers, from place to place. Like horned larks, they are strictly upland birds; at least I have never seen a specimen on the meadows or along the river shore. This, however, is inapplicable to them when in more southern localities.

When pipits are carefully approached they will maintain a safe distance by running, and if confident of your innocent intentions in drawing near, will often entertain you with a delightful song. It is a clear, flute-like warble, moderately varied, and seldom are the repetitions quite the same.

My experience makes them a bird of our open winters, lovers of dead grass and frost-nipped weeds, and never, like horned larks or arctic buntings, rejoicing in polar temperature and boundless reaches of untrodden snow.

In winter, as well as at other times, we have with us cedar-birds in abundance—every one trim as a dandy, neat as a shining pin. They are too lazy or too particular to sing, and it is said, probably with truth, that they die of nervous shock if their plumage be soiled. They never associate with others than their own kind, and under no circumstances are they demonstrative. I would be glad to become an enthusiast in their praises could I learn their merits. I fear they are but feather-deep; still I am thankful that they bear me out in my assertion that a birdless winter is a mere figment of the imagination.

Another feature of our woods in winter is the shrike, the foe of song-birds, but particularly a pursuer of the omnipresent tree-sparrow. It is a bird that suggests an essay, not a paragraph. Much as I hate him, I have one word in his favor. His presence proves that other birds abound. The shrike hates an uncertainty, and keeps a well-stocked larder ever before him. Is he crouching in some tall tree? The sparrows throng the tangled smilax at its base.

Although surly his countenance as an angry hawk, yet at times it lightens up; he sits up well upon his perch, spreads his tail, and gives his pretty wings a shake; looks almost as gentle as a nesting thrush, and attempts a song. I doubt if his mate, even, ever tolerates its repetition. A lamer effort at vocal music I have never heard, even among mankind.

And now we come to a long list of winter finches. All the world knows that in winter we have snow-birds. Some one has sung,

> "Better far, ah yes! than no bird
> Is the ever-present snow-bird;
> Gayly tripping, dainty creature,
> Where the snow hides every feature;
> Covers fences, field, and tree,
> Clothes in white all things but thee;
> Restless, twittering, trusty snow-bird,
> Lighter heart than thine has no bird."

But does all the world know as much of our other finches, the many sparrows of our " much be-sparrowed country?" If one dare brave the north wind, there is a pine-finch in store for him somewhere among the gloomy evergreens; and pine-finches are birds worth seeing, even with the temperature at zero. Purple finches, too, in flocks of several dozens, come trooping southward as our days grow short, and often sing merrily when in January there comes a royally bright day, filled with sweet winter sunshine. More ruddy finches haunt the cedars now, and two cross-bills, near akin, and alike in all their habits, climb like parrots, twitter like sparrows, and weary of gymnastics, hurry out of sight, to be gone, it may be, until another year rolls by.

Early and late, wherever trees are tall and weeds have been left for forage grounds, the pretty linnets are sure to be found. If not to-day, to-morrow; if not this week, next. Like all winter birds, save half a dozen, they are delightfully uncertain. If you see them when you walk, count it good-luck; if not, repeat your rambles until you have met them. That lemon-yellow and black finch that fed in summer on thistle-down, floated up and down as it flew, and twittered with every undulation, is now in a russet suit, and comes and goes in flocks of a dozen or a hundred, as the case may be. A near relative, the pine-finch, is now here, also, and in voice and habits they are as much alike as peas from the same pod. They chirp and twitter so earnestly that we listen with pleasure, even though they are high overhead, and we must bend our necks to see them dotting the naked branches of the tallest trees.

Coming back to the ground, if there has been a snow, one may count upon the arctic buntings. More beautiful birds it is seldom one's fortune to see; and seen at their best are they when trooping over the snow, seed-hunting among the upreaching stems of the tall weeds.

With them, it may be, will occur one or more Lapland long-spurs. Count it a red-letter day if you chance to see one. Many a flock of snow-buntings has one or more long-spurs, I am sure; but it is no easy task to single them out. I well remember the first and only flock of them I ever saw. It was a wild March day, and far more wintry than had been any of the days in February. I was crossing a wide field, covered with a thin and ragged sheet of snow. Up from the weeds they rose, like frightened larks, and sailing past me but little above my head, they twittered, one and all, most musically.

I stood watching them for several minutes, when they returned and settled very near their former feeding-ground. I approached cautiously, down upon all fours, and got near enough to see them plainly. There could be no mistake, they were long-spurs. But I need not have been so painstaking. As I flushed them the second time, one of them sang while on the wing. There was no mistaking that; no other of our winter birds has so sweet and artistic a song.

Not even the highest and widest of snow-drifts can drive a grass-finch from his native field. If needs be, it will burrow under it, and find many a meal of grass seed where other finches would starve. For years they puzzled me, but at last I learned their secret. When an unusual snow-fall occurs, the finches take refuge in the angles of the old worm-fences, and the bottom rail is sure to afford some shelter unless the drift forms here. From this vantage-ground the bird will work beneath the snow for several feet, and get at seed-bearing weeds that are quite hidden from birds flying over the fields. Let some such strange weather occur that every other bird would be driven away; I believe even then the grass-finch would not be dislodged.

Again, from autumn to spring we have white-throated sparrows that sing loudly if not well; and rarer to a degree, the even prettier white-crowned finch. Whether in the woods or fields, upland or meadow, it matters not, from October to April we are sure of these splendid representatives of the sparrow tribe.

And escape, if you can, the myriads of tree-sparrows. Over the snow they trip, as blithely as an arctic bunting, chirping pleasing notes at times, and ridding the winter's day of every semblance of dreariness. Not only here in treeless tracts, but up in the woods they are alike abundant; often in flocks of a hundred of their own kind, and not less frequently associated with birds of other species. When, as at winter, one does not expect elaborate love-songs, the united voices of scores of tree-sparrows are very welcome to the rambler's ear.

The social chipping sparrow does not always forsake us in winter, and the song-sparrow braves our coldest weather. They are now a bird of the willow hedges, in the marshes, and of smilax along the meadow fences. Here it is warmer than about the uplands, and so, finding warmth and food in abundance, they remain until nesting-time comes round again.

The fox-colored sparrow, largest and most beautiful of them all, is ever a feature of our winter landscape, and once seen, he is not likely to be forgotten; and when, as the winter closes, he sings among the hedge-rows, he is certain to remain in the memory of all who hear him.

With still another finch the long list closes; for happy are we in the presence of the acknowledged leader of the winter's choir, the brave and brilliant cardinal.

But let me give my country all her due; for there are yet other winter birds. The cow-bird, strange creature, with its gurgling rattle, can in nowise be omitted; and then the tuneful meadow-lark, that hidden aloft whistles half a day, yet is seen by no one. The purple grakle comes and goes, ever hoarse with overmuch chattering, and the only one of all I have mentioned meriting the charge of being tiresome. On the other hand, those equally noisy birds of the marshes, the red-winged blackbirds, are always welcome, the more so when their pleasant notes come floating over acres of dreary, ice-bound meadows.

Less musical than even a jay is our screaming, harsh-tongued kingfisher, and he, also, is no stranger in the land, even at Christmas, and at such a time his coarse rattling accords fairly well with the noise of chafing, icy branches stirred by the wintry winds.

Well the kingfisher knows the treacherous spring-holes in the meadows where frost fails in its handiwork and hosts of minnows linger until "April unlocks the icy rill."

It is ours, too, to boast of five or six woodpeckers, all of which, while having next to nothing to say, are so noisy at their work of tapping trees that we hear them often when they elude our search.

Lastly, in steps the chattering jay, quick-witted cousin of the cunning crow, and what he lacks in musical talent he endeavors to compensate the rambler for in vigorous declamation.

Let me recapitulate. An ordinary half-mile stroll beyond the city limits may enable you to see forty or more species of birds—possibly fifty. Fully one-half of them will be in flocks. Many will cluster in the thick-set cedars; others will be scattered over the weedy fields. Hundreds delight to lurk in the angles of a zigzag fence; others come boldly to the front and bid you welcome.

Divide these many winter birds in another manner, and we shall find that fully one-half may claim to be songsters; and better than all else, none are lazy, moping noodles, as are so many summer birds when the noontide heat is tropical, but, on the contrary, every feather of them is awake, alive, ready for fight or fun, and bubbling over with melody or loquacity.

Do you really think, then, a January jubilee a myth? The midwinter morning I was last here, the temperature was as low as ten, and never above twenty, degrees—that is, take the whole range of the fields and woods—but then scattered about were warmer, sheltered nooks, and such are the concert-halls affected by our winter songsters.

One doesn't buy a ticket for the roof when he goes to the opera. Why look for birds, then, on the north side of a hill? I found them yesterday on a sunny slope, and tarrying a bit I heard them.

The clear call of the crested tit opened the concert. The abundant tree-sparrows twittered; kinglets trilled a merry roundelay; snow-birds chirped; a cardinal performed an inimitable solo; and to all the downy woodpecker was alike attentive, and drummed a tuneful accompaniment on the most resonant tree in all the woods.

Then an interlude. Not mournful silence either, keeping one sadly shivering as the wind swept by, but only a brief waiting until a host of linnets dropped among the trees and sang a sweet hymn of thankfulness that such sunny nooks as this were vouchsafed by kindly Nature to our winter birds. Yet no sooner does November roll around than the poet's corner of the country weeklies, and the essayists' pages of the pretentious journals, teem with regrets at the sad silence of our woods in winter, or gush with nonsense about dreary snow-clad fields. Out upon such rot!

A somewhat striking feature of the creek shore near the bridge is the number of large catalpas, or Indian bean-trees. My neighbors persist in calling them "catawbas," and the boys say "candle-trees." In spite of its short-lived attraction when in bloom, it can scarcely be considered a fine growth. Its large leaves are coarse, the long seed-pods suggestive of broken and withered twigs. It has one peculiarity worthy of mention: except the hornbeam, no native tree is so apt to have angular branches. In one that I can see from the boat, every branch is either straight or bent at right angles. In one instance a long bough grows horizontally for some ten feet, then extends directly earthward for nearly three, when it turns inward, and grows horizontally towards the tree's trunk. Nothing in the present surroundings of the tree could have influenced this peculiar method of growth, hence our constant wonder why it should be so. Gray speaks of this tree as a southern species, and refers to its introduction into the northern States. If introduced and not native to New Jersey, the planting of the first specimens must have been long ago. I have positive knowledge of two that have shaded a little front yard since 1739; and is not this tree referred to when, in a deed bearing date of 1689, an "Indian bean-tree" is mentioned? After the first quarter of a century the growth appears to be very slow, and yet one that I was forced to cut down some years ago had one hundred and twenty-seven well-defined rings, and measured two feet one inch in diameter.

Considering that since earliest colonial times catalpas have been common, and are now an abundant forest-tree, it is probable that in central New Jersey the tree is native and not introduced. One strong proof of this is, I think, the fact that about a half mile from here there was, a century ago, a half-acre grove of very large catalpas. Their value as fence-posts was then known, and they were felled for that purpose. Many of the posts lasted sixty years, and one large gate-post was not wholly decayed when removed twenty years later. This is a better record as fencing material than that of the yellow locust.

As I was looking towards the crooked catalpa this afternoon, I saw issuing from it a blue-jay, chased by a score of smaller birds which it had doubtless been annoying. Jays are never happy except when in mischief, but as there are no birds'-nests now to rob, I cannot imagine his offence.

Under date of August 25th, Dr. Benjamin Smith Barton makes this curious entry in his field notes: "About this time the *Corvus cristatus*, called Blue-jay, having reared its young, appears in great numbers, waiting for the nuts of the Beech, Chinkapin, and Chestnut to feed upon when ripe, *and to store them up in its winter quarters.*" Who of late years has seen a jay's magazine of nuts, carefully stored for winter use? I take it this is a fancy on the part of the author, or a common impression then rife, but none the less erroneous. These birds, with all their cunning, are not so provident as this implies. Could they have been seen in winter, foraging on the supplies laid up by mammals, and so got the credit of storing for themselves? This is not improbable.

All this while I have been sitting in the boat, and quite unmindful of the world beneath me; but a loud splashing recalled the fact that the waters teemed with life, and looking in the direction of the noise, I saw a great number of small fishes rippling the water from shore to shore. It was a brood or hatching of young shad, wandering here to their certain destruction rather than making a seaward course down the river. Every perch and rockfish was aware of their presence, and on the alert to snap them up. They soon passed by, bound up the creek, and the waters were again undisturbed. Looking down into the stream near the pier, I could see small sunfish darting at, to me, unseen objects directly in front of them; and when I moved, they quickly darted into crevices among the large stones of the pier. Their vision serves them well, so far as seeing enemies, supposed or real, above the water. How fishes with eyes placed on the sides of their heads can see directly in front of them probably has puzzled a good many people. A recent explanation, which does not, however, differ from that of the older ichthyologists, but is couched in simple, non-technical terms, runs as follows:

"If a line extending through the centre of the pupil to the centre of the retina were the actual axis of vision, then such lateral-eyed fishes as the freshwater sunfishes would have separate fields of vision; but I am convinced that the true axis extends through the anterior margin of the ovate pupil to the posterior side of the retina. The spot of most distinct vision is this posterior portion of the retina, and on this spot the images formed in both eyes coincide.

"When the fish is quietly swimming in the water, this true axis is directed horizontally forward. This is true whether the fish has its body horizontal or not. The movement of the eyeball, to retain a horizontal direction of the true visual line, is a rotating one on the apparent optical axis; the rotation of the ball is not very noticeable, except in those fishes that have a dark band across the eye. One of those best marked for this purpose is the black-banded sunfish. There are quite a number of species marked with distinctness enough to show the rotation well, and the movement is an interesting one to watch. When the body of the fish is almost perpendicular, the eye retains its natural horizontal direction; this is true whether the fish is swimming obliquely upward or downward.

"The medium in which fresh-water fishes live gives them a chance to see a great distance only in the horizontal direction, and the proper adjustment of the eye would make, under usual conditions, the optical axis take this direction. To me it seems impossible to explain the constant revolution of the eyeball on any other hypothesis except that given, viz., that the optical axis extends forward instead of sidewise.

"When a fish wishes to eat anything, either at the bottom of the pond or at the surface of the water, it swims directly towards the object; and in this case the eyes are instantly adjusted in line with the body, so as to bring the image of the particle desired upon the posterior portion of the retina. In this case they lose their usual horizontal position.

"If a fish wishes to turn to the right or left in the water, the first movement is that of the eyes in unison with the direction of the turning. This would be entirely unnecessary if the apparent axis was the axis of most distinct vision, as one of the eyes would see all that was to be seen on the side of the turning. After this movement of the eyes the body turns enough to bring the eyes into their normal position; then there is again a movement of the eyes, and next a movement of the body. This causes a peculiar jerking motion of the eyeballs during the whole time of the turning of the body."

The little sunfish that I had been noticing made excellent use of their wits as well as eyes, and eluded my best-laid schemes to capture them. They knew perfectly well that when in the crevices of the pier they were safe, and that safety was an uncertainty under any ordinary circumstances. I waited many minutes for them to reappear, and found that they only purposed showing themselves after due precautions had been taken. They, at first, only peeped out and upward, and if I made the slightest movement away they went. At last I succeeded in refraining even from a wink, and very slowly they emerged from their stony caverns; but even now they would not venture beyond a few inches from the pier, and watched for movements on my part rather than food. These mere mites of fishes, scarcely three months old, had wise heads on their shoulders. How the old naturalists could suppose a fish passed a mere mechanical existence is indeed a puzzle. Did they never see living fish?

Quantities of eels kept passing in full view, all going up the creek. They were quite uniform in size, measuring perhaps a foot in length. I should be glad to know their errand, but it is too late in the day to follow them. Were they larger, and in shallower waters, probably they might be heard. A kindly disposed critic, referring to my essay on the voices of fresh-water fishes, says: "We own that we should much like to listen, on a still summer evening, to a nocturne performed by a school of catfish." So should I; and if by remaining to-night upon the creek I might be so fortunate, I should certainly stay; but the difficulty rests here. The vocal power of a catfish, if I mistake not, consists of but a faint humming sound, seldom if ever uttered except during the breeding season. It is otherwise with the eels; they pipe a single, half-metallic note at frequent intervals, and quite as often in August as in early spring. Most unsatisfactory, indeed, it is, as I know to my sorrow, to wait for hours until the eels have congregated and all seems favorable, and then bull-frogs in the marshes, katydids in the trees, and crickets everywhere, commence their fearful racket, drowning every other sound. Often and often I have had good grounds for believing that I should be treated to a nocturne performed by a fish, or a school of them, and such has been the result. Particularly disgusting is such an experience when you have brought a sceptical friend with you. He says provokingly little, but seems busy at measuring the length, breadth, and depth of your imagination. Often, when I have failed through such mishaps to hear the fishes that I knew were singing, I have, to misquote Tom Hood,

> Brought down my oar with a sudden slam
> That sounded like a watery " damn."

In conclusion, I clip the following from a recent magazine; its perusal gave me pleasure. The writer, who is wandering in Florida, writes: " What impressed me strongly were the mysterious sounds coming from the inland waters during this cruise. I had been sceptical as to vocal fish, but to-day I have not the least hesitancy in declaring that fish have voices which are just as distinguishable as if a man were singing in the room where I am writing. Now, I had been quite aware that certain fish (you can catch them off New York Harbor and all along the coast) emit sounds when out of their element, but I have never heard them before in the water. When off the Ten Thousand Islands, every quiet evening, for hours together, strange sounds were heard. Now they would burst forth on one side of the schooner, now on the other. Some fish was singing a solo for our benefit." And from another publication I clip the following, likewise for the benefit of those who doubt that certain fishes have voices: "The white perch of the Ohio are noted for the musical sounds they make. The sound is much like that produced by a silk thread placed in a window where the wind blows across it."

There is a gentle breeze that tiptoes by, an hour before sunrise, not rudely chilling animal or plant, but softly rouses each from its slumber, kisses it "good-morning," and is gone. It fanned my cheek as I passed over the meadow, hurrying to my boat.

As light a zephyr has rippled the waters at intervals this afternoon, with no intimation of its coming until the smooth surface was streaked with steel-blue bands that noiselessly shot from shore to shore, and as silently disappeared. I chanced in the path of one, and found it laden with the sweet odor of ripening fox-grapes.

The day closes. The shadows gather about the ancient bridge and soften its uncouth shapelessness until it is but a cloud in the horizon. My pleasant outings upon the creek are now but treasures of memory. With the perfumed breath of ripened summer, the song of a dreaming bird, and the flush of the evening breeze to cheer me, let me hurry away,

"Nor cast one longing, lingering look behind."

INDEX.

Acer rubrum, 103.
Acipenser sturio, 108, 142, 146, 220.
Adder's - tongue (*Erythronium Americanum*), 117.
Æstivation among mammals, 180.
Agelaius phœniceus, 49, 195, 223.
Alauda alpestris, 175, 287.
" rubra, 175, 287.
Alder (*Alnus serrulata*), 124.
Alisma plantago, 85.
Alnus serrulata, 124.
Alosa sapidissima, 105, 108, 142.
Amber, Occurrence of, in Crosswicks valley, 163.
America," "Travels in, La Hontan's, 157.
American Naturalist, quoted, 87, 129.
Amiurus catus, 108, 273.
Ampelis cedrorum, 49.
Ampelopsis quinquefolia, 44, 200, 205, 256.
Amphicarpœa monoica, 85.
Anas boschas, 283.
Anemone nemorosa, 117.
Anguilla rostrata, 254, 300.
Animals, Inquisitiveness among, 12.
Anne, The shallop, 225.
Anthus ludovicianus, 175, 287.
Antrostomus vociferus, 11, 220.
Ants, 36.
" brood of winged, 86, 88.
Apios tuberosa, 66, 271.
Apis mellifica, 16, 195, 241.
Araneina, 36.
Arctomys monax, 251.
Ardea herodias, 129, 177.

Arvicola riparia, 135, 200, 203.
Audubon, J. J., quoted, 118.

Baltimore oriole (*Icterus baltimore*), 57, 198, 237.
Barton, Benj. Smith, on migration of birds, quoted, 174, 277, 279, 296.
Bartram, John, quoted, 67.
" William, " 174.
Bascanion constrictor, 147, 264.
Bates, Henry W., on habits of Saüba ants, quoted, 89.
Bats (*Vespertilionidæ*), Æstivation of, 183.
Bats, 261.
Beaver - tree (*Magnolia glauca*), 147.
Beech (*Fagus ferruginea*), 297.
Bee-martin (*Tyrannus carolinensis*), 172.
Bell - wort (*Uvularia perfoliata*), 117.
Betula nigra, 38, 68, 103.
Bill - fish (*Tylosurus longirostris*), 217.
Birch (*Betula nigra*), 38, 68, 103.
Bird, Yellow (*Chrysomitris tristis*), 51.
Birds, Color sense of, 40.
" Migration of, 173, 178.
" Quarrels among, 12.
Bittern, Great (*Botaurus lentiginosus*), 127.
Bitter - sweet (*Solanum dulcamara*), 65.
Blackberry (*Rubus villosus*), 111, 256, 280.

Blackbird, Red-winged (*Agelaius phœniceus*), 49, 195, 223.
Black-capped tit (*Parus atricapillus*), 285.
Bluebird (*Sialia sialis*), 50, 255, 262, 284.
Bluet (*Houstonia cærulea*), 117.
Bolcosoma Olmstedi, 210.
Bonaparte, C. L., 18.
Boneset (*Eupatorium perfoliatum*), 79.
Bordentown, New Jersey, 171, 176, 187, 268.
Botaurus lentiginosus, 127.
Bowlders, 64.
Brainerd, John, Indian missionary, quoted, 235.
Branta canadensis, 9, 126, 144.
Brasenia peltata, 215.
Brewer, Thos. M., 55, 88, 172, 274.
Brinton, Dr. D. G., on Delaware Indian idols, quoted, 236.
Bristol, Pennsylvania, porpoises seen near, 215.
Bubo virginianus, 145.
Bufo americanus, 81.
Bull-frog (*Rana Catesbyana*), 11, 200.
Bunting, Bay-winged (*Poœcetes gramineus*), 51, 203.
Burlington, New Jersey, 68, 146, 215.
Burrows of mammals, how constructed, 245.
Butler, Amos W., on animal weather-lore, quoted, 28.
Butterflies, Migrations of, 80.
Butterfly Plexippus (*Danais plexippus*), 79.
Butterfly, Red admiral (*Vanessa atalanta*), 79.
Butternut (*Juglans cinerea*), 68, 145.
Button-bush (*Cephalanthus occidentalis*), 66, 85, 133.
Button-wood (*Platanus occidentalis*), 103.
Buzzard, Turkey (*Cathartes aura*), 42, 176.
Buzzard's Rest, 21, 38.

Caltha palustris, 118.
Calystegia sepium, 66.
Campanius, Thomas, historian of "New Sweden," quoted, 165, 214, 271.
Canis lupus, 145.
Cardinal-grosbeak (*Cardinalis virginianus*), 34, 53, 97, 293, 294.
Cardinalis virginianus, 34, 53, 97, 293, 294.
Carpenter-bee (*Xylocopa virginica*), 265.
Carpinus americanus, 2, 3, 38, 68, 200.
Carpodacus purpureus, 289.
Carya alba, 145.
"   *porcina*, 2, 38, 68.
Castanea pumila, 145, 198, 256, 297.
Castanea vesca, 146, 271, 297.
Cat, Domestic, as a weather prophet, 30.
Catalpa (*Catalpa bignonioides*), 82, 257, 295.
Cat-bird (*Galeoscoptes carolinensis*), 56, 105, 109, 206.
Catfish (*Amiurus catus*), 108, 273.
"   Stone (*Noturus gyrinus*), 59.
Cathartes aura, 42, 176.
Cat-tail (*Typha latifolia*), 137.
Cedar-bird (*Ampelis cedrorum*), 49.
Celastrus scandens, 78.
Centaury (*Sabbatia angularis*), 65.
Centurus carolinensis, 112.
Cephalanthus occidentalis, 66, 85, 133.
Certhia familiaris, 286.
Ceryle alcyon, 11, 38, 41, 293.
Chalkley, Thomas, Journal of, 153.
"   "   267.
Chat, Yellow-breasted (*Icteria virens*), 18, 56, 195.
Chestnut (*Castanea vesca*), 146, 271, 297.
Chewink (*Pipilo erythrophthalmus*), 202.
Chinkapin (*Castanea pumila*), 145, 198, 256, 297.

INDEX.   305

Chipmunk (*Tamias striatus*), 246, 261, 265.
Chordeiles popetue, 86.
Chrysomitris pinus, 175, 289.
" *tristis*, 51, 261.
Cicada tibicen, 83.
Cirsium lanceolatum, 261.
Cistothorus palustris, 253, 273.
Cistudo clausa, 149, 248.
Clay, 163.
Claytonia virginica, 117.
Clematis virginiana, 79.
Clethra alnifolia, 59.
Clover (*Trifolium pratense*), 138.
Coccygus americanus, 83, 193.
" *erythrophthalmus*, 84.
Colaptes auratus, 53, 195.
Collurio borealis, 281, 288.
" *excubitoroides*, 281.
Columba carolinensis, 177.
" *migratoria*, 177.
Condylura cristata, 246.
Cone flower (*Rudbeckia laciniata*), 67.
Contopus virens, 83.
Cook, Prof. Geo. H., State Geologist of New Jersey, quoted, 163, 165.
Corn-crake (*Crex pratensis*), 170.
Cornus florida, 2, 117.
Corvus americanus, 47, 56.
Corylus americana, 145.
Cougar (*Felis concolor*), 145.
Cowpen-bird (*Molothrus pecoris*), 55, 222, 293.
Cows as weather prophets, 25.
Coxcomb grass (*Panicum crusgalli*), 137.
Creeper, Brown tree (*Certhia familiaris*), 286.
Creeper, Virginia (*Ampelopsis quinquefolia*), 44, 200, 205, 256.
Crex pratensis, 170.
Cricket (*Gryllus sp.*), 220.
Crosswicks Creek, 144, 145, 170, 177, 214, 224, 226, 252, 268.
Crosswicks Sea-serpent, 81.
Crow (*Corvus americanus*), 47, 56.
Cuckoo, Black-billed (*Coccygus erythrophthalmus*), 84.

Cuckoo, Yellow-billed (*Coccygus americanus*), 83, 193.
Culex damnosus, 191, 241.
" *sp.*, 242.
Cumberford, Jemmy, adventure of, 225.
Cuscuta gronovii, 111.
Cyanospiza cyanea, 56, 262.
Cyanura cristata, 54, 293, 296.
Cynthia virginica, 118.
Cypress (*Cupressus thyoides*), 271.
Cypris sp., 211.

Dabchick. (See *Devil Diver*.)
Damsons. (See *Wild Plum*.)
Danais plexippus, 79.
Daphnia pulex, 213.
Darter, Tesselated (*Bolcosoma Olmstedi*), 210.
Datura stramonium, 261.
Dead Willow Bend, 116, 120, 127, 138, 140.
Delaware River, 64, 68, 144, 146, 167, 169, 187, 215, 268.
Dendrœca æstiva, 8, 41, 69.
" *discolor*, 198.
" *maculosa*, 8.
Devil Diver (*Podilymbus podiceps*), 177.
Dewberry (*Rubus canadensis*), 265.
Didelphis virginianus, 32, 96.
Diospyros virginiana, 272.
Dodder (*Cuscuta gronovii*), 111.
Dogs as weather prophets, 29.
Dog-wood (*Cornus florida*), 2, 117.
Dove, Turtle (*Zenædura carolinensis*), 177.
Drawbridge, The, 255, 267.
Ducks, Wild (*Anatidæ*), 144.
Duncan, P. Martin, quoted, 91.

Eagle-owl (*Bubo virginianus*), 145.
Ectopistes migratorias, 177, 224.
Eel (*Anguilla rostrata*), 254, 300.
Eel-crow, 176.
" grass (*Vallisneria spiralis*), 217.
Empidonax flaviventris, 15.
" *traillii*, 114.
Encyclopædia Britannica, quoted, 184.

Equisetum arvense, 118.
Eremophila alpestris, 175, 287.
Erythronium americanum, 117.
Eskimo, Traces of, in New Jersey, 77, 160.
Esox reticulatus, 106, 216.
Eupatorium perfoliatum, 79.

Fagus ferruginea, 297.
Fairthorne, Natty, 8.
Falcon, Winter (*Buteo lineatus*), 55.
Faxon's Brook, 65, 243.
Fedia olitoria, 232.
Felis concolor, 145.
Fiber zibethicus, 99.
Finch, Fox - colored (*Passerella iliaca*), 292.
Finch, Pine (*Chrysomitris pinus*), 175, 289.
Finch, Purple (*Carpodacus purpureus*), 289.
Finch, White - crowned (*Zonotrichia leucophrys*), 292.
Fire-fly (*Lampyrus sp.*), 220.
Fish affected by lightning, 186.
" hawk (*Pandion carolinensis*), 42.
Fish, Sense of direction possessed by, 136.
Fish, Vision of lateral-eyed, 298.
" Voice of, 300.
Florida cærulea, 129.
Flycatcher, Great crested (*Myiarchus crinitus*), 172.
Flycatcher, Green, black - capped (*Myiodioctes pusillus*), 8.
Flycatcher, Scissor-tail (*Milvulus forficatus*), 172.
Flycatcher, Traill's (*Empidonax traillii*), 114.
Flycatcher, Yellow - bellied (*Empidonax flaviventris*), 15.
Fossil - wood, Occurrence of, in clay, 163.
Fox (*Vulpes vulgaris*), 145, 251.
Fringilla melodia, 177.
Frog, Bull (*Rana Catesbyana*), 11, 200.
Frog, Green (*Rana clamitans*), 170.

Fundulus multifasciatus, 99.
" *ornatus*, 167.
Galeoscoptes carolinensis, 56, 105, 109, 206.
Gallinula galeata, 157.
" *carolina*. (See *Porzana carolina*.)
Gallinule, Florida (*Gallinula galeata*), 157.
Gar (*Lepidosteus osseus*), 142.
Gaunt, Uz, quoted, 263.
Geothlypis trichas, 104.
Gerardia flava, 78.
Godman, J. D., on habits of meadow-mouse, quoted, 203.
Gold, supposed occurrence in New Jersey, 165.
Golden Club (*Orontium aquaticum*), 118, 232, 271.
Goniaphea ludoviciana, 19.
Goose, Canada (*Branta canadensis*), 9, 126, 144.
Grakle, Purple (*Quiscalus versicolor*), 41, 56, 237.
Grape (*Vitis labrusca*), 44.
" (*Vitis cordifolia*), 256.
Grass, Coxcomb (*Panicum crusgalli*), 137.
Grass, Eel (*Vallisneria spiralis*), 217.
Grosbeak, Cardinal (*Cardinalis virginianus*), 34, 53, 97.
Grosbeak, Rose-breasted (*Goniaphea ludoviciana*), 19.
Ground-nut (*Apios tuberosa*), 66, 271.
Gum, Sour (*Nyssa multiflora*), 63.
Gun-slip, 69.
Gyrinus sp., 11, 180.

Harlan, Dr. Richard, 230.
Harporhynchus rufus, 56, 202.
Harvest-fly (*Cicada tibicen*), 83.
Haw, Black (*Viburnum prunifolium*), 85.
Hawk, Fish (*Pandion carolinensis*), 42.
Hawk, Hen (*Buteo vulgaris*), 35.
" Night (*Chordeiles popetue*), 86.

Hawk, Sharp-shinned (*Accipiter fuscus*), 205.
Hawk, Sparrow (*Tinnunculus sparverius*), 55.
Hawkweed (*Hieracium sp.*), 79.
Hazel (*Corylus americana*), 145.
Heckewelder, John, on habits of shrike, quoted, 280.
Helenium autumnale, 168, 171.
Hempweed (*Mikania scandens*), 137.
Heron, Blue (*Florida cærulea*), 129.
" Great blue (*Ardea herodias*), 129, 177.
Heron, Little green (*Butorides virescens*), 129.
Heron, Night (*Nyctiardea grisea*), 40, 129, 220.
Hesperomys leucopus, 180, 204.
Hickory, Pignut (*Carya porcina*), 2, 38, 68.
Hieracium sp., 79.
Hirimdinidæ, 35, 82, 192.
Hirundo horreorum, 279.
" *purpurea*, 278.
Honey-bee (*Apis mellifica*), 16, 195, 241.
Hopniss. (See *Apios tuberosa*.)
Hornbeam (*Carpinus americanus*), 2, 3, 38, 68, 200.
Hornbeam, English, 4.
Hornet (*Vespa maculata*), 37.
Houstonia cærulea, 117.
Hudson River, 144.
Hyla versicolor, 194, 256, 265.
Hypericum sp., 67.

Icteria virens, 18, 56, 195.
Icterus baltimore, 57, 198, 237.
Impatiens fulva, 252.
Indians, Delaware, 10, 18, 68, 74, 76, 106, 140, 145, 159, 165, 233.
Indigo-bird (*Cyanospiza cyanea*), 56, 262.
Ivy (*Rhus toxicodendron*), 256.

Jamestown weed (*Datura stramonium*), 261.
Jay, Blue (*Cyanura cristata*), 54, 293, 296.

Jefferies, Richard, on mating habits of English rook, 48.
Juglans cinerea, 68, 145.
" *nigra*, 145.
Junco hyemalis, 289, 294.

Kalm, Peter, quoted, 67, 145, 257.
Kingbird (*Tyrannus carolinensis*), 172.
Kingfisher (*Ceryle alcyon*), 11, 38, 41, 293.
Kinglet, Golden-crowned (*Regulus satrapa*), 285.
Kinglet, Ruby-crowned (*Regulus calendula*), 285.
King-rail (*Rallus elegans*), 70.
Krider, John, rare bird collected by, 171.

Lamb-lettuce (*Fedia olitoria*), 232.
Lampyrus sp., 220.
Landing, The, 222.
Lapland long-spur (*Plectrophanes lapponicus*), 290.
Lark, Red — titlark ? — (*Anthus ludovicianus*), 175, 287.
Lark, Shore (*Eremophila alpestris*), 175, 287.
Laurie's mill-pond, 74.
Le Sueur, C. A., discovers "ornamented" minnow; quoted, 167.
Lepidosteus osseus, 142.
Lepomis gibbosus, 137, 142, 297.
Libellulidæ sp., 80.
Lilium superbum, 58.
Linden (*Tilia americana*), 2, 68, 103.
Linden Bend, 2, 5, 8, 10, 16, 38.
Lindstrom, P., early survey of Delaware River, 165, 267.
Linnet (*Ægiothus linarius*), 290.
Liopeltis vernalis, 72.
Liriodendron tulipifera, 146, 186.
Lizard (*Sceleporus undulatus*), 255, 265.
Lobelia cardinalis, 59.
Lobelia, Scarlet (*Lobelia cardinalis*), 59.
Lockwood, Rev. Samuel, on mastodon in New Jersey, 129, 159.

Locust (*Robinia pseudacacia*), 68, 257.
Lophophanes bicolor, 51, 285, 294.
Loskiel, George Henry, on Indian fisheries, quoted, 106.
Louisiana, History of, Du Pratz's, 155.

Magnolia glauca, 147.
Mallard (*Anas boschas*), 283.
"Manahattan's Wägar," 268.
Maple (*Acer rubrum*), 103.
Marigold (*Caltha palustris*), 118.
Marmot (*Arctomys monax*), 251.
Marsh campagnol. (See *Meadow-mouse*).
Martin, Purple (*Progne subis*), 277.
Mastodon, Occurrence of bones of, in New Jersey, 159.
May-apple (*Podophyllum peltatum*), 2.
Meadow-comb grass (*Trichochloa capillaris*), 137.
Meadow-lark (*Sturnella magna*), 293.
Mechen-tschiholens-sipu, 2, 20, 129, 215, 219.
Melospiza melodia, 51, 105, 139, 202.
Melospiza palustris, 71, 105.
Mephitis mephitica, 246, 255, 260.
Mikania scandens, 85, 137.
Milfoil, Water (*Myriophyllum spicatum*), 137.
Mill Creek, 190, 215.
Milvulus forficatus, 172.
Mink (*Putorius vison*), 121, 255.
Minnow, Mud (*Umbra limi*), 216.
" Ornamented (*Fundulus ornatus*), 167.
Mississippi River, Catfish of the, 143.
Mniotilta varia, 41.
Mole, Star-nosed (*Condylura cristata*), 246.
Molothrus pecoris, 55, 293.
Monmouth Court-house, New Jersey, 269.
Morone americana, 106, 142, 273, 297.

Mosquito (*Culex damnosus*), 191, 241.
Mouse, Meadow (*Arvicola riparia*), 135, 200, 203.
Mouse, White-footed (*Hesperomys leucopus*), 180, 204.
Musk-rat (*Fiber zibethicus*), 99.
Mussel (*Unio sp.*), 101.
Mutilla occidentalis, 244.
Myiarchus crinitus, 172.
Myiodioctes pusillus, 8.
Myoxus sp., 184.
Myriophyllum spicatum, 137.

Nanemys guttata, 135.
Neun-toedter, 280.
New York, City of, 146.
North American Review, quoted, 78.
Notemigonus chrysoleucus, 7.
Noturus gyrinus, 59.
Nuphar advena, 59.
Nuthatch, Red-bellied (*Sitta canadensis*), 285.
Nuthatch, White-bellied (*Sitta carolinensis*), 285.
Nyctiardea grisea, 40, 129, 220.
Nyssa multiflora, 63.

Oak, Swamp white (*Quercus bicolor*), 68, 85, 99, 103.
Oak, White (*Quercus alba*), 257, 270.
Oats, Wild. (See *Wild-rice*.)
Oconio's leap, 69.
Œnothera biennis, 67.
Oporornis agilis, 8.
Opossum (*Didelphis virginianus*), 32, 96.
Ord, George, on habits of meadow-mouse, quoted, 201.
Oriole, Baltimore (*Icterus baltimore*), 57, 198, 237.
Orontium aquaticum, 118, 271.
Ortyx virginianus, 56.
Overfield, Miles, weather wisdom of, quoted, 21.
Owl, Barn (*Strix pratincola*), 54.
" Eagle (*Bubo virginianus*), 145.

INDEX. 309

Owl, Little red (*Scops asio*), 54.
" Snowy (*Nyctea scandiaca*), 226.

Packard, Dr. A. S., on habits of ants, quoted, 91, 244.
Palæolithic Man, Traces of, in New Jersey, 77.
Pandion carolinensis, 42.
Panicum crus-galli, 137.
Parus atricapillus, 285.
Pea, Climbing (*Amphicarpæa monoica*), 85.
Peach (*Persica vulgaris*), 271.
Peale's Museum, 159.
Pearson, Isaac, 269.
Pearson's Inn, 270.
Peewee (*Sayornis fuscus*), 272.
" Wood (*Contopus virens*), 83.
Pelecanus trachyrhynchus, 144.
Pelican (*Pelecanus trachyrhynchus*), 144.
Perch, White (*Morone americana*), 106, 142, 278, 297.
Persica vulgaris, 271.
Persimmon (*Diospyras virginiana*), 272.
Petrochelidon lunifrons, 273, 275.
Philadelphia, Pennsylvania, 145, 178, 278.
Philohela minor, 196.
Phleum pratense, 138.
Phytolacca decandra, 261.
Picidæ, 16, 262, 293.
Pickerel - weed (*Pontederia cordata*), 59, 109.
Picus pubescens, 294.
Pigeon, Passenger (*Ectopistes migratorius*), 177, 224.
Pigeon-woodpecker (*Colaptes auratus*), 53.
Pigs as weather prophets, 27.
Pike (*Esox reticulatus*), 106, 216.
Pipilo erythrophthalmus, 202.
Pipit. (See *Red Lark*.)
Platanus occidentalis, 103.
Plectrophanes lapponicus, 290.
" *nivalis*, 290.
" Plommons Udden," 271.

Plum, Wild (*Prunus americana*), 85, 271.
Poætquissings Creek, 4, 133, 214.
Podilymbus podiceps, 177.
Podophyllum peltatum, 2.
Poke (*Phytolacca decandra*), 261.
" Pons-pau-cloo-moose," 279, 280.
Pontederia cordatum, 59, 109.
Poæcetes gramineus, 51, 203.
Porzana carolina, 169.
" *jamaicencis*, 169.
" *noveboracencis*, 169.
Poultry in weather-lore, 33.
Primrose (*Œnothera biennis*), 67.
Princeton, New Jersey, 269.
Prinos verticillata, 283.
Printz, John, Governor of "New Sweden," 165.
Procyon lotor, 261.
Progne subis, 277.
Prunus americana, 85, 271.
Putorius ermineus, 255, 260.
" *vison*, 1, 21.
Pyrgites domesticus, 12, 56, 139.
Pyrites, Iron, occurrence of, in clay, 163.

Quail (*Ortyx virginianus*), 56.
Quercus alba, 257, 270.
" *bicolor*, 68, 85, 99, 103.
Quicksands, 160.
Quiscalus versicolor, 41, 56, 237.

Raccoon (*Procyon lotor*), 261.
Ragwort (*Senecio aureus*), 118.
Raia ocellata, 215.
Rail, Common, or sora (*Porzana carolina*), 169.
Rail, King (*Rallus elegans*), 70, 169.
Rail, Little black (*Porzana jamaicencis*), 169.
Rail, Little yellow (*Porzana noveboracencis*), 169.
Rail, Virginia (*Rallus virginianus*), 169.
Rallus elegans, 70, 169.
" *virginianus*, 169.
Rana Catesbyana, 11, 200.
" *clamitans*, 170.

Raritan River, 268.
Redstart (*Setophaga ruticilla*), 12, 104, 198.
Regulus calendula, 285.
" *satrapa*, 285.
Rhus glabra, 68, 82, 138.
" *toxicodendron*, 256.
Rhyacophilus solitarius, 195, 199.
Rice, Wild (*Zizania aquatica*), 109, 201, 253, 280.
Robin (*Turdus migratorius*), 284.
Robinia pseudacacia, 68, 257.
Roccus lineatus, 142, 273, 297.
Rockfish—striped bass—(*Roccus lineatus*), 142, 273, 297.
Rook, English, curious habits of, 48.
Rose, Wild (*Rosa lucida*), 280.
Rubus villosus, 111.
Rudbeckia laciniata, 67.
Rutland Beauty (*Calystegia sepium*), 66.

Sabbatia angularis, 65.
Salix Babylonica, 82.
" *sp.*, 63, 103.
Sand-piper, Solitary (*Rhyacophilus solitarius*), 195, 199.
Sand-piper, "Teeter" (*Tringoides macularius*), 195.
Sandy Hook, New Jersey, 252.
Sassafras (*Sassafras officinale*), 283.
Saüba ants, 90.
Sayornis fuscus, 272.
Sceleporus undulatus, 255, 265.
"Science," quoted, 142.
"Science Gossip," quoted, 46.
Sciuropterus volucella, 31.
Sciurus carolinensis, 16.
Scops asio, 54.
Scuttle-bug (*Gyrinus sp.*), 11, 180.
Seal (*Phoca vitulina*), 215.
Senecio aureus, var. *Balsamitæ*, 118.
Setophaga ruticilla, 12, 104, 198.
Shad (*Alosa sapidissima*), 105, 108, 142, 297.
Shark River, New Jersey, marl-pits at, 165.
"Sheep's-heads," 108.
Shell-bark (*Carya alba*), 145.

Shiner — roach — (*Notemigonus chrysoleucus*), 7.
Shrike, Northern (*Collurio borealis*), 281, 288.
Shrike, Southern (*Collurio excubitorides*), 281.
Sialia sialis, 50, 255, 262, 284.
Sitta canadensis, 285.
" *carolinensis*, 285.
Siurus aurocapillus, 6.
" *motacilla*, 5.
Skate (*Raia ocellata*), 215.
Skunk (*Mephitis mephitica*), 246, 255, 260.
Smilax (*Smilax rotundifolia*), 8, 205, 256, 280, 283.
Snake, Black (*Bascanion constrictor*), 147, 264.
Snake, Green (*Liopeltis vernalis*), 72.
Snake, Water (*Tropidonotus sipedon*), 11, 71, 81, 106, 136.
Sneeze-weed (*Helenium autumnale*), 171.
Snow-bird (*Junco hyemalis*), 289, 294.
Snow bunting (*Plectrophanes nivalis*), 290.
Solanum dulcamara, 65.
Sora (*Porzana carolina*), 169.
Sparrow, English (*Pyrgites domesticus*), 12, 56, 139.
Sparrow, Field (*Spizella pusilla*), 265.
Sparrow, Fox-colored (*Passerella iliaca*), 262.
Sparrow, Song (*Melospiza melodia*), 51, 105, 139, 202, 292.
Sparrow, Swamp (*Melospiza palustris*), 71, 105.
Sparrow, Tree (*Spizella monticola*), 292, 294.
Sparrow, White-throated (*Zonotrichia albicollis*), 126, 262, 292.
Spiders (*Araneina*), 36.
Spizella monticola, 292, 294.
Spizella pusilla, 265.
Splatter-dock (*Nuphar advena*), 59.
Spring Beauty (*Claytonia virginica*), 117.

Springs,"Boiling," 161.
Squirrel, Flying (*Sciuropterus volucella*), 31.
Squirrel, Gray (*Sciurus carolinensis*), 16.
St. John's-wort (*Hypericum sp.*), 67.
Stacy,Mahlon,on fisheries of Delaware River, quoted, 108.
Stork, European, 40.
"Striped-stockings." (See *Culex sp.*)
Strix pratincola, 54.
Sturgeon (*Acipenser sturio*), 108, 142, 146, 220.
Sturnella magna, 293.
Sumac (*Rhus glabra*), 68, 82, 138.
Sunfish (*Lepomis gibbosus*), 137, 142, 297.
Swallow, Barn (*Hirundo horreorum*), 279.
Swallow, Cliff (*Petrochelidon lunifrons*), 273. 275.
Swallows (*Hirundinidæ*), 35, 82, 192.
Swamp White-oak Bend, 93.
Swedes, early settlers in New Jersey, 123.
Sycamore (*Platanus occidentalis*), 68.

Tachquachcaniminschi, 76.
Tamias striatus, 246, 261, 265.
Tarm-fisk, 214.
Testudinata, 106, 220.
Thalictrum cornuti, 200.
Thistle (*Cirsium lanceolatum*), 261.
Thoreau, H. D., 17, 168.
Thrush, Brown (*Harporhynchus rufus*), 56, 204.
Thrush, Song (*Turdus mustelinus*), 10, 56, 204, 206.
Thryothorus ludovicianus, 53, 93, 255, 262, 263, 272, 283.
Tilia americana, 2, 68, 103.
Timothy (*Phleum pratense*), 138.
Tinnunculus sparverius, 55.
Titmouse, Crested (*Lophophanes bicolor*), 51, 285, 294.
Toad (*Bufo americanus*), 81.

Tortoise,Box (*Cistudo clausa*),149, 248.
Tortoise, Habits of young, 150.
Touch-me-not (*Impatiens fulva*), 252.
Tree-creeper (*Mniotilta varia*), 41.
Tree-toad (*Hyla versicolor*), 194, 256, 265.
Trifolium pratense, 138.
Tringoides macularius, 195.
Troglodytes ædon, 56, 118, 255, 262.
"   *americanus*, 118.
Tropidonotus sipedon, 11, 71, 81, 106, 136.
Tulip-tree (*Liriodendron tulipifera*), 146, 186.
Turdus migratorius, 284.
Turdus mustelinus,10,56,204, 206.
Turkey-buzzard (*Cathartes aura*), 61.
Turk's-cap (*Lilium superbum*), 58.
Turnbull, William P., on birds of New Jersey, quoted, 128, 144, 170, 173, 274.
Turtle, Spotted (*Nanemys guttatus*), 135.
Turtles (*Testudinata*), 106, 220.
Twin Islands, The, 153, 167.
Typha latifolia, 137.
Tyrannus carolinensis, 172.

Umbra limi, 216.
Unionidæ, 101.
Uvularia perfoliata, 117.

Vallisneria spiralis, 217.
Vanessa atalanta, 79.
Velvet ant (*Mutilla occidentalis*), 244.
Verbena hastata, 82.
Vervain (*Verbena hastata*), 82.
Vespa maculata, 37.
Vesper bird. (See *Bay-winged Bunting.*)
Vesper. tilionidæ, 183.
Violæ sp., 117.
Violets (*Violæ sp.*), 117.
Vireo, Red-eyed (*Vireo olivacea*), 104.

Vireo, Yellow-throated (*Vireo flavifrons*), 45.
Vireos (*Vireonidæ*), 56.
Virginia creeper (*Ampelopsis quinquefolia*), 44, 200, 205, 256.
Vitis labrusca, 44.
" *cordifolia*, 256.
Vulpes vulgaris, 145.
Vultures. (See *Turkey-buzzard*.)

Walnut (*Juglans nigra*), 145, 271.
Warbler, Black and Yellow (*Dendrœca maculosa*), 8.
Warbler, Connecticut (*Oporornis agilis*), 8.
Warbler, Prairie (*Dendrœca discolor*), 198.
Warbler, Yellow (*Dendrœca æstiva*), 8, 41, 69.
Water-flea (*Daphnia pulex*), 213.
" mite (*Cypris sp.*), 211.
" shield (*Brasenia peltata*), 215.
Water-thrush, Large-billed (*Siurus motacilla*), 5.
Water-thrush, "Oven-bird" (*Siurus auricapillus*), 6, 198.
Watson, Matthew, on early navigation of Crosswicks Creek, quoted, 68.
Watson's Crossing, 66, 82.
" Ford, 9.
Weasel (*Putorius ermineus*), 255, 260.
Weather-lore, Animal, English, 23.
" " " Swedish, 23.
Weather-lore, Animal, in New Jersey, 23.
Whippoorwill (*Antrostomus vociferus*), 11, 220.
"White Horse" tavern, 270.
Wild Bean. (See *Ground-nut*.)
Willow (*Salix sp.*), 68, 103.
" Weeping (*Salix Babylonica*), 82.

Wilson, Alexander, quoted, 84, 172.
Wind-flower (*Anemone nemorosa*), 117.
Winter-berry (*Prinos verticillata*), 283.
Woodcock (*Philohela minor*), 196.
Woodpecker, Downy (*Picus pubescens*), 294.
Woodpecker, Pigeon (*Colaptes auratus*), 53, 195.
Woodpecker, Red-bellied (*Centurus carolinensis*), 112.
Woodpeckers (*Picidæ sp.*), 16, 262, 293.
Wood-tattler. (See *Solitary Sandpiper*.)
Wood-thrush. (See *Thrush, Song*.)
Woolman, John, 267.
Wren, Carolina (*Thryothorus ludovicianus*), 53, 93, 255, 262, 263, 272, 283.
Wren, House (*Troglodytes ædon*), 56, 118, 255, 262.
Wren, Marsh (*Cistothorus palustris*), 253, 273.
Wren, Winter (*Troglodytes hyemalis*), 287.
Wren, Wood (*Troglodytes americanus*: Aud.), 118.

Xylocopa virginica, 265.

Yellow-bird (*Chrisomitris tristis*), 51, 261.
Yellow-fever, Epidemic of, in 1793, 18.
Yellow-throat, Maryland (*Geothlypis trichas*), 104.

Zenædura carolinensis, 177.
Zizania aquatica, 109, 201, 253, 280.
Zonotrichia albicollis, 126, 262.
" *leucophrys*, 292.

THE END.

www.ingramcontent.com/pod-product-compliance
Lightning Source LLC
Chambersburg PA
CBHW030743230426
43667CB00007B/824